ALAN MITCHELL

CLINT EASTWOOD

Other titles by Michael Munn

Trevor Howard
Charlton Heston: A Biography
The Hollywood Murder Casebook
Hollywood Rogues

CLINT EASTWOOD

HOLLYWOOD'S LONER

MICHAEL MUNN

Robson Books

First Published in Great Britain in 1992 by Robson Books Ltd, Bolsover House, 5-6 Clipstone Street, London W1P 7EB

British Library Cataloguing-in-Publication Data
A catalogue record for this book is available from the British Library

Typeset in Great Britain by Bookworm Typesetting, Manchester
Printed and bound by W.B.C. Print and W.B.C. Bookbinders Ltd., Mid-Glamorgan, S. Wales

For Trevor, Irene, Sarah and Kate

Contents

Acknowledgements

Before this book was finished, Don Siegel, who directed Clint Eastwood more times than anyone else, except Clint Eastwood himself, died. When I was planning to write a biography of Eastwood ten years ago, Don Siegel allowed me much of his time, for which I was and shall remain most grateful. It did not take me ten years to write this book. It just took ten years to pass before I was ready and able.

There are many to whom I owe thanks for allowing me to interview them over the years in connection with this subject. Among them, and now gone from us, are William Holden, Lee Van Cleef, David Janssen, Yakima Cannutt, Alan Jay Lerner and Lee Marvin.

My sincere thanks also to the following, some of whom spoke to me at length, some more briefly, and others who kindly wrote to me; Kay Lenz, Clive Mantle, Peter Barkworth, Ingrid Pitt, Ronald Lacey, Andrew V McLaglen, Charlton Heston, Bruce Dern, Doug McClure, Ennio Morricone, Eli Wallach, Derren Nesbitt, Brian G Hutton, Richard Brooks, Don Rickles, Telly Savalas, Stephen Longstreet, John Sturges, James Coburn, Franco Nero, Susan Clark, Fernando Cinquini, Jim Henderling, Elliott Kastner, Mariana Hill and Barry Brown.

Also thanks for their help to Brian Burton (Warner Bros), Carl Combs, Luciano Bayada (PEA Rome), and most especially to Dave Turner of the Clint Eastwood Appreciation Society (CEAS) whose help has been invaluable.

The lack of a bibliography is simply because there were so few books I found useful. However, mention should be made of Iain

Johnstone's *The Man With No Name*, by far the best published reference I could find on the films of Clint Eastwood up as far as 1980.

Articles referred to and journalists quoted are credited in the text. However, with regard to certain magazine articles, I have not given them credit since they were in fact written by me – it was because of the many articles and poster magazines I wrote on Eastwood that earned me honorary membership of the CEAS.

1
Drifting Around

On 29 October 1929, *Variety*, the film industry's trade paper, reported WALL STREET LAYS AN EGG. Wall Street had crashed. The Great Depression had begun. Millions became unemployed almost overnight. Soup kitchens opened up across the country in an attempt to ensure that the destitute had at least one hot meal of sorts inside them each day.

One man, no more significant than the countless others in search of work, was Clinton Eastwood, an accountant with a wife, Ruth, a daughter, Jeanne, and a son, Clinton Junior; he hated being named after his father and having to put up with being referred to as 'Junior' for years. 'I think a kid deserves his own name,' he said. The infant Clinton was born on 31 May 1930, in San Francisco.

Clinton Senior and Ruth were still very young when they began their family, 'quite the antithesis of my own situation with my children,' said Clint Eastwood who was to wait until he was in his late thirties before beginning a family of his own.

Clinton Junior's place of birth was due more to chance than choice. Eastwood Senior's job was selling stocks and bonds and he often moved from one company to another in order to better himself.

There were times when Eastwood Senior was so desperate he took on more menial jobs – waiting on tables, gas attendant, anything that could keep his family from starving. Through Junior's early years, the family moved up and down the West Coast, and both Jeanne and the younger Clinton were forever changing schools. 'I must have gone to eight different schools,' said Eastwood. In a sense the constant moving strengthened the family bonds, but not, said Eastwood, 'in the conventional sense. We moved around so much that the family was about all you had.'

He can't recall all the places they settled in – San Francisco, Spokane, Oakland, Redding, Pacific Palisades, Seattle and Sacramento – twice – are the locations he remembers. 'It seems to me now that we didn't live much in houses at all – we lived in cars.' For him, the most frustrating thing about spending little chunks of his childhood in so many places was 'constantly having to make adjustments.' Just as he began to settle, make friends and start making progress in his studies, Dad would get a new job and they'd be on the move again.

During those early years, there was never a sense of security in young Clint's life. He'd arrive at a new school to discover that the standards were different, or they would be working on different areas of any given subject. 'I always seemed to be behind and running to catch up,' he recalled.

He acknowledged, however, that there was a positive side to his life. 'It was hard,' he told Tom Snyder in a television interview in 1980, 'but I think you can find something good out of anything bad. I would have preferred to stay in the same place and enjoy the same people throughout the growing years. But I suppose there are benefits to it. You learn to get along with a lot of different people, in a lot of different places.'

When he could, Eastwood Senior spent as much time as possible with his children. A physically active man who enjoyed football and running, he loved the great outdoors and took his son on hunting and fishing trips. He also taught young Clint to swim, as well as a valuable lesson: 'Nothing comes for nothing, son, and don't plan on anything, because no one gives you anything in life. Of course, if you get lucky and something rolls your way . . . take it.'

Later, when Eastwood was old enough to drive the old jalopy his father bought him for $25, he drove himself and his sister up the Sierra Nevadas and Mount Lassen where they learned to ski. This was a pastime he pursued throughout his life.

The worst times were when Eastwood Senior had to leave the family behind in order to seek work. 'There were times when we had to be separated, when times weren't good,' recalled Clint who had to learn how to become independent as a boy. Even at such a young age, he was, and would in essence remain, a loner. But he didn't grow to resent his father. 'When I look back now, I know Dad had to think pretty fast at times because there were a lot of people out of work in America.' In retrospect, Eastwood acknowledges that he had 'great parents. I was lucky to have them.'

During those times of separation, the Eastwoods turned to other members of their family for help. This may well have been their only option, but it also ensured that Jeanne and Clint maintained a sense of 'family'. For a while they lived with their grandmother on her farm near Livermore in California. There Eastwood learned to love the country life, hunting in the woods and fishing and swimming in the lake that God had seen fit to put right on grandmother's doorstep. 'She was quite a person,' said Eastwood of his grandmother who obviously left her mark on the increasingly independent Clint, 'very self-sufficient, lived by herself on a mountain.'

He believes that his grandmother and his parents – their determination and sense of self-sufficiency – had more to do with the way he turned out than any educational process. His time on the farm benefited his later career as a film star in Westerns because his cousins had their own horses, stabled on grandmother's farm, and so Eastwood learned to ride. When he wasn't at school, or messing around in the lake, he was usually to be found on a horse, and usually riding alone. The lone cowboy of the screen was evolving. And taking off on his own into the wilds was something that Eastwood would continue to do into maturity.

He admits he was keen on girls at an early age. He said, 'I don't think there was a class I was ever in, right through from grammar, junior high and high school, where I didn't have a crush on some girl.'

He remembers his first major crush as being a stunning red-head called Joan, when he was at Glenview Grammar School. She was a 'little teenybopper – the most popular girl in the class.'

Joan, however, showed no interest in him. He sat far behind her in class, out of sight, out of mind. He was a compulsive daydreamer, often staring out of the window while he dreamed he was the world's greatest surfer, or a surgeon, saving more lives on the operating table than any surgeon in history. He even dreamed himself into the seat next to Joan. But that was as near to her as he got. He never could find the courage to ask her on a date, and as far as she was concerned he was, he said, 'a big zero.'

At high school he was a head taller than the other kids. He said he would gladly have lopped himself off at the knees in those days. He had to go through 'this male thing of handing it out as well as taking it,' although he says they weren't usually tough kids. He was just the odd man out – 'the big, silent guy.' He found he had to learn to defend himself. 'I was always a little big for my age so some other guy was always trying to punch me out.' Occasionally, he won.

But what he made up for by height, he lacked in confidence. He was introverted and unable to express himself. 'It was agony for me even to just ask a girl for a date.'

He noticed how the girls became hung-up on hero-types; football and track stars. 'You see them hanging around in groups, all mooning over the one guy. I could have done better at sports myself, I suppose. I had the physical qualities.' He would have been perfect for the school basketball team, for instance, but by his own admission, he was too introverted, too much a loner. He wished he could somehow become more of an extrovert.

'I was pretty scared of making a fool of myself,' he said. 'It was just being afraid of women, which is the way a lot of kids are in adolescence.'

Occasionally he did manage to pluck up the courage to ask a girl out. On one such occasion he was so nervous he couldn't stop talking. They were both nervous wrecks by the end of the evening and were glad to say goodnight to each other.

Determined not to repeat the same mistake, he kept quiet on the next couple of dates! He took one girl to an amusement park and said little more than half a dozen words to her all evening. 'She probably reckoned I was just too dumb,' he said. 'Somehow, I could never get it right.'

He did have some success however with a girl called Marge whom he met at Piedmont Junior High, in Oakland. He was invited to a birthday party which turned out to be quite a formal affair at which all the girls, including Marge, had parents along as chaperones. Eastwood managed to find the courage to kiss Marge when her mother wasn't looking, and asked for a date.

He had a newspaper-round then which earned him a few dollars to spend on Marge at the local drug store where they often hung out. He also took her to the local swimming pool and the cinema. Films had no great influence on him; they certainly didn't instil any desire in him to become an actor. He enjoyed Westerns and gangster films; he liked Bogart although James Cagney was more his hero.

Things between him and Marge were going just great until Marge's mother got the idea that he was perfect material for a future son-in-law, so he decided to fade out of Marge's life completely.

'I'm glad that I wasn't like some kids who rush into marriage today on the strength of a schooltime crush,' he said in 1969. 'They really don't know what they're doing. They ought to give themselves a chance to look around a bit and discover other standards. What looks good to you at fifteen or sixteen can look like crow-bait at twenty-one.'

Even though he was painfully shy and introverted, he was far more independent than most of his peers. His father, who was firm but never tyrannical, impressed upon his son the idea that he should learn to stand on his own feet as soon as he could. The younger Eastwood was earning some extra dollars by delivering groceries or newspapers, and when he was fourteen his father bought him his first car, 'an old rattle-trap'. That car took his mind off girls, and for the next couple of years his jalopy took priority in his life. Despite having only a learner's permit, he still drove himself around, and because he was over six feet tall, he looked old enough to fool the police who never bothered to stop him and check his licence.

As the Depression lifted, Clinton Senior's work stabilized and he landed a job with the Container Corporation of America in Oakland. The family were able to establish a permanent home at last. Eastwood, now fifteen, began attending the Oakland Technical High School. On his first day there he met up with another youth on his first day in that school. His name was Fritz Maines, and they became life-long friends.

'Clint hasn't really changed that much,' recalled Maines. 'He was always a tall, lanky kid and didn't necessarily dress the way the rest of the kids did. It was our first day in school and it was just one of those things – we instantly identified with each other. We weren't that excited about going to school, both being sort of non-joiners, non-members of the pack.' By then Eastwood had reached his full height; six feet four inches.

Another close friend was Harry Pendleton who shared one of Eastwood's most traumatic experiences as a youth. Their English teacher, Miss Jones, had decided to cast them in a one-act play, with

Eastwood playing the lead. 'The character in this little one-act play was an introverted kid,' said Eastwood, 'so she saw me and said, "Well, he's perfect." And this other kid, my buddy, had to play my father, and having one of your peers play your father is kind of ridiculous.'

He decided he had better things to do. 'I wanted to go out for athletics,' he said, although he was not a dedicated athlete during his school days, according to Fritz Maines who said, 'Clint had tremendous athletic ability all through school but not being a keen-spirited type of guy, he never really followed it through.'

Eastwood tried to avoid making his acting debut. 'Doing plays was not considered the thing to do at that stage in life, especially not presenting them before the entire senior high school, which is what she made us do.'

Miss Jones tried to convince him that he'd enjoy the experience, but as far as he was concerned, it wasn't possible for such an introverted guy like himself to be an actor. But she had been smart enough to cast him to type; the character he played was like him – an introvert and a loner. 'I can only guess Miss Jones wasn't such a bad amateur psychologist in her way,' Eastwood said. 'It was good casting. But it terrified me.'

His parents seemed delighted that their son was in the play, and hoped that it might draw him out of his shell. But the prospect terrified him, as it did Harry Pendleton. Throughout rehearsals they struggled through with a sense of foreboding; they knew it was going to be a disaster. The night before the performance, they went to the local drug store to share their anxieties.

'They'll laugh us off the stage,' said Clint.

'They sure will,' agreed Harry.

'You know what they're like. I know I'm going to freeze half-way through. I'm never going to remember all those lines.'

'Well, I won't go on if you don't,' Harry suggested.

Eastwood agreed. They went home that night, secure in the knowledge that neither would be laughed at the following evening. But the next morning Clint was on the phone to Harry, saying, 'We'll be murdered if we skip it.'

'Yeah, I guess it would be easier all round if we just did it,' agreed Harry.

That evening two terrified boys trod the boards for the first time.

They decided it would be the last. At one point the audience laughed and Clint dried. Then he realized that they were in fact laughing at the play itself, and not at him. 'I suppose it was the first time I realized you could act extroverted without really being so,' he said.

As for being an actor, the thought didn't occur to him at that time. In fact, it was almost enough to put him off for life. 'We muffed a lot of lines,' he recalled. 'I swore that was the end of my acting career.'

In retrospect, he conceded, 'It was a good laugh and a good thing to have behind you even though it wasn't till quite a few years later that I thought about being an actor.'

At that time of his life, he did think about a musical career. In 1945, at the age of fifteen, he went to one of the *Jazz at the Philharmonic* concerts. He recalled, 'Tenor sax players Lester Young and Coleman Hawkins were playing. But it was a young alto sax player, Charlie "Bird" Parker, who really caught my ear. I bought all his records, became a real Bird *aficionado* and, years later, when I'd started making movies, I determined that one day I'd make a movie about Bird.'

Eastwood was so impressed by Parker's music he began playing the trumpet although he became more accomplished on the piano. A musical career seemed a more attractive prospect for the young Eastwood than any routine job.

During the school summer holidays of 1945, he decided to take off in his car. He threw a few things together in a bag, kissed Jeanne and his mother goodbye, and set off for southern California. It was his first time away from home alone, and he was just going to drive as the mood took him.

He travelled deep into some big ranch country and eventually drove up to one of the big ranch houses. Finding the owner, he asked for a job, and was put to work baling hay. It was exhausting work, and each night he barely had the strength to crawl into his bunk. The moment his head hit the pillow he was, as he put it, 'dead to the world.' But that summer job toughed up the rangy, skinny fifteen-year-old.

The summer over, Eastwood returned home and to school. He was beginning to enjoy life now, no longer such a loner – although he still liked to take off on his own now and then – and with a number of close friends. Two of his best buddies were Bob Sturges and Jack McKnight, and together they set out to raise a little hell. They each had a car and spent much of their time customizing them. They entered drag races, sometimes reaching speeds of up to 110 miles an hour over just a few hundred yards. It was a dangerous pastime. 'Half the time we put these dragsters together with chewing gum,' said Eastwood.

Races were held at secret rendezvous where the dragsters would congregate at five in the morning every Saturday and Sunday. Each time they met, it was at a different location to foil the police who were forever receiving complaints from residents woken early by the roar of these souped-up cars.

During one race, Eastwood watched in horror as a friend's dragster spat flames at a hundred miles an hour. The car screeched to a halt and the driver jumped out just before the car became engulfed in an inferno. Sometimes the dragsters would be reaching up to 110 or 120 miles and hour when the skinny motorbike front tyres suddenly blew. Then the cars would career off the road and sometimes turn over and over. Clint considered himself lucky not to have had any bad accidents.

On one occasion the police were called and arrived before the dragsters had hardly started. Dozens of cops arrived in cars and wagons, blocking off both ends of the road. Eastwood and his buddies knew they were headed for jail – if they were caught. They scattered. 'It was like a scene from a mad movie,' recalled Eastwood. Dragsters careered over the fields in every direction, scattering cows, roaring across meadows, mowing down corn and tearing through fences, with the police in hot pursuit. Eastwood and his two pals escaped.

By the age of sixteen, his biceps were beginning to develop. He knew he looked good on a diving board because the women began taking notice of him. He and Bob and Jack – 'we were like the Three Musketeers' – spent much of their free time around the local swimming pool. 'In California you spend most of your life at the swimming pool,' said Eastwood. They all dived well and swam like fish, and were determined to impress the girls. Said Clint, 'I began scoring a few successes.'

At weekends, the trio gate-crashed swimming pool parties held at the homes of girls whose fathers were rich. They'd turn up in swimming trunks, figuring they looked like any other three guys in trunks, and once they were in, they became indistinguishable from all the other young male guests. They would help themselves to the generous buffet spread, but they weren't there for the food – they wanted girls.

During the next summer holidays, Clint, Bob and Jack took off together, heading for Sierra Nevada, now the biggest national park in America outside Alaska. They drove to Mount Lassen, a wild, picturesque live volcano, and landed themselves jobs as firefighters. When they arrived at the headquarters, they found the bunkhouse was full so they had to sleep in the garage among the firefighting trucks.

The daily work began each dawn as each gang climbed into their assigned truck and drove off, breathing in the clean mountain air. As they rumbled along, the forest animals scattered. They often saw deer and occasionally they spotted a grizzly. The gang's main task was to make fire-breaks to prevent any fire spreading. The day was spent clearing the ground of brush and small trees. It proved to be hard work – and very dangerous – scouting the foothills of Mount Lassen where the dry timber in summer was like a tinder box.

After their first day out with the firefighting gang, Clint, Bob and Jack didn't care where they slept as they bedded down in the garage once again. But as they became used to the hard work, they joined in with their companions in the bunkhouse, gathering round a big log fire and swapping stories. At weekends they drove into town looking for a little excitement.

The day came when Eastwood discovered just how dangerous this job could be. His gang was busy, as usual, clearing an area. The kind of undergrowth he was clearing – known as manzanita, which is particularly dry and burns fast and furious – caught fire. Within minutes the whole area was a sea of flames which swept through the forest.

Despite the thick smoke and almost unbearable heat, the firefighters stood by waiting to see if their fire-break held back the inferno. As the flames licked at the fire-break, the wind carried sparks across the clearing, and in no time at all the brush and trees on the other side of the break were engulfed. Reinforcements were called and they fought the fire throughout the night and into the next day. They hacked and cut ferociously, digging out new breaks and widening old ones in a desperate attempt to halt the blaze. They'd not slept and all they had to eat was dried-up sandwiches and oranges.

The sky was black with smoke as the exhausted firefighters slowly retreated, trying to hold back the swiftly spreading fire with hoses. On the fourth day Eastwood's gang found themselves in serious trouble when their hose became entangled in a tree. The fire was moving so fast that they had no time to do anything but leap into the truck which the driver had already put into gear. Suddenly the truck jerked to a halt. The entangled hose was holding them back. The truck's wheels strained and spun but they were held fast. The fire was advancing almost as quickly as a man could run. Sparks were flying over their heads and the manzanita was sizzling all around them. Unless the hose was cut, they would all perish.

Eastwood suddenly jumped from the truck with an axe in his hand, and began laying into the hose while the truck's engine roared and strained. He hacked and cut until the truck was free and already running away, picking up speed as it headed down an incline. The men called to Eastwood to run, but even before he was racing after them, the truck was a hundred yards away. He was suddenly alone in the inferno, knowing he had less than a minute before being burned alive.

To his right, he saw a large clearing on the other side of a hedge, and in the middle of the clearing a house. He tore through the hedge and found himself running through a pumpkin field. Sparks were tearing through the smoke-filled air. With his eyes stinging and his lungs bursting, he fell to the ground. He lay there terrified, fighting for his breath until he was able to scramble to his feet again and stagger on towards the house where a farmer and his wife stared in disbelief at the smoke-blackened, exhausted young man who stumbled towards them. They took him into their kitchen and fed him coffee and pumpkin pie. They'd lived in that forest for years and knew how to deal with the sparks which, in that clearing, were the only threat to them.

After an hour he had the strength to leave them with much thanksgiving, and found his way through the vast area of burned and smouldering stubble to the truck. His friends didn't seem too surprised to see him, figuring he'd manage to fend for himself. He was, to all who knew him, an independent man who could handle himself in any situation. He was, in a real sense, becoming very much like the steely-eyed hero of the films that would later make him the world's number one box office star.

It took four days to put out the fire which left hundreds of acres of once green woodland looking like a desert of blackened stubble. The firefighters arrived back at base and ate ravenously. Then they fell exhausted into their bunks. But Eastwood, even though he'd not slept for three nights, was unable to sleep. The forest fire kept playing over in his mind like the rushes of a film. He finally fell asleep around dawn and woke up a day-and-a-half later.

He loved being up in the high country and in the forest. He was sixteen and had just two years left at school, and he had to decide what he was going to do for the rest of his life. While making fire-breaks and sucking in the clean mountain air, he thought long and hard about his future. He wondered if he should go to college, or find a job. 'I hadn't any definite ideas,' he said. 'Kids around my age were making their plans. They were going to be doctors or lawyers or dentists or were taking business courses.'

Although he didn't know what he wanted to do, he knew what he *didn't* want. 'I couldn't see myself clerking or arguing court cases or peering down somebody's throat all day. What I wanted was an outdoors job.'

He admired those of his friends who knew what they wanted to do. 'I had a friend who always wanted to be a dentist from the time he was eight years old. He went ahead and worked his way through by bartending at night and working in restaurants after school. I never saw my father in a specific profession and so I was never really raised with the idea that you grow up thinking you want to be a druggist or a physician or whatever.'

He'd even decided that a musical career wasn't for him, although when he was seventeen he landed a job playing piano at the Omar Club in Oakland. But he didn't earn any money. 'I got all the beer I could handle and all my meals.'

In 1948, at the age of eighteen he left school with a satisfactory academic record and a fine athletic record. But the idea of lumberjacking appealed to him. He'd heard that there were good prospects in lumbering in Oregon, and when his family moved to Seattle, he decided it was time to take off on his own. His father was supportive. 'I guess Dad thought a little drifting around would be good for me. He helped me with some ideas.'

He packed his bags again and drove off to Springville, Oregon.

2

Greetings from the President

Clint spent the next year lumberjacking near Springfield for the Weyerhauser Company, as well as working in their pulp mill. It was a rigorously tough job but with very good pay. Unfortunately there was no town nearby in which to spend his well earned salary; the nearest place was Eugene several miles away. 'Around Eugene, in the Willamette Valley, it's beautiful,' he said. 'But in the winter it socks in. You can go six or seven months without seeing blue sky. Finally the dampness got to me and I moved on.'

He 'bummed around,' doing three or four other different jobs in the Seattle area, close to his family. 'I worked for Bethlehem Steel on the graveyard shift, in front of a furnace.' It was a short-lived job. He worked as a lifeguard for King County, and then as a swimming instructor in Renton. He also worked at the Boeing plant in Renton in the parts department, a particularly non-stimulating job for the outdoors type; he received orders for parts which he supplied and filled out the relevant forms. It was enough to make him work for the Color Shake organization driving trucks, which was a little more to his liking.

This 'bumming around' actually helped him later as an actor, giving him the kind of insight into people and their motivations that no drama school could have supplied. 'I think it helped me judge what audiences like in the way of entertainment as an escape from that kind of existence. I believe that's probably the secret to my whole career. The choice of material – and the judgement of whether an audience will buy the material – is what makes an actor, or a director, a success.'

At the time, however, he was frustrated with the constant drifting from one job to the next with no prospects for the future, and he decided that he would go back to school and major in music. Uncle Sam had different plans though for Clint Eastwood, and just as he had satisfied himself about his future, he received his call-up papers in 1949; or as he put it, 'I got this notice from the Government: "Greetings from the President." '

Checked by medics, shorn by the Army barber and supplied with a uniform, Private Eastwood was sent off for basic training at Ford Ord for sixteen weeks. The rigours of Boot Camp were a lot tougher on most of the other recruits than they were on the fit Eastwood. It also supplied him with a basic knowledge which he found useful later in life when he starred in war films and Westerns. Said Eastwood, 'I didn't realize then that the knowledge of guns I picked up in the army was going to be so valuable to me later.'

The Korean War was on and the United States and Great Britain were shipping their soldiers overseas to fight a war which a lot of Americans, as well as Britons, believed wasn't theirs. Eastwood expected to be among the forces fighting in Korea, a prospect he objected to.

'Is it best to bring up a child and not discuss war, and have wars anyway?' wonders Eastwood. 'Or discuss it and *still* have wars. Okay, so I shoot, and I own some guns, but that's just my little thing. I don't like the idea of getting killed – of *anybody* getting killed, but especially *me*. I'm against war, *period*. When I was in the Army I was against the Korean War.'

Learning to handle guns didn't prove particularly useful to Eastwood while he was actually in the army as they seemed to have other ideas for him. Not that they made it clear to him, as he watched his buddies being shipped off to war while he gratefully remained at Fort Ord. So he decided to take his fate into his own hands when he heard that they were looking for swimming instructors at the camp pool. He promptly volunteered, telling them that he was a great swimmer and had taught swimming in Renton. He got the job. 'When we started out, there was this buddy of mine and me, a master sergeant and four sergeants over us, and a lieutenant over them.'

His main task was to prevent the recruits from drowning during their initial swimming tests. Anyone who sank was pulled out by him. Gradually, his buddy, the master sergeant, the four sergeants and the lieutenant were shipped off to Korea.

He considered himself lucky not to go, as about ninety per cent of his company were shipped off to war. When Tom Snyder asked him if he had felt lucky not to be getting shot at, Eastwood replied, 'Oh yeah, I thought about that every night.'

The Army seemed to be running short of swimming instructors because they seemed agreeable to Eastwood's idea of running the pool himself. He told the captain, 'Look, I'm only a private, but I think I can handle this swimming pool thing.'

'Well, I don't even know how to swim,' said the captain, 'so go ahead and run it. You're wearing a sweatshirt so nobody will know you're just a private.'

So Eastwood found himself in charge of the pool, and then found four other men to work for him so that they had a decent swimming instruction programme running smoothly. 'I was a private with a swimming pool, wearing khakis and a sweatshirt, and a year and a half later I was a corporal.'

During this time he met a number of actors whose careers had been interrupted by National Service, including Martin Milner, Norman Bartold and David Janssen. Janssen once told me, 'I think Clint was a little fascinated by people like myself who were actors before we were soldiers. Like most people, he was interested in our work, and I guess that had some effect on his decision to become an actor when he got out the Army.

'I remember Clint. He lived in a hut down by the swimming pool, and he wore shorts and a T-shirt. I kinda thought he had a pretty good deal there.'

When I asked Janssen if he and the other soldiers resented Eastwood's somewhat cushy job while they were off fighting a war, he replied, 'Resent it? Hell, no. Given half the chance I'd bet we'd have all swapped places with him.'

When Eastwood was able, he spent weekends with his family in Seattle. One weekend there, he found himself in a fix when he became stranded with no money to pay for the fare back to camp. He'd hoped to find a lift back at the local Navy air base, but there were no military flights going anywhere near Fort Ord. With just a few hours to go before he would be on a charge of absent-without-leave, he discovered that a torpedo bomber was leaving for San Francisco. He asked the pilot for a lift, but was told, 'Sorry, buddy, I've no room for you.'

Eastwood persevered. The pilot pointed out that not only was there no room but it would be illegal for him to hitch a ride. Eastwood still persisted, turning on every ounce of charm he possessed, until the pilot allowed him on board. The only space big enough to hold Eastwood was in the cramped radar compartment in the tail.

They took off and Eastwood breathed a sigh of relief now that he was on his way. As the plane climbed to 6,000 feet, the pressure of his body against the door caused it to suddenly spring open. There was a great rush of air as the pressure tried to suck him out to certain death. He managed to grab a part of the structure and, finding a strap, he was able to lasso the door handle, pulling it shut. Then, to his horror, he found that the handle had broken. He held onto the strap as the door fought to open itself.

He reached for the intercom and told the pilot to return to base, only to find the intercom wasn't working properly; he could receive messages from the pilot, but the pilot couldn't hear him. Shortly after, the pilot told Eastwood to put on his oxygen mask. That was when he found that his oxygen mask wasn't working. He cried in vain on the intercom that he had no oxygen, but the plane rose higher. It grew colder and Eastwood began to believe that he would now freeze to death. He began to black out.

Unfortunately for the pilot, though luckily for Eastwood, the pilot's oxygen mask didn't work either, so he dropped down under the clouds allowing Eastwood some semblance of consciousness. Below was dense fog and, fearing he might hit a mountain or land on a town, the pilot turned out to sea. The plane soared along the coast at just a few hundred feet. Just as it seemed that matters couldn't get any worse, the engines began to cut out and Eastwood heard the pilot's voice on the intercom saying, 'Am experiencing engine failure. Will bring the plane down in shallow water.'

'Shit, I've no life jacket,' cried Eastwood.

The plane dropped lower, gliding close to the choppy Pacific. It skipped over the surface of the water and then came to a sudden halt as the nose dipped down into the sea and the tail rose up.

Eastwood now pushed open the door that he'd battled to keep shut, and scrambled on to the wing. The pilot joined him. They could see nothing through the fog, so they made an educated guess which way the coast lay, and dived in as the plane sank out of sight. In the dense fog they lost each other. Eastwood's ability to swim well was now a life-saver for himself. It took about an hour for him to reach the coast, but he found his way barred by a pool of jellyfish. He carefully manoeuvred his way through them, avoiding the paralysing stings, and then found himself battling against a heavy undertow. Totally exhausted, he managed to drag himself ashore, then passed out. He then came to, finding himself lying on a flat rock. He had no recollection of getting there.

Struggling to his feet, he began searching among the rocks for the pilot, calling for him as he waded in the shallows. But there was no sign of him. He could only hope that the pilot had managed to make it to land further up the coast.

In the distance he saw the lights of a radio communications relay station, and headed for it. It was a five-mile hike, at the end of which he burst in through the door of the station, cold, hungry, damp and looking like a man who'd looked death in the face. Or, as one of the men at the station told him, 'You look like a survivor from the *Titanic.*' He never did discover the pilot's fate.

During a day off, Clint took himself to the village of Carmel, ten miles away. Its beautiful white beaches and immaculate streets struck him as being the perfect place to live. He determined to settle down there if he could ever afford it. But he had no idea he'd one day be the Mayor of the town.

His jaunts into civilian areas were, more often than not, outings in search of a few beers and a woman. He was no longer the shy, introverted lanky kid of a few years earlier, but a muscular, six foot four, good looking man radiating an innate charm that was irresistible to girls. His close friend of many years, and one-time business partner, Robert Daley said, 'He was always the type that people would turn around and stare at. I know from experience that in the days when he was totally unknown, he was still noticed by people.'

His taste in women seemed to run to blondes, although he insisted he didn't fall for bimbos. He said, 'I'm not turned on by a dumb chick - for anything. What's that old joke? "What do you talk about afterwards?" There's an awful lot of afterward, very little during. Before and after, there have to be many other things. And I think friendship is important.'

To help finance his nights out with girls, he worked behind the bar at the non-commissioned officers' club. He also moonlighted at nights by carting sacks in the warehouse of the local sugar plant, a job which could have led to charges if the Army had found out.

Around this time, something happened to him that came close to the scenario of *Play Misty for Me* (in which a woman becomes obsessed with him and insanely jealous). Eastwood has never spoken of this episode of his life at great length, but has said, 'The girl who wrote [*Misty*] based it on a real-life story, on a girl she once knew. It appealed to me, too, because I've had this situation happen to me in my own life, this thing of having somebody clinging and clutching at you, not allowing you to breathe.

'The *Misty* sort of thing happened to me when I was very young, 21 years old, before I was married. Sick jealousy isn't confined to any particular age, but most people I know, male or female, who have gone through that type of insane jealousy had it happen at a very young age.'

His definition of insane jealousy is 'when people start threatening to kill themselves and do all kinds of silly things.'

One weekend, his friend Don Kincaid - the one who later became a dentist - convinced him to forgo his Seattle trip for once and come with him to San Francisco where he had a girl friend who was a student at Berkeley, who had a friend, Maggie Johnson, an attractive blonde who was much admired by the campus males. As a favour to her friend, Maggie agreed to be Eastwood's blind date. The two buddies arrived in San Francisco on a warm day in May and went to the sorority house at Berkeley, and there Clint first set eyes on Maggie. In her he found everything he liked in a woman.

'Physical attraction is the basis of so many young relationships,' he said, 'though I don't think it was in ours. I mean, we were physically attracted, but we also had everything in common. We both liked the same kind of music - jazz and classical, like Bach - and we'd go to the same kind of places.'

Like Clint, she loved the great outdoors, and she had a great sense of humour which especially appealed to him. 'There was nothing phoney about her,' he said. They began meeting regularly, which may have surprised some who knew Maggie to be an intelligent type of girl who wasn't usually particularly struck by the tall, lean and handsome type. What appealed to Maggie about Clint was his soft-spoken manner, his charm and a quiet wisdom which she found in him. In June she graduated from Berkeley and went to work for Industria Americana, a small firm based in Los Angeles supplying automobile parts.

Toward the end of Eastwood's Army service, a film unit from Universal Studios set up camp near Fort Ord and began filming. While out on a march, Clint was attracted by what was happening and when the assistant director spotted him, he was struck by what he thought were natural movie star looks. He coaxed Eastwood into coming to meet the director who gave him a script and asked him to read a few lines. There was something in his easy manner that impressed the director who told Clint to look him up when he got out of the Army.

He did. His Army service at an end, he took himself off to Hollywood and called in at Universal Studios, asking to see the director. He was duly informed that the director had moved on. Eastwood promptly gave up the idea of becoming an actor. 'When I came out of the Army, I didn't know what to do, so I figured I'd better fill up some of the holes in my education and enrolled at Los Angeles City College,' he said. He used the money issued to him under the GI Bill to enrol and took to studying Business Administration. It was a course which he admitted to being 'for any student who hasn't the faintest idea of what he wants to do when he graduates.'

He found himself an apartment in Beverly Hills and subsidized his rent by managing the whole block for the landlord. Now close to Maggie, he took her off to Newport beach, often mingling there with a crowd of friends. He began enjoying a whole new life on the beach - the kind had by every Californian kid according to the Hollywood beach-party pictures - playing basketball and partying round campfires. He and Maggie also went to jazz and classical concerts, the cinema and the theatre.

While going to school he worked at a Signal Oil station on Santa Monica Boulevard, and delivered cars to General Service Studios where he spotted film stars.

This constant exposure to the film industry got him thinking again about going into movies. He was stimulated further when he met up with some of his actor friends from the Army, including David Janssen, who had returned to their profession. 'I was curious about it,' said Eastwood, 'I wondered what it would be like.'

His curiosity finally got the better of him. 'There was a stills photographer named Irving Lasper - he's dead now - who was a friend of mine, and he tried to encourage me to become an actor.' Lasper worked at Universal. 'I went to see him one afternoon and he introduced me around. He called a guy at the studio and said he should run some film on me.'

It was Arthur Lubin, who would direct Eastwood in some of his early films, who gave him his screen test. 'There are two types of film test,' Eastwood explained. 'There is the kind where you do a scene and they shoot it like it's part of a movie or there's the kind where you just stand in front of the cameras and look like an idiot. I did the latter kind.

'When I saw it I thought it was awful. I had never seen myself on film before. I had to stand in an office set and just walk around. They were talking to me off camera trying to get different expressions, but the only expression I could register was one of stark terror.'

To his total surprise, the studio called him the next day and asked him if he'd be interested in their training programme. They said they'd pay him $75 a week. 'That was an enormous amount, it seemed to me then,' he said. 'I'd been going to school on the GI Bill at $110 a month, plus working in the afternoons at a gas station and night managing the apartment house I lived in, so $75 a week sounded great. They signed me up as a contract player - which was a little lower than working in the mail room.

'I still don't know what they saw in me.'

His prospects might have not looked too good, but when he proposed to Maggie she accepted, and they married on 19 December 1953, just six months after meeting.

3
The Universal Years

'That first year of marriage was terrible,' Eastwood told *Photoplay* in 1963. 'If I had to go through it again I think I'd be a bachelor the rest of my life. Just knowing myself like I think I do, to have to start over from scratch...I'd really hate to do it again.

'It's so foreign, you know, moving in together, having to trip over somebody else's things and so forth. Never having lived with someone before, I didn't know what to expect. I lived at home with my family, but it wasn't the same. I just wasn't used to having to share my life with anyone.

'I'd had room mates before, but if two guys are sharing an apartment, each has his own things, and you stay out of each other's way. With a wife, it's another thing again.'

He was full of misgivings about marriage. 'I liked doing things when I wanted to do 'em. I didn't want any interference. I just didn't like to be pressed down, or having to go out of my way to cater to somebody, which I don't do. I'm not going to be that way. I never have been. You see, I'm a person who's never been gifted with a particularly easy going temperament and I have lived by myself since I was about seventeen years old.'

He made it clear to Maggie that there were going to be limitations to their marriage partnership. 'I wasn't about to give up my life entirely. I was willing to enter into the partnership, but I wasn't necessarily willing to sell myself, give myself away, you know – be dominated in any form.' His fear was of becoming totally 'submerged by the whole thing, so that being married was everything in the world. Because it isn't everything in the world. The whole marriage relationship consisted of learning about one another. One thing Mag had to learn about me was that I was going to do as I pleased. She had to accept that – because if she didn't, we wouldn't be married.'

All this may make one wonder why Maggie married him at all. But she is very much a bright, capable woman, never given to being particularly docile, possessing a high spirit and a mind and will of her own. While Clint's attitude towards marriage might have been enough to send some prospective brides running tearfully back to their mothers' arms, Maggie recognized Clint's need for independence and for the space he needed. She didn't see it as being any kind of a hindrance, and the fact that their marriage lasted as long as it did was due probably more to her understanding and tolerance than anything else. Eastwood agreed, and said, in 1973, 'I'd say I'd have to give Mag a lot of the credit. We were married very young. I don't really recommend getting married that young. But you can't say exactly – the right age for one person isn't the right age for another. The luck, I guess, is in getting the right partner. There are so many things that can go wrong. It had to be something of a crap shoot.'

A great deal of the trouble during that first year was due to Eastwood's insistence on being 'the man of the house.'

'I'm going to run the show, you know,' he told *Photoplay*. 'That's pretty well laid out. That's cut and dried. She's stuck with it. A man either runs the show or not. If I'm staying home and she's supporting me or something, then I shouldn't be running the show.'

Considering how their marriage started out, with Clint on a low income, this wasn't perhaps the best law for Eastwood to lay down. 'It was tough at first,' Maggie recalled of the days, weeks and months following their marriage. 'We went through periods when Clint was out of work for weeks at a time. It's why I took up modelling – swimsuits and sportwear mostly – not as a career, but simply because we needed the money.'

As Eastwood recalled, 'She helped support us.' She worked for Industria Americana, as well as for swimming suit manufacturers Caltex and Catalina, as a model. Recalled Eastwood, 'She was a good bathing suit type.'

Trying to get his points across to Maggie without either of them heading for a divorce lawyer wasn't accomplished without some fireworks. The sparks flew when Maggie discovered that Clint hated the idea of his wife opening any mail addressed to him. 'Women have a fantastic curiosity,' he said. 'This is a thing that has always been a bug with me. It's not a question of getting anything special. Probably most of the time it's just bills or something, but I just don't like to have anybody open my mail. Mag did it twice, and then we put the ceiling back in the building.'

There was a difference of opinion between the couple over his newly chosen career. 'Everybody recommended against it, including Mag,' he said. 'She didn't want any part of it. She was always reading in the columns about actors and actresses getting divorced. I guess she didn't want her marriage exposed to that kind of thing.'

Having determined to become an actor, Eastwood began attending the studio's drama classes. Established actors would occasionally come and give the students the benefit of their experiences. Among these was David Janssen who had been under contract to Universal since 1952, reviving his screen career with one of the studio's colourful swashbucklers, *Yankee Buccaneer*. He and Eastwood would work together in a couple of films. Another visitor was Marlon Brando, then one of the top box office stars. He could have had no idea that one of these students would become an even greater movie star, especially since the majority of Eastwood's class mates never amounted to anything. Starlets being groomed at that time included Jane Howard, Myrna Hansen and Dani Crayne, none of whom became a major star and only played small parts in several of the studio's grade-B movies.

Although not a paupers' studio, Universal was nevertheless struggling. Following the war, audiences became a lot more choosy about what they paid to see. By 1946 the cost of a cinema ticket in America had almost doubled since the outbreak of war, and in an attempt to give the public their money's worth, Universal merged with International Pictures in 1946, thus becoming Universal-International under the leadership of Leo Spitz and William Goetz. They decreed that no feature would run less than seventy minutes, and that serials, B-features and Western programmers would be axed while more films were to be shot in Technicolor. Unable to compete with MGM, who boasted having more stars at their studio than there were in heaven, Universal-International maintained a relatively small group of major stars, including Donald O'Connor, Deanna Durbin, Abbott and Costello, and Marjorie Main and Percy Kilbride as the continuingly popular Ma and Pa Kettle (there were nine Ma and Pa Kettle comedies in all).

But in 1949 the studio was deeply in the red. Budgets were cut and the number of films reduced. Deanna Durbin's career came to an end. A new era at the studio was ushered in with studio manager Edward Muhl taking control of the studio's output and effectively halting its decline. Into Muhl's reign came Clint Eastwood as a hopeful young actor. It was not a good time for young hopefuls in the studio's drama class. Universal had a small crop of young stars it had already spent much time and money on grooming, such as Tony Curtis, Rock Hudson and Jeff Chandler. There was little room for any more. Nevertheless, after his initial six months' training course, the studio felt Clint was ready to work and his contract was renewed.

He became a member of a large group of contract players who all prayed for their big break. 'You always hoped for any kind of part in a picture, small, medium or large,' said Eastwood. He was one of about fifteen male contract players. There were far more women – about forty.

Oddly enough, considering that Eastwood was the perfect cowboy type, being so tall and rangy, it didn't occur to them to put him into Westerns. There were a number of horse operas coming out of Universal, although they had room, and funds, for only one regular cowboy star, and that was Audie Murphy. However, James Stewart, while making fewer Westerns at the studio than Murphy, made better ones, usually with director Anthony Mann, establishing Stewart as a leading saddle star. Joel McCrea had been a popular cowboy star at the studio, but just as Eastwood was beginning there, McCrea said *adios* to Universal. Other contract stars, including Hudson, Curtis and Chandler, all made Westerns, and why it didn't occur to Universal to try Eastwood out in the saddle is a mystery. Just what to do with Clint Eastwood was a question the studio found hard to answer. In an effort to find a solution they put him into several different kinds of films.

The first of these was *Revenge of the Creature* in 1954, a sequel to the 3-D horror flick *The Creature from the Black Lagoon*. Apart from the Gill-man, the star of the film was John Agar, better known as the former husband of Shirley Temple than for anything else. He had in fact begun his career as a regular supporting actor to John Wayne in films like *Fort Apache*, *She Wore A Yellow Ribbon* and *Sands of Iwo Jima*, but failed to cash in on these successes and was swiftly relegated to below average routine pictures, of which *Revenge of the Creature* was probably the worst. The leading lady was Lori Nelson who came from the Universal stable of starlets. Her career survived only a further two years following her role as the Beauty to the Gill-man's Beast.

It was not an auspicious start to Clint Eastwood's career but he was nevertheless excited when the studio sent him to meet the film's producer, William Alland, who had made the original creature feature. Alland was looking for someone to play a lab technician, and he thought Eastwood would fill the role adequately. Clint, delighted to get his first acting role, followed Alland down onto the film's set to meet the director, Jack Arnold, who had also directed the original creature film. To his surprise, Eastwood discovered upon meeting Arnold that the director hated the role Eastwood was to play. In fact, Arnold hated the scene and he seemed to hate William Alland. An argument ensued between the producer and director, and before long they were throwing punches at each other.

The next day Eastwood turned up on the set to do his single scene. All it demanded of his acting talents was to enter a lab in search of some missing white mice, only to discover them in his pocket. Arnold was still seething from the day before, but told Clint, 'Go ahead and do the scene. I'll shoot it but I don't like it.'

This tension, along with the fact this was his debut, was enough to turn Clint into a nervous wreck, but he went through his paces. Arnold took about five takes, and Eastwood left feeling that he'd be lucky if the scene was included in the final cut. To his happy surprise, it was. 'It was pretty dumb stuff,' he said of it, 'but I guess they were short on time and just wanted to pad the script.' In fact, the film barely ran more than eighty minutes. It emerged as the comedy of the year.

There must have been something about Eastwood that pleased Jack Arnold because he had him back for another small role in another creature feature, *Tarantula*, again produced by William Alland. John Agar was again the star and this time the creature of the title role was a giant spider, and the obligatory Universal starlet part was taken by Mara Corday. Interestingly, Corday's career, typically, came to a virtual end when Universal dropped her a couple of years later, but was revived again in 1977 when Clint Eastwood cast her in *The Gauntlet*. When Eastwood first read the script of *Tarantula*, he was enthusiastic about playing the part of the jet pilot who bombs the giant spider that terrorizes Arizona. But then, as he said, 'I was enthusiastic about anything that would increase my experience.'

When he arrived on the set he was given a helmet, goggles and a mask and suddenly realized that he would be totally unrecognizable in the scene. He didn't even so much as see a real jet plane. It was purely a mock-up on a sound stage with back screen projection. Films like *Revenge of the Creature* and *Tarantula* turn up often on American television, and have in a sense become famous as Clint Eastwood movies. 'My parts ranged from one-liners to four-liners,' he says of those early films, 'but to look at some of the billings in *TV Guide* these days, you'd think I co-starred in those films.'

Universal were making quite a few costume adventures and decided to try Eastwood in one of them, *Lady Godiva*. It starred Maureen O'Hara as the famous eleventh-century lass who had the bare-faced cheek to ride naked through Coventry. But before that much awaited event in this Technicolored adventure, the audience were treated to numerous court intrigues and some swordplay between the Normans and the Saxons. Clint Eastwood found himself playing a Saxon warrior with a very unusual American drawl.

Then came *Francis in the Navy*, the sixth in the hugely successful comedy series featuring Francis the Talking Mule and his human compatriot Donald O'Connor. David Janssen had a major supporting role as did Eastwood's classmate, Jane Howard. For the first time, Eastwood was given on-screen billing, and there followed several other films which he's all but forgotten about.

'I think I played in about thirteen or fourteen films over the year and a half I was there. None of them were top-rank movies. But I learned a lot. There were classes every day, and I went to them, and I'd hang out on sets, behind the scenery somewhere, trying to be unobtrusive and watch people operate.'

Despite the often dreadful results that came out on screen, Eastwood found it was all invaluable experience. 'I think you learn from seeing a bad movie as much as you do from seeing a good movie. It's just like acting in a picture with a bad director. It gives you some point of reference, some comparison, so that when you meet someone who is half-way adequate, you see what makes the difference.'

His future suddenly began to look uncertain in the movies when Universal decided he wasn't worth the amount of money they'd promised him. His salary had risen to $100 a week after his first six months, with a promise of a further increase by $25 six months later. Those six months were up and Eastwood was summoned to the office of some studio executive who told him they didn't feel he was of any value to them at $125. 'But we are willing to keep you on at your current salary,' he was told.

'At first I was mad, of course, and I said, "What the hell, if they can't give me a raise, I'll take a hike." Then I decided I'd better hang in there another six months and get a little more experience.'

Around this time, Rock Hudson was becoming firmly established as a star of glossy 'women's pictures,' one of which was *Never Say Goodbye*, a remake of *This Love of Ours*. Hudson played a Californian physician in search of his long-lost wife. David Janssen had a major supporting role, while way down far below him in the credits was Clint Eastwood as another laboratory technician.

'The director decided I'd look more like a laboratory technician if I wore glasses,' recalled Clint, 'so they gave me about ten pairs to try on, and I picked out the pair that I thought suited me.'

Upon seeing Clint in his glasses, Hudson said, 'Where's mine?'

'You're the leading man,' said the director, 'you don't wear glasses.'

'Well, I think I ought to wear them,' said Hudson, and began trying on all the glasses Eastwood had rummaged through. Liking none of them he took Clint's pair, tried them on and decided he would wear them. 'So he got the glasses and I didn't,' recalled Clint.

If he figured his future in movies looked bleak, he didn't show it. He said, 'The number of people who had faith in me that I'd make it in show business, I could name easily on one hand – and have a few fingers left over.'

At last Universal decided he would be perfect for a part in a Western, and he appeared, albeit briefly, in *Star in the Dust*. The cast was headed by John Agar, Richard Boone, Leif Erickson and Mamie Van Doren, and was shot in just twelve days. The result, however, under the direction of Charles Haas was a superior B Western in which all the action took place between sun-up and sundown as Sheriff Agar battled to prevent gunmen from freeing a killer due to be hanged at sundown.

Now earning a hundred dollars a week, Eastwood was able to live up to his own edict of being the man of the house, even though Maggie continued to work. He felt strongly that no man should ever be dominated by his wife. 'Nowadays, it seems a lot of girls come from a family where the mother might be the dominating factor,' he said in 1963.

'They just grow up to think this is the way it's supposed to be. Then, when they marry some guy and he rebels – they can't understand it. They think something's wrong with *him*.'

His opinion, at least in 1963, about women who do take charge would not have pleased feminists. 'I definitely feel I would never have been married this long if I had been wishy-washy. When women are running the ship completely, they might think they like it. But really, underneath, they're pretty unsolid about everything. If they feel they're running the show, they wonder "What happens if something goes wrong?" Then they're left by themselves.'

Not that he was a total chauvinist. From the beginning of their married life, they shared the chores. 'She'd come home tired and I'd come home tired, so we'd split it all down the middle. When I had time off, I did the housework. When she had time off, she did it. I'd cook half the meals. It was strictly fifty-fifty, so far as that type of thing went.'

Some of the wrinkles of early marriage were by this time ironed out. Clint was to concede, 'I married young, and there were all the petty hangups. Maybe it would be different today.'

But there were some things that were basic. 'The worst thing is owning people,' he said. 'It brings you down. Clauses. I don't want to be owned by anybody – maybe share, but not owned lock, stock and barrel.'

An important aspect in Eastwood's life was, and remains, the ability to be able to take off on his own. He never got over the deep-seated feeling of being a loner, and the occasional need to be on his own. He also sometimes needed to get away just to calm down, for as he conceded, 'I have a very bad temper, and I do what I want to do. If I want to go somewhere, I go somewhere. If I want her to go, I want her to go. If I don't want her to go, I don't. She can go anywhere she wants to. If she wants to go away for a weekend, she can go. I trust her. If she feels fed up, if she feels like getting away by herself, I'm not so egotistical that I think I'm the greatest person to be around all the time.'

It's fortunate that this need for space was something Maggie agreed with and she took the opportunity to mould her own life. She told *Photoplay* in 1970, 'What Clint really likes in a woman is independence. To have someone who was just a housewife sitting around the house would drag him down. He doesn't want someone around him all the time, watching every move he makes, devoid of all interests except him.

'And I think a woman should have her own interests and not be content to be just involved in the home, cooking, cleaning and dusting. One of the things I do quite well is paint.'

During 1956 Clint came to realize just how much he needed Maggie in his life – if not for every minute of the day – when she became gravely ill with hepatitis. 'She got it very badly,' he recalled. 'About as badly as you can get it without ceasing to exist.' She was treated in hospital, and no matter how late Clint worked, he visited her every evening. He was deeply worried he might lose her and phoned the hospital at all times of the day and night.

Maggie's hospital room was full of the flowers he kept sending. It was a distinctly uncharacteristic thing for him to do. 'I'm not terribly sentimental,' he said. On anniversaries and birthdays, he would buy an expensive present – maybe a Cadillac or mink coat – but he always covered up his emotion by making a joke about how long he expected his present to last her. But it was difficult for him to hide his worry over her illness. 'You don't appreciate some things until they look like they might be shaky,' he said of that time. 'And she was pretty shaky, I guess. When she came out all right, it was pretty good.'

Following her discharge from hospital, she was ordered to convalesce for a year and had to give up both her regular job and her modelling. They now had only Clint's income to live on. Having been on Universal's payroll for a year and a half, the studio decided he wasn't worth even $100 a week to them, and dropped him.

4

The TV Years

All Eastwood had, when he left Universal in 1956, was a few meagre credits to his name and an agent in whom Clint had little faith. 'Everybody knows agents don't give a damn about young unemployed actors,' he said. Fortunately for him, Arthur Lubin, the man who gave him his first screen test, hadn't forgotten him.

Lubin had directed scores of movies, including many of the Abbott and Costello films, and a number of the *Francis* pictures (including the one Eastwood had appeared in). He'd also directed *Lady Godiva*, proving he might not have been one of Hollywood's most prestigious directors, but he was certainly one of the most often employed. He left Universal at the same time Eastwood did and moved over to RKO. Not the wisest move, in retrospect, since the Howard Hughes-owned studio was on its last legs. However, Lubin produced and directed a western, *The First Travelling Saleslady* at RKO. It was a comedy starring Ginger Rogers as a corset designer who finds herself out of work when a Broadway show, featuring her corsets and little else, is closed. With her secretary, played by Carol Channing, she heads out West to try and sell barbed wire to antipathetic Texans. Heading the male contingent were Barry Nelson, David Brian and James Arness. Looking for a handsome cowboy type to supply Carol Channing's love interest, Lubin cast Clint Eastwood, giving him his biggest role up to that time.

The idea for the film, originally intended as a piece of 'Americana' as opposed to a comedy, came from screenwriter Stephen Longstreet. He wrote the original screenplay which was added to by Devery Freeman. Longstreet explained, 'I got the idea from a true item: the law that called for the fencing in of the West – no more open range in certain parts of the country. Ranch owners actually killed a few barb-wire salesmen, or so the story goes. I invented a smart seller who decided to hire sales*women*. The West respected women, didn't it? Fuck 'em, don't hang 'em. My agent sold the idea to RKO and I wrote the screenplay.'

The film earned Eastwood his first press notice. 'Clint Eastwood is very attractive as Carol Channing's beau,' noted the *Hollywood Reporter*. The film, though, was a bomb and just another nail in RKO's coffin. Longstreet explained the reason for the film's failure: 'The director wasn't much of a big-timer – his best credits were the Francis the Talking Mule films. Ginger Rogers, our top-billed star, seemed pleased, but I wasn't sure Carol Channing was for real. The studio seemed to think it needed comedy, and another writer added to my script. Many of us felt what should have been a bit of Americana and history was turning to slapstick.

'I do not think the picture was ever actually released as a major film in theatres. It may have been shown here and there, but I don't recall any reviews or major advertising. It sank without a bubble until TV, where it can now be seen on the Late Shows. It has not improved with age. I would say we can all take group blame: the final overgrown script far from my original, direction, acting, studio-added ideas and casting all helped with kicks in the ass.'

Lubin and RKO had Eastwood back for another supporting role in an engaging children's adventure film, *Escapade in Japan*, playing an American pilot. Filming took Eastwood off to Japan where Lubin photographed the picture very handsomely in Technicolor and Technirama. Clint began to believe he had some kind of future at RKO. But even before the film was finished the news broke that Howard Hughes had decided to close down the studio. There were still a number of films to be completed, as contracts had been signed, but the distribution of these films would be handled, ironically, by Universal-International. *The First Travelling Saleslady* was the last to be released by RKO's own distribution unit.

Unemployment for Eastwood loomed large and ominous. He decided to make a change of direction in his career. 'Television was going pretty good then, so I figured there'd be some opportunities for me,' he said. 'So I got out there and tried the cold world.'

The 'cold world' of freelancing was almost enough to make him want to give up acting. Most actors then considered television was a step down from making movies. But Eastwood considered it a logical step in his career to learn his trade. 'Most of the people in television were doing the newest things,' he said, 'and in TV you had to work twice as fast, twice as hard to get half the credits. I learned a hell of a lot.' He also earned very little money, so to subsidize his irregular income he took to digging swimming pools for the United Pool Company. It's said that in 1957 and 1958 he earned more money digging swimming pools than from acting.

'Digging swimming pools certainly wasn't mentally stimulating,' he said. 'I'd put down my shovel and sneak off in the middle of the day, get to a public phone and call my agent: "Anything? Anything?" '

If he was lucky his agent had a job for him. In fact, Eastwood turned up in many of the most popular TV series of the time, although he only had supporting roles. He appeared in *Navy Log*, *Men of Annapolis*, *Highway Patrol* and *Maverick*. It was his growing reputation as a man of action that kept him in work as an actor. He was more than willing to perform stunts. 'I could ride a motorcycle, jump off a building or some crazy thing,' he said. 'They didn't have to pay for a stunt man. They'd be two or three or four-day jobs, and then I'd be collecting unemployment again or digging more swimming pools. Sometimes I was out of work for up to six months at a time, and I got pretty depressed about it.' Years later, when asked if he was against unemployment insurance, he replied, 'No. I've collected it often enough. Although when I see what it is today (in 1973) – something like $85 a week – I wonder what the hell I'm doing working! But I suppose with inflation it's not worth much more than the 20-something a week I used to get.'

While digging pools he observed the lives of working men. 'On those kinds of jobs you run into some wild characters,' he said. 'I'd like to make a movie about some of them.' His observations while digging pools came to an end when, one day, his friend George Fargo was fired. Eastwood began taking off his work overalls. 'What are you doing?' asked the boss.

'Well, George is my friend,' replied Clint, 'and he hasn't got a ride home.'

Eastwood took his friend home and didn't return to work. His days of digging pools were over. Fortunately, he landed a regular role in a series called *West Point*, as one of a number of young cadets at the Military Academy. It was a short-lived series, its failure, in Eastwood's opinion, due to the fact that nothing ever happens in real life to West Point cadets. 'They march, go to classes, play football, study, and go to bed,' he said.

In 1957 he was given his biggest part to date, in a minor western, *Ambush at Cimarron Pass*. He was billed third, after popular cowboy star Scott Brady and unknown starlet Margia Dean. Below Eastwood were billed actors of no renown whatsoever, apart from Irving Balco, then aged 64, who specialized in played doleful simpletons. To add to the total lack of prestige, the film was directed by one Jodie Copelan in something called Regalscope.

The story revolved around a cavalry sergeant, played by Brady, transporting a prisoner across Apache territory. Along the route he meets a band of Confederates, led by Eastwood making a rare appearance as a heavy. With the help of the rebels, Brady bravely fights off the Apaches, leads the men on a seven-day march to the fort and finally fights Eastwood for the attention of Margia Dean. It was, said Eastwood, 'the low point of my movie career,' and added, 'it may have been the worst Western ever made.'

Variety, however, proved more lenient than Eastwood, giving some praise to Copelan's direction in spite of the low budget, and noted that 'fine portrayals also come from Margia Dean, Frank Gerstle, Clint Eastwood and Dirk London.'

Since it was produced at a quality studio, Twentieth Century-Fox, Eastwood could have been forgiven for believing that the picture should have been injected with some quality. He discovered just how awful it was when he and Maggie went to see it at their local cinema. He was dumbstruck by the total ineptitude of the whole thing. The production values were cheap and the photography uneven. After ten minutes, he slumped down in his seat in the hope that nobody would recognize him.

(The film returned to haunt him during the sixties when it was reissued with top billing given to Eastwood, following the success of the *Dollars* films.)

He made his next film, and his last for seven years, for Warner Bros. It was *Lafayette Escadrille*, directed by tough old Hollywood boot William Wellman, one of the most colourful characters in the film colony who enjoyed a hero's status because of his roisterous personality and the memory of his World War One exploits. He had joined the French army's Foreign Legion as an ambulance driver, and when America entered the war he became an ace pilot with the famed Lafayette Escadrille which became the subject of his last film.

Originally called *C'est la Guerro*, it starred new screen heart-throb Tab Hunter, portraying a true life character and close friend of Wellman's who died in the war. David Janssen and Clint Eastwood played, respectively, real-life heroes Duke Sinclair and George Moseley. However, all the script required of Eastwood was to lend his taciturn presence and he had no significant dialogue.

Once again, the film was much less than Eastwood had hoped for when it was released in 1958. Wellman placed the blame for its failure well and truly on the shoulders of Jack L Warner.

'That dumb Warner, my great hate,' said Wellman, 'he raped my *Lafayette Escadrille*, the story of a very dear friend. I had made it as a tragedy. It was previewed as a tragedy. It was the only preview I ever had where people stood up as the picture ended and said nothing. Then there was a beat and a beat and a beat and then they suddenly started cheering. And that dirty, rotten bastard decided that killing Tab Hunter was impossible. At the time, he'd made a record that had sold two million copies, so they changed it to a happy ending and called it *Lafayette Escadrille*. It didn't have a damn thing to do with *the* Lafayette Escadrille. All the guys that were still alive from the Escadrille thought I was nuts. I shot the happy ending, came away and went home and said to my wife, "Dotty, I'm tired. I've worked too hard and I made a deal with a man I hate, knowing he's wrong. I'm never going to make another picture." And I never have.'

As the fifties began drawing to a close, Western series began flooding the television market. By the end of the decade there were thirty Western series being aired on American TV. When CBS announced a new series, *Rawhide*, based on the great cattle drives of the 1870s, Eastwood's agent tried to get him a screen test to play the leading role of the trail boss. They told the agent they were looking for someone older than Eastwood.

It so happened that one day he went to the CBS studios to have coffee with friend Sonia Chernus who worked in the CBS script department. According to one source, it was Sonia Chernus who took Clint to see Robert Sparks, executive producer of *Rawhide*, who in turn introduced Eastwood to Charles Marquis Warren, creator of the series. That was when Eastwood learned they were looking for a second, younger, lead for the show.

But according to Eastwood, 'It was a fluke. I'd been trying for months to get a screen test at the studios, but was getting nowhere. I went down and visited a friend, Sonia Chernus, who was in the story department at CBS-TV. Anyway, we were sitting there talking by this coffee wagon in the basement at CBS and this guy came up and said, "Are you an actor?" And I said, "Yeah." He said, "What have you done?" So I listed a line of credits, increasing the importance of the roles by about fifty per cent, praying to God the guy would never ask to see *Ambush at Cimarron Pass*. Which, of course, he did. I was taking the whole thing kind of lightly because my agent had told me the lead had to be older than me – about 39 or 40. So the man – I didn't know who the hell he was – called me into an office and another guy came in wearing old clothes. Looked like he'd just been pushing a broom in the back room. I didn't know whether he was going to sweep under the chair or what.'

The 'cleaner' turned out to be Charles Marquis Warren. Eastwood continued to play it cool and asked, 'So what's the lead like?'

'Well, there are two leads,' replied Warren, 'and one is a young guy in his early twenties.'

Clint recalled, 'My agent wasn't bright enough to find that out. So I started perking up, straightening out the wrinkles in my T-shirt – I was wearing Levis – and finally the guy said, "Well, we'll get in contact with you." I kind of half wrote it off because I figured once they'd seen *Ambush at Cimarron Pass* that'd be the end of it.'

That very afternoon Eastwood received a call from the studio, telling him to come down and make a screen test. He did, and followed it with a further screen test the next morning. 'The big wheels at CBS liked it,' he recalled, 'and I was picked, and Eric Fleming was picked for the other lead. That was a great day in my life. The money looked to me as if I'd be in a league with Howard Hughes!'

A great day it might have been, but according to his friend of some years, Bob Daley, who had been his neighbour during his days under contract to Universal, Eastwood was hardly jumping for joy. Daley went over to congratulate Eastwood but couldn't get an answer at his apartment door. Then he went outside and discovered Eastwood washing one of his two old cars – 'never more than one of them would run at any given moment' – dressed in his old clothes and behaving as though it were any other day. 'Congratulations on getting the TV role,' Daley told him. According to Daley, Eastwood just shrugged it all off. 'He thought it was just too good to be true and wouldn't count on it.'

Eric Fleming, who was to play trail boss Gil Favor, was, like Eastwood (playing ramrod Rowdy Yates), relatively unknown and CBS were relying on a succession of major guest stars to attract audiences. It was thought that they could either make a single pilot show and air it before deciding whether or not to go ahead with the series, or take the risk and film thirteen episodes. While the studio executives thrashed it out over a period of some weeks, Eastwood and Fleming were kept on tenterhooks.

Finally the decision was made to go ahead with the thirteen episodes and the cast and crew were transported to Arizona for two months' work. Rodeo cowboys were hired to portray the hired hands and thousands of cattle were rounded up to give the series a taste of authenticity. For two months Eastwood enjoyed the routine of film-making day after day and the opportunity to live the outdoors life. He and Fleming became firm friends. The storyline had the herd being moved from Texas to Sedalia, Missouri with plenty of opportunity for incidents along the way. In fact, each episode was titled I*ncident of the* ... or I*ncident at the* ... The drovers were all veterans from the Civil War, having fought for the Confederacy.

With the completion of the first ten episodes, disaster struck. The unit was recalled to Hollywood where CBS announced to the stunned cast and crew that they were shelving the series. 'Here was my career,' said Clint, 'lying in the basement of CBS because the word was that hour-long shows were out.' It's possible that CBS also had cold feet because of the immense competition from all the other Western series saturating air time.

In a fit of depression, Eastwood and Maggie caught a train from Los Angeles to go and visit his parents who had moved from Seattle back to Oakland. En route a telegram arrived for Clint informing him that the series had sold and he was to be ready to report for work. He recalled that to celebrate he and Maggie 'did a little champagne trick and yelled a lot – I stuck my head out of the window and shouted a lot of profane things!'

Work on *Rawhide* continued and the first episode was aired in America on Friday 9 January 1959 at eight o'clock. The series was highlighted by certain trademarks to make it accessible to audiences: the theme song written by Dimitri Tiomkin, who had written the score for *High Noon* as well as countless other films, and sung by Frankie Lane; the familiar pre-credit sequence in which Gil Favor looks out over the vast herd and yells, 'Head 'em up, move 'em out.' *Rawhide* was a hit.

As the series progressed, a succession of star names guested included Lon Chaney, Julie Harris, Brian Donlevy, Shelley Berman, Peter Lorre, Margaret O'Brien, Victor McLaglen, Kim Hunter, Leslie Nielsen, Vera Miles, Cesar Romero, Dan O'Herlihy, Woody Strode, Robert Culp, John Cassavetes, Jack Lord, Jock Mahoney, Dan Duryea, Ralph Bellamy, Richard Basehart, Burgess Meredith, Ed Wynn, Barbara Stanwyck, James Coburn, Walter Pidgeon, Keenan Wynn, Claude Rains, Frankie Avalon and even title-song singer Frankie Lane.

Years later Eastwood noted that in his movies, 'I haven't worked with many actresses. Once in a while on *Rawhide* you'd get an actress who'd be looking in the make-up table all the time. But we did have some sensational actresses like Julie Harris and Geraldine Page.'

Among the directors were R G Bud Springsteen, who began in the business directing Wild Bill Elliott and Allan Lane Westerns for Republic, Jack Arnold from Eastwood's early Universal Monster Movies, Tom Post who cut his directorial teeth on numerous TV shows – *Wagon Train*, *Gunsmoke*, *Peyton Place* – and B-Westerns of the fifties, and Andrew V McLaglen. McLaglen, son of actor Victor, had worked as assistant director to Budd Boetticher and John Ford and had turned out his own first feature, *Gun the Man Down* in 1956. He had signed a long-term contract with CBS-TV and directed episodes from numerous series, including *Have Gun Will Travel* and *Gunsmoke*.

Of his stint on *Rawhide*, McLaglen told me, 'I directed several episodes from *Rawhide* and even did an episode in which I directed my own father who was the guest star for that week. I did two or three of the first ten episodes after which the studio decided to shelve the series because there were too many Westerns on TV. Then the word got around that this was a superior cowboy show, and it was put back on the schedule.

'At that time Clint Eastwood was known only for *Rawhide*, but he was absolutely perfect for the role. He could ride a horse well enough and he wasn't afraid to try a few stunts, although he couldn't do too many because he was the major co-star and couldn't afford to get injured. Even when he wasn't on call for a scene, he'd be hanging around, watching, and I guess even then he must have been thinking about directing films.'

Working with so many directors was bound to teach Eastwood a great deal. But being interested in all aspects of film-making, working on *Rawhide* was invaluable. 'When you do 250 hours of television,' he said, 'you learn what makes one prop man good and another fair and another lousy, and what makes one cameraman better than another one. You learn about leadership, how one week a crew can move very fast and efficiently and next week drag. About ninety per cent of the time, it's the fault of the director. And you just store those things up in your head.'

Unlike a lot of actors who get their break in TV, become big stars and try, not always successfully, to break out and do other things, Eastwood was happy to stay the eight-year course to learn everything he could. It was also a steady job, which he valued. 'Acting is strictly a feast or famine business. You are either collecting unemployment and knocking on doors or you are making pretty good money. The only thing an actor can do is to try and set himself up so that he can take care of himself later on in life.'

He was proud of the show's historical approach and its lack of glamour. 'We did honest stories,' he said, 'pretty much the way they happened. Now and then we may have rearranged things to heighten the drama. But in general, we respected historical truth.'

As one of TV's favourite good guys, he (or perhaps the studio) cultivated his image in every way, and he even gave his dietary advice in *TV Guide*, saying, 'Stay away from carbohydrates, especially rich desserts. Keep a scale in your bathroom. Proper rest, not midnight to 4 am. Try to be optimistic. Eat fruits and raw vegetables. Take vitamins. Watch the amount of liquids you consume and skip beverages loaded with sugars. Avoid alcohol in excess.' If we didn't know that Eastwood did in fact take care of what he consumed, this might read as just a mere publicity gimmick to heighten his image as Mr Nice Guy.

However, he eventually grew bored with playing the ever-nice, boringly traditional Rowdy Yates for so long. 'I did get awfully tired of playing the conventional "white hat"; The hero who kisses old ladies and dogs and was kind to everybody.'

He has also said, 'Everybody gets sick of it. But I hesitated bitching about it because you get into a series, you hear actors complaining and you think, "Wow, what's this guy bitching about? He's making $50,000 a year!" So I didn't have any real beefs.'

He found that having the security of being in a series each week gave him the flexibility to experiment with the character. If he made a mistake one week, he didn't lose his job but simply made sure he didn't repeat the same mistake. The worst thing was to get three or four bad scripts in a row, but whenever he received a bad script he rewrote bits of it and tried to improve on it. 'If you can take crap and make it adequate, make it palatable to the public, then you feel you've accomplished something,' he said.

To keep himself in shape he worked out every Saturday morning by running and walking alternate hundred yards along the banks of the Los Angeles River. He did press-ups every day, and took care to eat fresh vegetables. But filming *Rawhide* proved exhausting work.

'Six days shooting, Sunday off, then straight into the next one,' he said. 'You'd be learning next week's script while shooting this week's.'

During its early days, the original six-day a week schedule became a seven-day a week schedule. Work began at 5.30 am and often didn't finish until around midnight. Eastwood recalled, 'After a few months of that, I was beat. So was Eric. So were the steers! The horses would have been in the same shape but for the guardian presence of the SPCA. As I crawled to my car one night, I told Eric, "One of the things that gravels me is that there's no Society For The Prevention Of Cruelty To Actors. I'll tell you the truth, my friend, I've had it." '

Fleming told Eastwood, 'I'm glad to hear it because I'm with you.' The following morning Fleming announced to the producer and the director, 'Gentlemen, I'll be through at 6 o'clock this afternoon – and at 6 o'clock *every* afternoon hereafter.'

Eastwood recalled of Fleming, 'There was always something about Eric's delivery – easy, pleasant, laconic – that gave people an idea he could be manipulated. A mistake! That night, when the whistle blew, "Mr Favor" decamped for home. The result was one big *megillah*, but Eric was prepared to take the matter all the way to Washington if necessary. His ruling that work stop at 6.00 pm stuck. That's about all that kept the actors alive.'

Eastwood's friendship with Fleming was a close one. They became stars together and acknowledged each other's contribution to the show. Eastwood said while making *Rawhide*, 'When I hear about the rivalries and animosities and tensions that are standard on a good many of the production stages in Hollywood, I just draw a deep breath and say, "Thank God for Eric Fleming."

'That old smoke-pot about billing. There always seems to be a certain amount of such fumes rolling off the sets. We never had that problem. When the story dealt with Gil Favor's headaches, Eric was given top billing. If the story happened to deal with Rowdy Yates, I got top billing. No sweat.'

He always maintained that without Eric Fleming, the show couldn't survive. He once said, 'The series will last as long as Eric is Gil Favor. When he goes ... ' and he left the sentence unfinished.

Stardom didn't sit easily on him. Even though fan mail was pouring in for him, he dismissed his own importance to the show with, 'Yeah, but I'm the kid in the series. I get patted on the head – if they can reach that high.'

The Eastwoods were then living in a modest ranch-style house at Sherman Oaks overlooking the San Fernando Valley. It had four bedrooms, four bathrooms and an extra room which they had built on. Now financially secure, they bought a second home in a more up-market part of Los Angeles. It included a games room where the couple played table tennis and pool. 'Clint's pretty good at pool and even better at table tennis,' said Maggie.

He appeared on TV chat shows and did countless newspaper interviews, and in the second year of the series, *Rawhide* appeared in the top ten shows of the year. It went on to be shown in almost thirty countries, including Japan where its popularity reached almost fanatical proportions. In 1960 *Rawhide* was at the height of its success. It was also the year Clint's private life became too hot to be made public. Few people knew then of the secret which he kept for almost thirty years.

5

Hellsapoppin Out West

'Sex is a small part of life,' said Clint Eastwood in 1970. 'It's a good thing; *great* – but 99.9 per cent of your life is spent doing other things. And if you accept a guy, you have to make that guy important, so he gets satisfaction. It's selfish – you give love to get love. Women are always saying, "Why wasn't this going for me?" a question of want, want, want. Men, too. Woman's got the toughest role – it's easier to be on the offensive than the defensive.'

As Maggie had learned long before, Eastwood's attitude to sex and women was somewhat cavemanish. Since the day they married, Maggie had accepted that he needed his own space and tolerated his jaunts off on his own. 'I throw my golf clubs in the back of my car and I'm off,' he told *Photoplay*. 'One time, I was tired of working. I jumped in the car and went into the country. I have a nature, when my mind's made up. I just do what I want to do.'

Maggie believed independence in their marriage was important to them both. There were no children in their lives to keep her occupied, and she didn't have to work now that Clint was earning enough to 'run the show,' so she continued to paint and allow him his space. But he wasn't always necessarily taking off to the backwoods or swinging a golf club. He had found another interest in his life. Her name was Roxanne Tunis.

She was an extra on the set of *Rawhide*. She was 29 and, according to her friend Frances Stevenson, 'She adored the man and would do anything for him.'

Under Eastwood's influence, Roxanne was given larger roles. She even became listed in the American actors' bible, the Academy Players' Directory. It's said that on the set their affair was common knowledge and that they were openly affectionate.

If, as some have claimed, Maggie knew about the affair, she was keeping it a secret. She even chatted to Roxanne on the set. Always Eastwood made it clear to Roxanne that he was not going to leave Maggie for her.

By 1961 he was in some demand by other TV series to guest star, as well as appear in feature films. He even had offers from Europe at that time. But his contract prevented him from accepting anything. Despite his own rule not to complain about his frustrations with *Rawhide*, he told the *Hollywood Reporter* in July of 1961, 'I haven't been allowed to accept a single feature or TV guesting-off since I started the series. Maybe they figure me as the sheepish nice guy I portray in the series, but even a worm has to turn sometimes. Believe me, I'm not bluffing – I'm prepared to go on suspension if necessary, which means I can't work here, but I've offers to do features in London and Rome that'll bring me more money in a year than the series has given me in three.'

His outburst was not lost on CBS-TV and they duly gave him all deference due to a major star, allowing him to work elsewhere during the summer hiatus. One odd job Eastwood landed himself was to make a record, *Unknown Girl*, released by Gothic Records in America. He had previously sung in an episode of *Rawhide*. No doubt, it was decided that if pop stars like Fabian, Paul Anka and Frankie Avalon could make films, then an actor like Eastwood could make records. In the event, Clint's recording career was short-lived.

He said, 'Singing has never been my foremost thing. I did make an album and about four singles. They weren't the talk of the airways particularly, but I had taken lessons. Like every actor, I thought I'd try singing, so I made a few records. I hoped they might make the top of the record charts, which they didn't.' He didn't appear again on record for almost ten years when he sang on the soundtrack album of *Paint Your Wagon*, and later on a single, *Bar Room Buddies*, from the film *Broncho Billy*. However, his love of music and somewhat secret talent for composing the odd tune would manifest itself in the future.

The more Eastwood learned about the process of film-making, the more he knew he wanted to direct. During the shooting of a cattle stampede, he noticed that it was being filmed only from the sidelines. They had around two thousand head of cattle running hell for leather, with Clint and the rodeo hands riding through the midst of them. He thought it would make for a better scene if there were some shots taken from the middle of the stampede.

He told the director, 'I'd like to take an Arriflex, run it on my horse and go right in the middle of this damn thing, even dismount or whatever. But let me get in there and really get some great shots because there are some beautiful shots in there that we're missing.'

He was told, 'You can't get in there with a camera because it's against union rules.'

He knew that wasn't true and recalled, 'If you're doing a shot which the normal camera operator can't do, if he's not a horseman, then there's no reason in the world why you can't do it. In fact, I've done it lots of times and there is no union rule against it.'

Finally the desire to direct became enough for him to take Eric Fleming aside and ask, 'Would you be averse to my directing an episode?'

'Not at all,' Fleming told him. 'I'd be for it.'

Eastwood went to the producer and put forward the proposition. The producer told Eastwood, 'Tell you what, Clint. Why don't you direct some trailers for us – coming attractions for next season's shows?'

Eastwood was so delighted he said he'd do them for nothing, providing he could direct a whole episode of *Rawhide*. He recalled, 'The producer said "great." Evidently he didn't say "great" behind my back but he said "great" at the time.'

He went ahead and made the trailers, getting his first taste of directing, and he looked forward to directing an episode. But the network were having problems with another TV star who was directing an episode of his own series and making a pig's ear of it, and it was enough to give them cold feet over Eastwood and any other actor with aspirations of directing. They made a firm company policy that no actor could direct an episode of a series they were in. Eastwood was disheartened.

He continued seeing Roxanne. If Maggie did know about her, she was keeping quiet. Everyone assumed that the Eastwoods had the perfect marriage. He avoided questions from journalists about his private life, but he said in 1963, 'We still argue now and then. We have some beauts. And when we do, you can hear it a mile away. But she's as good a wife as you can get.'

When he and Eric Fleming were sent on a personal-appearance tour of the Orient, he wasn't disappointed to learn that CBS were unprepared to foot the bill for Maggie coming along, so she stayed home. 'To tell you the truth,' he told *Photoplay*, 'I just didn't want her along. I felt like going myself. We were going to be in parades all the time, and they had a terrifically tight agenda set up, and I just didn't want to be involved with somebody else. It might be a pleasure for her, but it wouldn't be a pleasure for me.'

Eric Fleming spent months polishing up on his limited Japanese vocabulary for this tour, and bought a Japanese-English dictionary, memorizing dozens of words and phrases, particularly those he felt would be useful in answering questions about American television. Upon their arrival in Japan, a party was thrown for them in Tokyo by Suntory Products, their Japanese sponsor. As the party progressed, Clint noticed that Fleming was deep in conversation with the son of Suntory's president, combining English and Japanese. Eastwood noticed that the young Japanese listener was having trouble keeping a straight face. When somebody told Clint the reason for the mirth, he approached Fleming, made a polite excuse to draw him away, and said, 'Knock off the Japanese phrases. I've just learned that your friend holds a master's degree from Yale.'

Fleming swore in English! Eastwood saw the funny side of it but Fleming felt totally embarrassed. 'I laughed my head off half-way across the Pacific,' said Clint. 'Eric finally got around to grinning, and then he bust his buttons with a roar of laughter.'

In 1964, as the summer hiatus approached, his agent called him and asked if he'd be interested in going to Spain to make a low budget Western; an Italian/German/Spanish co-production.

Eastwood said, 'For six years I've been doing a Western every week. Hell, no. I'm not interested in it, especially not a European Western. It would probably be a joke.'

'Well, do me a favour,' said his agent. 'I promised the Rome office that I'd get you to read the script.'

Eastwood read it, and recognized it as a Western version of Akira Kurosawa's Samurai film *Yojimbo*. He had seen the film with a friend and they were both of the opinion that it would make a good Western, in much the same way *Seven Samurai* had been turned into *The Magnificent Seven*. Reading the script, then called *The Magnificent Stranger* – making it sound very much like *The Magnificent Seven* – he was struck by how atrocious the dialogue was. 'It was in English, but very strange English,' he said, 'because it had been written by an Italian group of people who didn't speak English that well; especially English with a Western kind of slang. It was like an Italian concept of what Western slang might be, so a lot of the dialogue was on the shaky side.'

But he was impressed with the structure of the story.

'Usually the hero rides into town, sees a horse getting beaten, sees the schoolmarm, rescues the horse and you know who he's gonna get hitched with at the end – and it isn't the horse! But in this, he rides into town on a mule and wearing a black hat, sees a kid being shot at and kicked about, sees the maiden in distress, and then he just turns around and rides away. You're never really sure if he is the hero until about half-way through the film. And then you're not sure because he's only out to get whatever he can.'

It was the birth of the anti-hero. The story opens with a stranger, known in the original script as Joe, riding into the border town of San Miguel to find that it is run by two gangs – the corrupt Sheriff Baxter and his men, and the Rojos, a band of ruthless Mexicans. Joe decides to play each gang against the other, joining one side and then the other in order to make as much money as he can. And each gang is pleased to think he is on their side because he uses a gun with lightning speed. However, he becomes involved with a poor Mexican family broken apart by the Rojos when the wife, Marisol, is taken hostage by the sadistic Ramon Rojo. While trying to recover gold which the Rojos have stolen from the American Army, Joe winds up rescuing Marisol and getting a severe beating from the Rojos for his trouble. He escapes town while the Rojos set about destroying the Baxters, and then returns to save his friend, tavern owner Silvanito, by killing Ramon Rojo in a showdown.

After reading the script, he asked Maggie to take a look, because, said Maggie, 'Clint says I'm good at spotting the woman's angle to a story, and I liked this one of the loner. Women want to be looked after and protected and a man who can dominate the scene, handle himself against the odds, has instant appeal to a woman.'

When she put down the script, she told Clint, 'This is really interesting. It's wild.'

Eastwood called his agent and said, 'Okay, go ahead. I've really got nothing to lose on this deal, because if the picture turns out to be a bomb, it won't go anywhere.'

His fee for the picture was $15,000, a meagre amount compared to what he was making on the series, but he saw it also as a chance to go to Europe where he'd never been. Whether he knew it or not, he was in fact far from being the first choice for the role. The director, Sergio Leone, had wanted Charles Bronson, then a major supporting actor in films like *The Magnificent Seven* and *The Great Escape*. He was not yet a major star, fitting the mould of many of the American actors who chose to make European films during the sixties, like Steve Reeves and Gordon Scott. Bronson found no redeeming features in the script. He said, 'Sergio Leone wanted me to star in his first spaghetti Western. The script was so bad that I turned it down. It was just about the worst script I'd ever seen. What I didn't understand was that the script didn't make any difference. It was the way Leone was going to direct it that would make the difference. So then Clint Eastwood got the part.'

In fact, when Leone was unable to get Bronson, he made a pitch to James Coburn before trying to hook Eastwood. Coburn also turned it down and told me why; 'I didn't know who Sergio Leone was, and I'd heard nothing but *bad* about Italian film makers. I read the script and it wasn't anything great – just a stylized version of a Japanese film, as *The Magnificent Seven* was. But I didn't know who Sergio was until he came down to Almeria in Spain where I was making a film, and he wanted me to do a film with Charlie Bronson, *Once Upon a Time in the West*. I turned *that* down as well and it made a star of Charlie Bronson! And I'd turned down the first film, making Clint a millionaire – and he's never thanked me!' In good jest, Coburn added, 'Ungrateful millionaire!'

Sergio Leone was not, at that time, an established director, which is why his name impressed neither Bronson nor Coburn. His only previous credit as a director was the sword-and-sandal epic *The Colossus of Rhodes*. Prior to that he had collaborated on the screenplays of *Sign of the Gladiator* and *The Last Days of Pompeii*, and had worked as assistant director and second unit director on international spectacles including *Sodom and Gomorrah* and *Ben-Hur*.

Leone co-scripted *The Magnificent Stranger* with Duccio Tessari. He wanted it to be something totally different from all other Westerns and believed the key to a new style could be found in the kind of music used on the soundtrack. He said, 'The first Westerns were more or less tied to using the same type of music. Recent composers have translated folk music to a modern sense, for example Dmitri Tiomkin with *High Noon*. The Western to us European film makers was forbidden ground until a few years ago, even musically. When thinking about making Westerns I forbade myself to think about such legends as the OK Corral and Doc Holliday. I wanted to transmit a new image, so the music had to be exact.'

To supply him with that music, he approached Ennio Morricone, his friend since childhood. Said Leone, 'Musically, I have made an indestructible partnership with Ennio Morricone. Maybe I couldn't work with any other composer if I have a film in mind. Calling Ennio before the filming was arranged, I told him the whole story. For three or four months we would row violently. But in the third or fourth month after listening for the three hundredth time to every small detail of my film, Ennio began to bring from the piano keys the first three or four bars of the film score. At last I had my drug. Now I could shut myself in a room knowing what Ennio, with sacred patience, had prepared for me. All the scenes and the photography now began to take shape. The characters were all moving with the correct style and I put in the finishing touches. A film was born.'

Much of the originality in the film was due to its rich mixture of realism, brutal violence and black humour. '*Stoic* was the word,' said Eastwood. 'It was stoicism against comedic things. It was comedy and yet it was played dead straight. I personally don't think of it as violent, only, perhaps, as black humour.

'These were satirical movies,' he said of the film and its sequels. 'Unless you've got a sense of humour you won't really enjoy them. The fact that I play the hero, for instance, doesn't mean I wait for the bad guy to draw first. I go with my gun out, let 'em see me, and then plug 'em. You might say that we carry a lotta dead weight in these movies!'

What he didn't know at the time was just how much reaction there would be to Leone's style of violence. 'I knew they were tough films,' he said. 'I'm not a person who advocates violence in real life, and if I thought I'd made a film in which the violence inspired people to go out and commit more violence, I wouldn't make those films. But I don't believe they do. I believe they're a total-escape type of entertainment.'

As to how the character Eastwood played was fully developed – the visual style and the laconic nature of the man – is something that Leone and Eastwood disagreed over. Said Eastwood, 'I kind of devised it. I even picked out the costumes. I went into Mattsons', a sport shop up on Hollywood Boulevard, and bought some black Levis and bleached them out, roughed them up. The boots, spurs and gun belts I had from *Rawhide*. The hat I got at a wardrobe place in Santa Monica. The little black cigars I bought in Beverly Hills. The poncho I got in Spain.'

He also said that he exerted some influence over the final script, saying, 'The Italians were a little bit panicked by my interpretation of the part because they are not used to silence in films. But I felt the less he said, the *stronger* he became and the *more* he became in the imagination of the audience. I insisted that all the long dialogue of the explanatory scenes was cut. You never knew who he was, were he came from or what he was going to do next.'

Leone, however, claimed that *he* decided on the strong, silent approach, and in fact described his pictures as 'silent films' because of the lack of dialogue. He also took credit for giving the character a cigar to chew on between clenched teeth. According to Christopher Frayling, who is an authority on the Italian Western, the cigars were actually Italian cigars called Toscani. He also said that Leone wanted Eastwood surrounded by actors from what Clint himself described as the 'hellsapoppin school of acting' so that there was plenty of shouting, belching and all sorts of noise going on while this strong silent man strode through the middle of it all.

Whoever thought of the cigars, the fact was they tasted so awful that they had a particularly valuable effect on the non-smoking Eastwood who said, 'The unpleasantness of them sometimes put me in the mood for the scene. If I had to be in an unpleasant frame of mind, I took a couple of draws and, boy, I was right there.'

It was only after Eastwood signed the contract to make the film that Leone was able to find a producer – or, to be exact, *two* producers, Arrigo Colombo and Giorgio Papi, suggesting that Leone in fact had no backing at all when he first approached Eastwood, or any of the American actors he initially sought. Managing to cast a major TV Western star in the film hooked the producers, neither of whom was impressed by Eastwood's pruning of the script, or Leone's concept of the silent hero. 'I had more faith in the film than the producers did,' said Eastwood. 'They thought it was going to be an absolute disaster when they saw the dailies. They wanted me to play a more expressive character.'

In the film Joe was simply a soldier of fortune. His only motivation was money. However, contrary to general agreement among film buffs, critics and *aficionados*, Joe (he wasn't called the Man With No Name until the film was released in America) did have a soft spot. When he rescues the heroine – eventually – it isn't just because he wants revenge on the Mexican bandit keeping her captive. When the woman asks him why he has done this, he tells her, 'Because I knew someone like you once. Only there was no one around to help.'

The Magnificent Stranger was made on a shoe-string, $225,000, on location in Spain, in Almeria where a complete authentic-looking border-type town – half white adobe Mexican-style, half American-Western-style – had been constructed. The terrain beyond was an arid expanse of plains rolling up to jagged, snow-capped mountains. There were few other major exterior sets. A small hamlet was built, consisting of only two adobe houses, where the opening scene of Eastwood riding in on a mule was filmed. The only other exterior set was a small cemetery. Everything else was shot on natural locations; the Spanish terrain served very well as the Wild West.

The town itself was constructed in such a way that many of the buildings, such as the saloon, had actual interiors as opposed to being mere fronts so that Leone could film as much as possible in Spain. Other interiors were later filmed at Cinecitta Studios in Italy after location shooting was completed.

The blazing Almerian sun beat down, but Leone still had bright arc lamps set up for every exterior shot to give his actors a constantly sweaty look. At the best of times Eastwood's blue eyes were sensitive to light, causing him to squint from time to time, but the uncomfortable mixture of bright Spanish sunlight and hot arc lamps caused him to squint permanently in the exterior shots. The squint became a Clint Eastwood trademark.

He found himself the only English-speaking actor on the set. Gian Maria Volonte, as the sadistic Mexican bandit Ramon, was a leading Italian actor. Marianne Koch, as Marisol, the damsel in distress, came from Germany. The other actors were either Spanish or Italian. Each actor spoke his dialogue in his own native language, so Eastwood found himself speaking English to Volonte who replied in Italian and Marianne Koch who spoke in German.

Like all Italian films, it was actually shot silent, and all the dialogue and sound effects were dubbed in later. As Eastwood said, 'It was all kind of hysterical. There was a lack of wardrobe and to some extent of technical knowledge. Sergio, by the way, while working always wears a ten-gallon hat, boots and sideburns. I suppose it puts him in the right frame of mind.'

Clint spoke hardly any Italian and Leone knew only some very basic English. For instance, he would say 'Clint, watch me.' Then

Leone would mime what he wanted Eastwood to do. Apart from that, all communication had to be done through an interpreter.

Eastwood was able to perform most of his own stunts. He also knew how to draw a gun at high speed, fire off five or six shots by fanning the hammer with his left hand, and twirling his gun before putting it back in the holster, all adding realism to the gunfight scenes. One of the few stunts Eastwood didn't do himself was when, having set Marisol free, Joe races Ramon's men back to town by riding his horse up and down rocky slopes. Eastwood was perfectly able to ride a horse, but an experienced stunt man and stunt horse were used for this particular sequence since the whole thing was filmed in long shot.

The lack of money caused constant problems on the set. One day Eastwood found Leone and the crew, part Spanish, part Italian, arguing loudly. Clint didn't understand a word of what was going on but he figured it was over money – again. In many respects he was thankful that the budget was small; if there had been a lot more money, he wouldn't have been the star of the film. 'They'd have gone for James Stewart or Bob Mitchum if they'd been loaded,' he said, 'so I figured I'd have to put up with some disorganization.'

He just waited silently throughout most of the morning for the argument to die down until, eventually, Leone's interpreter said, 'Okay Clint, you can start making-up.'

The scene they were to shoot called for him to be beaten to a pulp; the film portrayed violence in a far more brutal way than any American Western, and Clint knew he was going to be in the make-up chair for a long time as the make-up artist applied fake blood and plastic padding to his face. He finally emerged into the strong Almerian sun feeling hot and uncomfortable under layers of realistic make-up that made his face look bloody, bruised and swollen. One eye, made to look closed up, was completely covered over, so he was looking at life for that afternoon through just a single eye. But when he arrived on the set he could see clearly enough to know the place was deserted except for the camera and the huge arc-lamps. 'I'd always been a loner,' he said, 'but now I was literally the most alone man in all Spain.'

It turned out that the crew hadn't been paid for two weeks – hence the argument that morning – and while he was being made-up, they had finally decided they were going home until somebody paid them. 'This wasn't the first time this had happened. It was just one foul-up after another,' said Eastwood, and this time he'd had enough; he informed the production office that he was heading for the airport to fly home.

He arrived back at his hotel and began packing. Before he left for the airport, Leone and his interpreter arrived, apologizing profusely for the ordeal he'd been put through and promising it would never happen again. Eastwood gave Leone the benefit of the doubt and returned to the set. 'Things ran a little smoother after that,' said Clint, 'but they were far from perfect.'

During the eleven-weeks shooting schedule, Maggie was with Clint for some of the time, and during his free time they toured the Iberian peninsula. They sampled as many of the local dishes as time allowed; they ate paella at Club del Mar, clams at the Castellana Hilton, and they raved about a Mexican restaurant that served magnificent avocados stuffed with shrimp and huge artichokes stuffed with ham.

They spent hours in the Prado Museum and toured the Royal Palace with all its priceless paintings, unique collections of gold plate, tapestries and timepieces. They went to the Plaza de Madrid to see El Cordobes and followed that by dining on sweetbreads and Spanish wine at the Jockey Club. They visited the Valley of the Fallen, where thousands of Spaniards died in the Civil War, and the Alcázar in Toledo and the Alcazár in Segovia. 'Spain is for a man what Paris is for a woman,' said Eastwood.

He was able to roam unrecognized because of the rough beard he had grown for the film. He was generally welcomed by the Spanish because he behaved with courtesy and made the attempt to speak a little Spanish, which the people appreciated.

When the location filming was over, the unit moved to Rome for interiors, and Maggie flew home. Eastwood was taken to the dubbing studio at Cinecitta where there was a bunch of American actors he'd never met before, all supplying voices for the other characters in the film.

He spoke very little Italian and purposely had a little fun with the language problem. 'In Italy they have *cornettas*, little sweet rolls that you have in the morning with coffee,' he said. 'And I used to go into a store and put on a typical American accent – a kind of Texas-cowboy drawl – and say, "Ah'll have one of them thar core-noodos. Raht." '

He was relieved to finish the film and somehow thought that *The Magnificent Stranger* might never be heard of again, although he felt he had been involved in a movie different from anything he had ever seen and that, if given the chance, could make an impact. But somehow he thought it would never be given that chance. He headed back to America and *Rawhide*. And more than he expected.

6

Circles and Cemeteries

Even before Clint had gone off to Spain and Italy, Roxanne was nursing a secret which he knew nothing about. She was pregnant and Eastwood, who had so far refrained from starting a family with Maggie, was the father. She was, it was said, too terrified to tell him. If so, then presumably Eastwood had not seen Roxanne for quite a while for if he had, he couldn't have failed to notice Roxanne's condition. He had been away filming during May and June, and it was on 17 June 1964, that Roxanne gave birth to a daughter, Kimber, at the Cedars of Lebanon Hospital in Los Angeles. The child's surname on the birth certificate was shown as 'Tunis', but the father was named as Clinton Eastwood Junior.

According to Frances Stevenson, 'When he came home and visited Roxanne, he saw the child crying.' He said to Roxanne, 'I see one of your sisters finally had a blonde baby.' Then, according to Stevenson, when the truth began to dawn on him, he stormed, 'Goddammit! Don't tell me this child's *mine*.'

Decisions had to be made. Clint said that he would take care of Roxanne and the baby. But he would *not* leave Maggie. He began sending regular cash sums to his secret family. But in return, he wanted total secrecy from Roxanne.

In the meantime, he went back to work on *Rawhide* and kept checking out the trade papers for news of *The Magnificent Stranger*. Then, one day, he saw an item in *Variety* in which the correspondent in Rome wrote, 'Westerns have finally died out here.' It was a blow to Clint who by now felt that *Rawhide* had just about run its course and he was in need of a boost to his career.

Two weeks later another article appeared indicating that the whole situation had changed in Italy regarding Westerns; producers were falling over themselves to make cowboy pictures after the phenomenal success of *A Fistful of Dollars*. Clint read it and shrugged. He'd never heard of the film. Two days later he read another item from Rome that said, '*A Fistful of Dollars*, starring Clint Eastwood, is going through the roof here.'

'*Clint Eastwood*!' he exclaimed. He was suddenly a star in Italy in a film that had been retitled *Per un Pugno di Dollari* which literally translated meant *For a Fistful of Dollars*. This was the first Eastwood knew about the title change, or the success of the film. In fact, he said, 'The producer hadn't bothered to write me since I left, saying thank you or go screw yourself, or whatever.'

The fact was that the producers, Arrigo Colombo and Giorgio Papi, had got cold feet about putting out their film as an authentic Italian Western, and had tried to disguise it as an American-made film. For the screen credits, they changed their own names to Harry Colombo and George Papi respectively, and changed most everybody else's name. Sergio Leone became Bob Robertson. Cinematographer Massimo Dallamano became Jack Dalmas. Ennio Morricone became Dan Savio, and other names were sprinkled throughout the credits to erase any hint of Latin connection – Unit Manager Fred Ross, Assistant Producer Peter Saint, Film Editor Bob Quintle, Make-up Sam Watkins. Even Italian star Gian Maria Volonte became John Welles. Hefty Mario Brega became Richard Stuyvesant.

Almost hoping that nobody would notice the film, the producers opened it in a small cinema in Naples in its English-language version with Italian subtitles. But before long word of mouth got around and people began queuing to see it.

Leone and Morricone went together to watch the film when it first opened and again a year later when it was still in its first run. Said Morricone, 'Then we both realized that although it was a good film, perhaps it could have been much better. Sergio felt he could do much better and I thought I could do much better.' So they decided to collaborate on a sequel. Leone already had a story called *Two Magnificent Strangers* which he had written with Fulvio Morsello. They retitled it *Per Qualche Dollari in Più – For a Few Dollars More*.

They needed two important ingredients – a new producer and the return of Clint Eastwood.

Leone secured a new producer, Alberto Grimaldi. He had been an attorney who began in the film business as a legal counsel. In 1962 he established his own production company, PEA through which *For a Few Dollars More* would be produced. Eastwood was eager to make another film for Leone and duly reported for duty. Leone needed a second leading actor since this film was primarily about *two* magnificent strangers, and he approached Charles Bronson again. Said Bronson, 'This time I turned it down because I said it was just like the first movie. It *was*, but what I didn't understand was that everybody *wanted* it to be just like the first movie. Lee Van Cleef got the role.'

Lee Van Cleef had been a major supporting actor in Westerns since his debut as one of the gunmen in *High Noon* in 1952, in which he made a huge impact without uttering a single word of dialogue throughout. He went on to co-star in many major films and B-Westerns including *The Man Who Shot Liberty Valance*, *The Bravados* and *How the West Was Won*. He'd also appeared in *Rawhide*. But by 1965 he was out of work and broke. That's when the offer came from Sergio Leone. The story goes that Leone and Van Cleef met in a coffee shop to discuss the matter, and two days later the contract, guaranteeing him a fee of $17,000, was signed. 'Because I had nothing more exciting to do,' said Van Cleef, 'I accepted the offer.'

He told me, 'We signed a contract that was thirty per cent more than anything I'd made before. The production manager opened an attaché case containing thousands in greenbacks. I shelled out 10 per cent to my agent and went home. I just walked in and threw my wife an envelope. The rubber band broke and there were greenbacks all over the room. It was two weeks' advance pay. She was crying and laughing and she counted it four times. The day before was our wedding anniversary and I couldn't give her anything. We were living on TV royalties and unemployment and what she made as a secretary. I didn't even have money to pay the phone bill.

'I had seen *A Fistful of Dollars* and liked it, and I thought Clint was mesmerizing in it. So I knew this was going to be an enjoyable ride. I only knew Clint from when I was in *Rawhide*, but I figured that between the two of us we could find some chemistry. We got along famously. Not everyone likes his style, but everyone's got their own thing, and he sure as hell been successful.

'The funny thing about the film was that there are these two men at first pitted against each other and then working with each other. But you never know if the time will come when they must face each other down in a gunfight. Now, in just about every film I ever made I was killed off by John Wayne or Gregory Peck or Gary Cooper. Now here I was with Clint Eastwood who was supposed to be the fastest gun in the Italian West. Well, I'll tell you, I believe that in actuality I'm faster on the draw than Clint. I'm probably the fastest draw of them all. They discovered it took three frames of film for me to draw, cock and fire. That's one eighth of a second.'

The rest of the cast were a similar mixture as before; Italian and Spanish actors all speaking the dialogue in their native tongues. Gian Maria Volonte was again the chief villain, only this time he was even more sadistic, and brilliantly so, and received equal screen billing, under his own name this time, with Lee Van Cleef. Another notable actor was the Polish star Klaus Kinski, father of Natasha Kinski.

This time Eastwood's stranger is identified as a bounty hunter who finds himself competing with another bounty killer, Colonel Douglas Mortimer (Lee Van Cleef) for the head of Indio (Gian Maria Volonte). The two hunters join up for an uneasy partnership and formulate a plan to capture Indio and his gang by having one of them join the outlaw band. 'Why do you look at me when you say "one of us"?' asked Eastwood. And so he rescues one of Indio's men from jail and joins the band of outlaws. But Indio is not as stupid as he is psychotic and he succeeds in capturing the two hunters and then, in an effort to escape with all the money from a bank robbery, he sets the hunters free to wipe out his own men while he escapes. But his plans go wrong and he is finally killed by the Colonel, not for the bounty, it turns out, but to avenge the rape of his sister by Indio and her subsequent suicide.

The filming of *For a Few Dollars More* had to be scheduled to fit in with Eastwood's March to June hiatus of 1965 from *Rawhide*. His salary this time was raised to $50,000. The film's budget was $600,000. Leone and producer Grimaldi took advantage of every dollar, spending it economically but wisely to give the film a superproduction look. The Simonella Company, which specialized in building chariots and wagons for the Italian sword-and-sandal epics, now turned to constructing authentic-looking stagecoaches and buckboards. Pompeii, the shoemaking company famed for its Roman sandals, began making leather boots for the entire cast. A collection of Winchesters and pistols were dispatched from Jaeger, a skilled craftsman in firearms, in Milan.

Filming began at Cinecitta Studios in Rome where interiors were shot. As before Leone chose to film some of the interior scenes in fully constructed buildings on location, but some scenes needed the control of a studio-built set such as the scene in which Eastwood makes his first appearance in the film, entering a saloon in the town of White Rocks in search of outlaw Red Cavanagh. Leone didn't want the traditional Hollywood-style saloon but a bustling, seedy, smoke-filled den of iniquity. Before he allowed Eastwood to pass through the swing doors into the saloon, he ordered technicians to turn on the smoke machines. Thinking they'd pumped the air full enough of choking smoke, they turned the machines off. 'No, no,' shouted Leone. 'We need more smoke. It's got to look like a man could choke in there.' Before the smoke machines were turned off again, the air was thick with smoke. Leone placed strong arc lamps to beam through the fog, making the faces of Eastwood and the other actors shine while the background faded into a bluish smog.

Another interior scene that needed special control was the 'prophet's' house. Here Eastwood comes to visit the prophet to find out about the mysterious Colonel Mortimer, but all the prophet does is rant and rave about the railroad which runs right past his house. As a train passes by, the whole house shakes. Leone had his set builders construct a 'rocking' set so that everything shook violently, while once again the smoke machines got to work to send a thick cloud of smoke billowing in through the window. To add to the comedy, Eastwood tried lighting his cigar as the train passed, but was unable to put the match to the cigar with all the rocking.

Maggie came with Clint and spent ten days with him in Rome, and then another ten in Grottaferrate. This time round Eastwood was mobbed everywhere he went; *A Fistful of Dollars* had made him a superstar in Italy. Children, dressed in ponchos, called him 'El Cigaro'. The infamous Italian paparrazi were hot on his heels wherever he went.

One afternoon, while Maggie was shopping, photographers found him seated at a sidewalk café and took the opportunity to introduce him to a beautiful oriental model.

'Would Mr Eastwood please pose with the beautiful model?' they inquired. Mr Eastwood obliged them. Several months later, an American magazine published the pictures complete with captions indicating that there had been a bitter-sweet romance between the couple. 'Would this, *could* this love affair end in marriage?' asked the headline. Maggie told him, 'Never mind, this is all part of what is called *fame*.'

Eastwood had become a cult figure and everybody started jumping on the bandwagon. Westerns were being made in every studio in Italy and all featured strong, silent, cigar-smoking and mysterious strangers Eastwood-style. Franco Nero was *Django*, which spawned a series of no fewer than thirty films. Giuliano Gemma carried *A Pistol for Ringo* and returned in a superior sequel, titled, appropriately, *Return of Ringo*. Lee Van Cleef later became *Sabata*. One actor even called himself Clint Westwood. American actor Tony Anthony came up with the best of these imitations by actually spoofing *A Fistful of Dollars*, which itself was something of a spoof, in *For a Dollar in the Teeth*. Imitation being a form of flattery, Eastwood just smiled a little sideways at these attempts to emulate his screen persona, but he didn't take kindly to an Italian producer who pirated a couple of episodes of *Rawhide*, spliced them together and released a brand new Clint Eastwood feature film called, appropriately, *The Magnificent Stranger*. Eastwood sued and the film was withdrawn.

Filming completed in Italy, the unit moved to Madrid and Almeria in Spain where a number of new frontier towns were constructed. Tucumcari came complete with a mile or two of railway track and a fully working steam train. A full-scale replica of El Paso was built, as well as the Mexican village, Agua Caliente, where the film's climactic shootouts occur. Leone used high-stepping Spanish horses. Eastwood again donned the same hat, gun-belt and jeans, and of course the poncho which was a one-of-a-kind. Normally every piece of film costume has a duplicate in case of accident. But there was no 'double' for the poncho, and Eastwood conceded that he never allowed it to be washed. There was one addition to his wardrobe – a leather wrist support for his gun hand.

Although it was clear that Eastwood was portraying the same character from *Fistful*, Leone didn't bother with conventions like continuity between one film and the other. In the former movie, Eastwood was known only as Joe, and he rode into town, and out again at the end, on a mule. If he had any profession at all, it was a mercenary. In *For A Few Dollars More* he was a bounty hunter, bringing in criminals, usually dead, for the reward. He also rode a beautiful chestnut horse as opposed to a mule, and he was identified, if only once, by name in an early scene in which the black-clad bounty hunter, Colonel Mortimer, inquires about a particular outlaw. The Sheriff tells him that another bounty hunter is after the same man. 'I never seen him before,' says the Sheriff. 'His name is Manco.' However, the name is never referred to again and in the British release print the name was completely deleted.

This time there were no strikes by the crew, no lack of funds, and much more organization. But despite being a much smoother operation, it was still far from perfect for the two American actors.

Said Van Cleef, 'I understand when Clint made the first film he and Sergio conversed hardly at all. Well, I can't say that on this they managed to string too many words together in conversation but Clint assured me that Sergio was speaking better English than he had done a year before. Although we managed to get by during filming, I had to wonder how they managed to get the first film made if Sergio's English, and Clint's Italian, had been even worse. Actually, I think Clint and I found it easier to get by on a little Spanish which helped Sergio.

'But it was all very strange at first, standing in front of the camera, speaking to actors who replied in either Italian or Spanish, and not only that but also Greek, French or German sometimes. And all the time knowing that no matter how well I said a line – I could have said the most impressive line of dialogue in the history of movies – none of it mattered because it was all shot silent, and we had to dub it all in later. The simple trick of it, of course, was to just memorize everybody's dialogue. I got used to it.'

When filming was over, Van Cleef and Eastwood returned to Italy for the dubbing at the RCA Italiana studios in Rome. Van Cleef went home to America, hoping that someone somewhere might see *For a Few Dollars More* and offer him more work. Eastwood, before heading home, was offered a small part in a film called *The Witches* produced by Dino de Laurentiis and directed by Vittorio De Sica. He was in just a short sequence which he described as 'a funny dream sequence showing the various stages of marriage. I come into a bedroom, go behind a screen, and leap out on to the bed half naked, then fully clothed, and then I just crawl out on to the bed. Very funny!'

He was much in demand by Italian producers by now, but he could only spare the time to work briefly for De Sica before returning to continue with *Rawhide*. 'I don't know what I've got going for me,' he said of his popularity in Europe, 'but Vittorio De Sica thought I appealed to foreign audiences because I depicted *their* idea of a rangy American, the same way I guess Gary Cooper might have done.'

The Witches was never shown outside of Europe; it would seem that United Artists bought the film when Eastwood began earning them millions of dollars, although their purpose was not to release it but to bury it in the vaults to protect the Eastwood image.

Clint returned to America, still predominantly a TV star. But not for much longer, it seemed. He discovered that Eric Fleming had resigned from the series. CBS bosses begged Eastwood not to throw in the towel. He had always said that without Fleming, there was no series. 'There's nothing in the script to make Rowdy look big enough to fit Gil Favor's shoes,' he argued. 'Modesty had nothing to do with it; common sense has.' He finally agreed to continue in the series, with Rowdy as the new trail boss, if only out of loyalty to the studio that gave him his big break.

Kimber was now a year old. He saw less of Roxanne, but she remained hopeful that he would one day leave Maggie for her. Sometimes she waited months for a visit from him. He continued sending the money.

Meanwhile the series, propelled by eight years of momentum and viewer curiosity about what would happen, managed to keep going, but after a few months the ratings had dropped. 'It just kind of quietly died in 1966,' said Eastwood. (The last series was never shown in the UK, even after he became a major movie star.)

He was suddenly out of work, although not exactly broke. His big problem was that as far as Hollywood was concerned, he was a *television* actor. The success of *A Fistful of Dollars* and *For A Few Dollars More*, neither of which had been seen by American audiences because of copyright problems over the first film, meant nothing to the major American studios.

'Not only was there a movie prejudice against television actors but there was a feeling that an American actor making an Italian movie was sort of taking a step backward,' said Eastwood. He was now as *out* of demand as was Lee Van Cleef. But not for long. Sergio Leone had another proposition for the two actors. A bigger, better and ultimately more successful venture than the two previous outings.

It was called *Il Buono, Il Brutto, Il Cattivo*, translated as *The Good, the Ugly, the Bad*. It was an original story by Leone, Luciano Vincenzoni and Age Scarpelli, and, like *For A Few Dollars More*, was not written specifically as a sequel to *A Fistful of Dollars*. In fact, this new story was set during the American Civil War whereas the previous two films were set after the war. Since the screenplay was fashioned as another vehicle for Eastwood in his mysterious stranger role, the film became a *prequel*.

Due to the success of the previous two films, *The Good, the Ugly, the Bad* enjoyed a budget of $1,200,000, and for the first time Eastwood, as well as receiving a flat fee as *il Buono*, was put on a percentage deal. Lee Van Cleef had a new role, *il Cattivo*, a cold blooded hired killer. 'The only reason they brought me back,' he joked, 'was because they forgot to kill me off in *For a Few Dollars More*.' In Italy children called him *Il Collonello*. As *il Bruto*, a treacherous but somewhat comical Mexican bandit, Leone once again courted Charles Bronson who this time would have accepted the offer but had to turn it down because he had signed to do *The Dirty Dozen*. In his place, Leone wooed and won noted stage actor Eli Wallach.

Set during the Civil War, the three men find their paths crossing time and again as they search for army gold buried in a grave in Sad Hill Cemetery. Eastwood forms an uneasy alliance with Wallach which eventually breaks down, due mainly to Wallach's continual scheming to try and kill Eastwood off. Later Eastwood unwillingly teams up with Van Cleef, but deals with that situation by wiping out Van Cleef's gang, and joins up again with Wallach. Finally arriving at Sad Hill after getting caught up in the Civil War – they spend time as POWs and take part in a battle – Eastwood and Wallach find Van Cleef has followed them, and there the trio engage in a showdown in which Van Cleef is killed. Leone ensured the film, running almost three hours, was generously laced with violent action and a fine sense of comedy.

Throughout this Western trilogy, Leone had developed his own unique style accented by extreme close ups (e.g., eyes, guns about to be drawn), exaggerated sound effects (cocks crowing, spurs tinkling, wind blowing, guns cocking) and the unsurpassed musical talents of

Ennio Morricone. His collaboration with the composer had become essential to Leone's concepts. By now Morricone was writing and recording some of the score prior to filming so that Leone could virtually compose the visuals to match the music almost note for note. The films became something of a ballet as characters moved in time to the music (most notably in Leone's *Once Upon a Time in The West*). An example of this was the scene in which Eli Wallach races through Sad Hill Cemetery looking for a specific grave. On paper the scene had no impetus whatsoever. But the superb music, called 'The Ecstasy of Gold', in conjunction with Leone's visual genius, results in one of the film's most memorable scenes. Leone's style would influence Eastwood's own method as a director of Westerns.

This film had something of a new look about it. Costumes were far more authentic-looking, and many of the characters, including Eastwood, wore long brown cattle duster coats. Army scouts wore their hair and beards long. There was a slower pace, usually building up to quick, violent bursts of action.

Not all the towns in this film were dry and dusty. For the scene in which Eastwood first brings Wallach in for the reward, Leone ordered the streets to be hosed down so the ground would be turned into a slippery, muddy street. El Paso in *For a Few Dollars More* was transformed into a town full of fleeing Confederate soldiers.

There was another difference; one that was a considerable improvement for English-speaking audiences. Every actor this time, regardless of his or her nationality, spoke the dialogue in English. This meant that many of the actors had to learn their dialogue parrot-fashion so that American actors could later dub in voices that were more accurately synchronized with the lip movements. This allowed the Italian and Spanish actors, who had portrayed Mexicans previously, to play Americans. Mario Brega, for example, had been a hefty Mexican bandit in the previous films. Now, with his hair cut, wearing a Union uniform and with a voice supplied by an American actor, he made a convincing burly Yankee sergeant.

Again Eastwood proved he could handle his own stunts. In one scene he had to ride his horse after Eli Wallach and hoist him up into the saddle. Wallach, as a stage-trained actor unused to action roles, had a stunt man double for him. It was a simple enough stunt, except that the stunt man had his hands tied, so he had to depend on Eastwood to get it right. Some of the most dependable and sturdiest of cowboy stars would have refused to do this and leave all the action to a stunt man, but Eastwood had no qualms about doing it himself; he swept the stunt man up onto his running horse with ease.

Leone invested his budget wisely and turned the film into the first Italian Western Epic as the Civil War content opened the way for scenes of towns under siege, prisoners of war, trench warfare and a battle with hundreds of extras. It told the audience more about the soldiers of the Civil War than *Gone With the Wind* ever did. Yet all of this was portrayed merely as a backdrop to the story of the three protagonists searching for lost gold. The war never emotionally involves the audience as it is viewed through the eyes of Eastwood, Van Cleef and Wallach who are merely observers more than participants.

Leone injected the war scenes with a startling realism, basing them on actual photographs by Matthew Brady and his agents whose original photographs of the war have provided history with the most graphic of visual records. The Union prisoner of war camp was little more than a rambling stockade filled with hundreds of extras portraying Confederate POWs for whom there was no proper shelter. The sparse wooden buildings were to house the Union guards and officers only.

Recalled Lee Van Cleef, 'The prison camp that Sergio had built didn't have much to it – just a few houses and lots of fences – and it was overcrowded, but you had the feeling that it was how it must have been in the Civil War. It was like pictures I'd seen of Andersonville.'

For the battle scene, deep trenches were dug into a hillside overlooking a river across which spanned a 200-yard bridge. Hundreds of extras lined the trenches. 'It looked just like a Brady photograph,' said Van Cleef.

But there was, it seems, much for Leone to learn about the filming of such a spectacular sequence, while Eastwood had his own doubts about the way it would work. For the scene in which a 200-yard bridge is blown up, Leone had his special effects men rig it with plenty of dynamite. A number of cameras had been set up to capture the moment. Eastwood watched curiously as the dynamite was set and then asked Leone, 'Where are Eli Wallach and I going to be?'

Through his interpreter, Leone explained that Clint and Wallach would run towards the first camera, and that as they came over the ridge the bridge would blow up. Eastwood took a second look at the bridge, and then at how far – or close – the first camera was to the bridge. 'Sergio, where are you gonna be?' he asked.

'I'll be right behind the camera waiting for you,' replied Leone.

'If you'll be behind the camera, I'll do it,' said Eastwood, causing Leone himself to take a second look at the distance.

When they were ready to begin filming, Eastwood noticed two stunt doubles in his and Wallach's wardrobe. He asked his assistant why they were using doubles, and was told, 'Well, Sergio has decided he wants to be up on the hill so he can get a better look.'

Eastwood recalled, 'When they blew the bridge up, rocks and stones were coming up from the bridge and almost killed the assistant cameraman on the lower camera where we would have been standing.'

About that same sequence, Eastwood told *Photoplay*, 'They spent a week preparing to dynamite a 200-yard bridge, and finally it went up with three cameras shooting it. But none of them worked! Not one!' The bridge had to be rebuilt and re-dynamited.

Wallach appreciated Eastwood's knowledge of film-making. Although he had appeared in a number of films, such as *Baby Doll*, *The Misfits* and *The Magnificent Seven*, he was primarily a Broadway star, and the thought that he might have been injured, or even killed, by fragments of the exploding bridge hadn't occurred to him.

Wallach told me, 'I was very grateful to Clint because, unlike a lot of movie stars, he wasn't bothered by the fact that the focus of the film would be more on my character than on his. He even came up with ideas and bits of business that made my character even better. He also helped me get through the confusion of making an Italian film. He guided me through it all.'

Wallach was dead right about Eastwood being aware that Wallach was to be the focal point of the film. At the beginning of filming, Clint commented, 'In the beginning I was just about alone. Then there was two. And now there are three of us. I'm going to wind up in a detachment of cavalry.'

The fact was that Leone, who had always dreamed of directing a major American star, now had one – Eli Wallach. Following *The Good, the Bad, and the Ugly*, Leone only featured big Hollywood stars in his films, such as Henry Fonda, Rod Steiger, James Coburn and Robert De Niro.

But most importantly in the third and last of the *Dollars* films, Leone was far more interested in Wallach's character, a fact not lost on either Eastwood or Van Cleef. 'Tuco is the only one of the trio the audience gets to know all about,' said Lee Van Cleef. 'We meet his brother and find out where he came from and why he became a bandit. But Clint's character and mine remain mysteries which I felt made us more interesting. But it was clear the public would go for the Wallach character.'

Critic Louis Seguin, writing in *Positif*, May 1968, noted, 'Leone gives the best part of the most foolish, most awkward, most devious, most fortunate, most greedy, most treacherous, in other words, the most human of his characters. Stuck next to a shaggy and belching Eli Wallach, slimy and splendid, granted a total freedom in which he luxuriates at every opportunity, gobbling up each shot with joyfully entertaining greed, Clint Eastwood and Lee Van Cleef come across as expressionless characters with poker faces.'

Leone made full use of the various terrains offered by the Spanish landscape. Eastwood found himself in familiar territory from time to time, riding into frontier towns that had been slightly altered from previous films or through rocky passes he and his horse had ridden before. However, for the desert scene Leone filmed in the tiny but impressive patch of actual desert in Almeria, where Eastwood and Wallach walked up and down what director Franklyn Schaffner had called the 'peanut dunes' when he filmed *Patton* there a few years later.

To establish the Eastwood character as being the same as in the previous two films, Leone came up with a clever if simple solution by having Eastwood cover a dying soldier with his long brown cattle duster coat and swapping it for an article belonging to the soldier – a poncho. The last fifteen minutes of the film features Eastwood in the full regalia of poncho, jeans, bandanna, dark brown hat and cigar. After filming, Clint gave the poncho to a friend of his who owned a Mexican restaurant in Carmel, and there on the wall the legendary poncho was left to hang.

The climactic scene was filmed in a huge cemetery. Unlike the small graveyard in *Fistful*, this was Sad Hill Cemetery, burial ground of the war dead; hundreds of graves were laid in great circles. 'Sergio had a thing about circles,' said Van Cleef, 'and he had this cemetery built as a circle, in the middle of which he placed Eli, Clint and me for the final showdown. He'd done something like this before in *For a Few Dollars More* where he had Clint, myself and Gian Maria Volonte face each other in a circle. So there we were in the middle of this cemetery and Sergio was taking one close-up after the next of each of us, and taking close-ups of our hands wavering near our guns, and all sorts of unusual angles. I said to Sergio, "I could take Clint, you know. Shoot him down." "I know," said Sergio, "and that's why the audience will wonder just who will walk away from this gunfight alive." He made that scene last, what, five minutes? And all we do is stand there and look at each other across this great circle, with the music blaring on the soundtrack. It's one of the most impressive scenes I've ever seen, let alone be involved in.'

This time round Eastward's stranger was known as Blondie, and only by Eli Wallach whose character, Tuco, was the only one of the three protagonists to be identified by a real name. Although the official cast list released by United Artists names Lee Van Cleef's character as Sentenza, he was never called that; he was only ever known as 'Angel Eyes'; it was a joke of Leone's to give such a nick-name to the steely-eyed and merciless killer. The same cast list also credits Eastwood's character with the name of Joe, which was odd since by then United Artists had decided to call him the Man With No Name.

As this third of Leone's Westerns went on to become even more successful in Europe and Japan than its predecessors, Alberto Grimaldi began negotiating with United Artists for the release of the trilogy in America and Britain. The first of the films to be viewed by the United Artists brass was *The Good, the Ugly, the Bad*. They were suitably impressed but felt that, at three hours, the film was too long. *A Fistful of Dollars* was the film that least impressed them but they liked *For A Few Dollars More*. Grimaldi wanted to sell the films only as a single package, and United Artists agreed to take all three. The publicity department got to work on marketing the films. They found themselves faced with the problem of selling a series of films featuring an unidentified hero. Some bright spark came up with the idea of promoting him as 'The Man With No Name.'

They set about advertising *A Fistful of Dollars* as 'the first film of its kind' and promising, 'it won't be the last.' The film opened in New York at eighty cinemas on 2 February 1967. Audiences flocked to see it; critics slated it. The *Post* said, 'They simply made this picture out of 1,001 Westerns they have seen and admired.' The *Daily News* thought it a 'straining-hard-to-be-off-beat almost pop Western; not bad enough to be bad or good enough to be good . . .

a washed-out imitation (of *Yojimbo*).' Ballsy critic Judith Crist decided it was an 'ersatz Western dedicated to proving that men and women can be gouged, burned, beaten, stamped and shredded to death.'

For A Few Dollars More followed in May. 'The Man With No Name is back,' proclaimed the posters. 'The Man In Black is waiting.'

The films opened in Britain that same year, but only after United Artists battled with the British censor who wanted *A Fistful of Dollars* banned because of what he considered to be excessive violence. It was passed with an X certificate – which meant only the over-sixteens could see it – but only after a few arbitrary cuts which caused abrupt jumps in the film. A number of times the audience heard what appeared to be the beginning of a gun firing while the image made a sudden jump to a body lying dead. No wonder the critics thought the film crudely made, mistaking the censor cuts for bad editing.

Clint Eastwood travelled to the UK to promote *A Fistful of Dollars* which opened on 8 June at the London Pavilion. He arrived at Heathrow Airport on 1 June to be met by United Artists representatives, photographers and three girls wearing Carnegie Ponchos – 'a snappy idea for the beach.' He'd hardly stepped off the plane before he found himself posing for the cameras with the girls and holding a couple of toy guns in his hands. Then he was whisked away to begin an exhausting nine-day publicity tour. For him the greatest pleasure while touring was to stop off at the small towns and villages to taste the beer in the pubs. He was impressed by some of the 'crazy names they all had.' Jack Straw's Castle on Hampstead Heath in London was a particularly favourite haunt of his, and he was able to visit these public houses relatively unnoticed.

The censor was even more brutal to *For A Few Dollars More*, destroying Leone's careful use of flashbacks (which he was to make an art form in later films, particularly his last, *Once Upon a Time in America*), by cutting the final flashback which made it clear exactly why Lee Van Cleef wanted to wreak vengeance on Gian Maria Volonte. Happily, the scene is restored on the video version, as too is the great chunk cut from the severe beating Van Cleef and Eastwood receive at the hands of Volonte's men. This was another carefully constructed scene in which the sounds of beating are mingled with the ever growing laughter of the sadistic Mexican bandits.

In 1968 the third of the trilogy was released. For a while United

Artists had considered changing the title to incorporate the word 'Dollars' but decided instead to rearrange the original title so it was released as *The Good, the Bad and the Ugly*. In America the film was cut to around 160 minutes and in Britain it was reduced to 148 minutes – over half an hour of the film was missing. Some of the cutting was due to censor cuts, such as Wallach's beating by burly Mario Brega in the prison camp. (This was again a skilfully crafted scene in which the violence is contrasted by the prison orchestra and choir performing, through their tears, a haunting song, 'Ballad of a Soldier'.) Again the video version of the film restored some of the missing scenes but the complete version has never been seen publicly in either America or Britain. (Perhaps with the recent vogue for restoring films, as with *Lawrence of Arabia* and *Spartacus*, somebody might see fit to restore *The Good, the Bad and the Ugly*.)

By today's standard the violence of the *Dollars* films is tame. They certainly set a precedent that other film-makers tried to imitate, a fact not lost on Eastwood who said in 1970, 'Since *Fistful* there've been some 250 films in Italy about violence. Producers getting on the bandwagon – cut somebody's ear off, make him chew on it . . . crap! Just trying to be sensational.'

He was not impressed by the violence of Sam Peckinpah's *The Wild Bunch* which was something of a Hollywood attempt to emulate the Italian Western. 'A lot of critics interpreted Sam Peckinpah's *The Wild Bunch* as a statement against violence; it was so violent they saw it as anti-violence. I don't think that's true at all. I think Peckinpah just wanted to make a super-violent flick. I don't think he showed how bad violence is; I think he showed how b*eautiful* it is, with slow motion cameras and everything. I liked the picture, but when you have that many shootings, you lose the horror aspect of it and it just becomes comedic.'

He was heartened to learn that inmates at San Quentin had told a journalist for the *Los Angeles Times* that their favourite movies were the *Dollars* films. They said that watching the films allowed them to release any pent-up emotions. After a screening of a *Dollars* picture, everything in the prison would be very calm for the next few days.

Censor cuts and distributor cuts notwithstanding, the films were hugely successful both sides of the Atlantic and established Clint Eastwood as a major star. Suddenly Hollywood was interested.

7

First Bad Steps

The initial success of *A Fistful of Dollars* in the States was not enough to send major Hollywood executives rushing to Clint's front door with offers. Nor did *For a Few Dollars More.* Meanwhile, impatient film distributors in France, Italy, Germany and Spain were asking Hollywood when they were going to make a film starring Clint Eastwood. It was only when *The Good, the Bad and the Ugly* took America by storm that the studios took a second look, and were very soon knocking at his door.

Now that he was suddenly in demand, he decided to take a step back, catch his wind, and decide how best to deal with this overwhelming love and devotion suddenly poured upon him from every studio in town who previously had shown no interest in him whatsoever. Despite the success of the *Dollars* films, he knew his future could prove to be just fleeting. He figured his best hope was to take control of his own destiny. So, like many a film star before him, he set up his own company.

'My theory was that I could foul up my career just as well as somebody else could foul it up for me, so why not try it?' he reasoned.

He decided to call his company Malpaso for reasons that are not at all clear. Malpaso is Spanish for 'bad step' or 'bad pass.' On the one hand, he has said that he decided on the name because when he went off to Italy to make the *A Fistful of Dollars*, someone told him that he was making 'a bad step.' 'It was the best bad step I made in my life,' said Eastwood. That would seem the most likely reason for the choice of name, although he has pointed out that in the Big Sur Country, a portion of which he was to buy later, is a creek called Malpaso Creek. 'I guess it runs down a bad pass in the mountains,' he explained.

He held the controlling stock in Malpaso but no actual office and gave the presidency of the company to his friend Irving Leonard. In fact, the company at the start was little more than just Eastwood and Leonard. Their prime task was to find suitable vehicles for Eastwood that would allow them a certain amount of control over the product.

As this turning point in his career came, so too came a turning point in his private life when Maggie fell pregnant. As far as the public, and even many who knew Eastwood closely, were concerned, Clint was about to become a father for the first time. But at Roxanne's home was Clint's three-year-old daughter Kimber. Eastwood played a delicate balancing act between his secret family and public family. His visits to Roxanne were occasional, but he regularly sent her cash sums reputedly ranging from $2,000 to $5,000 in hundred-dollar bills. Roxanne would have loved Clint to leave Maggie, but he was determined to hang on to his marriage.

Despite the complications of Eastwood's private life, Maggie seemed satisfied with their lives together. She had wanted a child for years and friends said that she had to fight to have her first baby. Clint put it down to 'planned parenthood.'

He explained, 'I think it felt better for me at this age than it would have when I was 21, trying to start a career. I wasn't broke, like my father was when he had me. I suppose that's the reason we had children late in life.'

Other plans in his life were taking shape. Since his army days he had wanted to live in Carmel. Now he had the money to realize his dream so he and Maggie drove up to Carmel and began searching for their new home. They found an old house sheltered by cypress and pine trees on a five-acre piece of land that stretched down to the ocean where, jutting from its own sandy beach into the Pacific, sat a rock point. The land was perfect; they fell in love with it and promptly laid down a deposit. Plans were drawn up to erect a redwood timber, rock and glass ranch house complete with gym, art gallery and a main bedroom that would jut out over the Pacific. A keen golfer, Eastwood figured the new house would be 'about a driver and a tee-wood straight south on the coast from the 18th hole at Cypress.'

Another important feature would be a Japanese bath. 'Clint says the Americans are the biggest people in the world with the smallest baths,' said Maggie, 'and the Japanese are the smallest people with the biggest baths. He wants a big, big bath tub.'

United Artists were still busy counting the receipts of the *Dollars* films, and were now particularly enthusiastic to have another Clint Eastwood Western. United Artists are not a studio, as some people assume, although they do partly finance films which they exclusively release, and it seemed to Eastwood that he could possibly make a film for release by United Artists without having the kind of interference that major studios often imposed.

Leonard Freeman, a former member of Universal's story department during Clint's days at the studios, came up with a screenplay he'd written with Mel Goldberg, called *Hang 'Em High*. With it, United Artists saw the prospect for a major box office winner in what they hoped would be an American imitation of an Italian Western. And it had the kind of ingredients Eastwood was looking for: action, violence, romance, all in a Western setting. Freeman wanted to produce the film himself but, because of his inexperience as a producer, had little chance of interesting any of the major studios without relinquishing control. Eastwood and Irving Leonard agreed to co-produce the film with him, although Freeman would receive sole credit as producer. Irving Leonard would be billed as associate producer and the film would be a Co-production of Leonard Freeman Productions and the Malpaso Company. Had Freeman or Eastwood approached a major studio at that time with this kind of set-up, they would most likely have been turned down flat. But this was precisely the kind of deal that United Artists was happy to agree to, and so the project was signed and sealed.

Although Irving Leonard was the face at Malpaso that United Artists executives saw, Eastwood was involved in every aspect of the deal. A budget of $1,600,000 was set, a modest sum then for a major Western. Eastwood's salary was $400,000 plus 25 per cent of the gross profits. In consultation with Freeman, he managed to secure Ted Post as director. Post had not made a feature film in almost ten years but had worked a good deal on TV, notably on several episodes of *Rawhide*. Of all the directors who had worked previously with Eastwood, Post was one of the most efficient and technically proficient. And because he was not in demand for major motion pictures, he was not expensive. All this helped enormously as Eastwood wanted to prove that a successful film could be produced without spending millions on it. He'd learned that lesson working with Sergio Leone.

Even before cameras had turned on *Hang 'Em High*, he had negotiated a contract with Universal, the studio that had hired and fired him more than a decade ago. Producer Jennings Lang had writers working on a script, *Coogan's Bluff*, in which he interested Eastwood even before it was completed. It was a contemporary story of an Arizona deputy sent to New York to bring back a prisoner. As Coogan, Eastwood would be able to maintain his Western persona, complete with ten gallon hat and cowboy boots, as he turns the Big Apple upside down in the course of his duty. This new deal with Universal would be worth a cool $1,000,000 for Eastwood. Alex Segal would direct.

Late in 1967, filming began on *Hang 'Em High*. Although there were no other star names in the film, Eastwood was surrounded by a sterling cast of major supporting actors, including Pat Hingle, Ed Begley, Ben Johnson, Inger Stevens and Bruce Dern.

Eastwood played Jed Cooper, an ex-lawman trying his hand at raising cattle. After buying a small herd from what turns out to be the killer of the real owner, Eastwood is captured by a group of men, led by Captain Wilson (Ed Begley), and then hanged for the murder of the cattleman. Their big mistake, however, is not to finish the job, for Eastwood is cut down by a Marshal (Ben Johnson) who takes him in to be interrogated by Judge Fenton (Pat Hingle). The judge swears Eastwood in as a deputy and allows him to go after the men who hanged him. En route, he falls for an attractive widow (Inger Stevens) who checks out every man brought to the local jail, searching for the man who killed her husband.

Filming was based at MGM studios where the boom town of Fort Grant was created, or rather converted from an older Western set, on Lot Three by art director John Goodman. The company took over 'Boomtown Street' and 'Billy the Kid Street' for the scenes of a mass hanging which involved hundreds of extras. The United Artists publicity claimed that this was the largest crowd scene filmed in Hollywood since *Gone With the Wind*. This may have been a little over-enthusiastic of the United Artists publicity department, but it was an impressive scene as the crowd gathers to watch six men being hanged simultaneously.

To achieve the mass hanging, a huge gallows was built, authentic in every detail. Art Director Goodman designed it as an exact working replica of the gallows then used in Fort Smith, Arkansas, although the original gallows was built to hang *twelve* men simultaneously. Veteran stunt man Harvey Perry co-ordinated the scene, setting up special 'hanging harnesses' for the six stunt men whose job was to make the executions look as realistic as possible.

The unit moved off to Las Cruces in New Mexico where they set up headquarters at the Ramada Inn. Not far from there the film's opening sequence was shot at the Rio Grande in which Eastwood found himself in a familiar role: a cowboy herding cattle. The small herd was borrowed from New Mexican A B Cox whose 40,000 acre ranch was used in the film.

Ted Post worked in the way Eastwood had expected him to, quickly and efficiently. Each scene was filmed with very few takes. Location shooting in particular had to be kept within schedule, and there was no room for movie-star tantrums. But, as has been noted, there were no other movie *stars*, only highly professional major actors. This would be the pattern for virtually all of Malpaso's films. As Bruce Dern told me, 'Clint was the star, but he worked hard and didn't let up for a minute. And because we were all professionals, and just wanted to do good work, we were happy to work at the rate he set.'

They couldn't afford to spend weeks out on location. One day Dern found himself on Organ Range, which rises directly above Las Cruces, for the scene in which he is found and arrested by Eastwood. The next day they were traipsing through White Sands National Monument, 176,000 acres of constantly shifting dunes that reach heights of fifty feet. It was the first time filming had been permitted there since 1945.

Said Dern, 'There was Clint, the two boys who have joined up with me, and me – and a small crew – and we had to get on with the work. Besides the economies of the thing, it was an uncomfortable location. We were filming a fight between Clint and myself, and we didn't use doubles. Clint was happy to trust me not to really kick him when I laid into him with my boots. I had to leap on him and push his face into that sand. Now that was no ordinary sand. That stuff was almost pure gypsum and it was very powdery. It gets up your nose, in your eyes, your mouth, your ears. And there's Clint Eastwood paying me to push his face in this stuff. "Go ahead," the director's telling me, "make him look like he's having a bad time." Bad time? I pushed his face in that sand and he came up spluttering and trying to blow the sand out of his mouth, and he just got on with the scene. He won the fight, of course. He ended up pushing *me* down in the sand. We didn't shoot that scene too many times, but we got everything on film we needed and got the hell out of there.'

Swedish actress Inger Stevens supplied an almost obligatory love interest role. The part really had little to do with the story, and was just the kind of thing Clint had always hated about Westerns. 'I think, on the screen, men like Westerns better without a female; and sometimes women do, too. Westerns are designed as men's shows. I haven't worked with many actresses – and I've been lucky not to have too many turkeys.' In time, he would become enthusiastic about developing strong roles for women in all his films, including Westerns.

Inger Stevens was one of Eastwood's favourite leading ladies, but a tragic one. A runaway as a youngster, she had been married for just four months to her agent in 1955 and she'd had fractured romances with some major stars (including Bing Crosby). Her unhappy private life led her to attempt suicide in 1959 by swallowing twenty-five sleeping pills, washed down with ammonia, after which she remained blind for two weeks. In 1961 she secretly married black musician Isaac Jones. She confessed to a friend, 'I often feel depressed. I come from a broken home, my marriage was a disaster, and I am constantly lonely.' Her role in *Hang 'Em High* was a tragic one, as a woman looking for her husband's killers; it was hardly a cheerful film for her to work on, and she was clearly unhappy in her life at that time. She threw her whole being into work between 1967 and 1968, making six films in the space of a year. But in May 1970 she took an enormous quantity of barbiturates and was discovered, still alive, by the woman who shared her Hollywood home. She died on the way to hospital. It was only after her death that the public learned of her secret marriage.

Following her death, Clint said, 'I loved her. She was a doll, a real good woman to work with.'

Their one real major scene in *Hang 'Em High* was the picnic scene. This was filmed at the Albertson Ranch in the Conejo Valley, forty miles from Hollywood. They filmed the whole scene in just one day, during which Stevens and Eastwood were soaked by sprinklers simulating rain. The remainder of the scene, which takes place in an old abandoned house where Stevens attempts to keep the fever-struck Eastwood warm with her body – *á la* Jane Russell in *The Outlaw* – was filmed back at the MGM studio.

The film was completed and rushed into release by United Artists early in 1968. It was considered an American attempt to imitate the Italian Western because of its brutal violence. But in fact, Ted Post's direction had little style and it seems evident that certain moments in the film – zooms into close-ups of Clint with cigar clenched in his teeth – were probably due more to Eastwood's own influence rather than Post's creativity. The film's biggest flaw was that it had no real ending. After a not very climactic shootout, during which Ed Begley hangs himself, Eastwood returns to town, throws in his badge and is persuaded to pick it up to go after one more of his would-be killers. Certainly the ending was in there somewhere as per script, but Post gave the audience the feeling there was more to come. As Eastwood rides out of town to bring in one more man, you get the feeling that something more is going to happen. Then, suddenly, the end titles roll. The film was a huge success nonetheless.

The music of Dominic Frontière had a slight spaghetti taste to it, particularly when accompanying Eastwood riding into town, alighting from his horse and lighting a cigar as camera zooms into close-up – very Leone-ish. But for much of the time the score was purely conventional with a particularly awful love theme. The whole look of the film was decidedly 'Hollywood'. It was photographed in Deluxe Color, so everything looked bright and colourful, counteracting the rather grim atmosphere Post was clearly trying to achieve. And the main street of the town was very nice and clean; the kind of place a frontier couple would be glad to raise their kids. Even Eastwood was clean-shaven and nicely dressed. But then, Eastwood had not intended to make an imitation Italian Western (even though United Artists seemingly hoped to). 'It was a Western in the old tradition, only tougher,' he said. 'It was not a *Dollars* picture. It wasn't satiric. It had a comment on law and justice and capital punishment. Not a pro or con statement, but it analysed these things and let the audience draw its own conclusions.'

Audiences flocked to see it and it broke even almost immediately, becoming United Artists' fastest profit-making movie ever.

Critics slated it for its violence. Eastwood was becoming increasingly connected with screen violence, a subject that columnists and critics have vigorously pursued him with over the years. Many mistook the on-screen violence displayed by Eastwood to be a reflection of his real self. Time and again Eastwood asserted that he was anti-violence. 'If a guy wants solid violence, he can go to a prizefight and call it a day,' he said in 1970. 'I don't arbitrarily enjoy violence – violence is much more fun to watch on film than to do anyway; the doing is technical – but, look, you've got violence in life. It's nothing new. Like guns are better than being hacked to death with a sword like in medieval times. Now the world is bigger, riots get out of control, groups get together and become rioters, and 90 per cent of those guys aren't really interested in rioting; they just get swept along with the feeling of the thing.

'Me? I take out all my anger, feelings, in a film – as the audience takes out all theirs in viewing it.'

He did admit to *Photoplay* in 1963, 'I have a very bad temper,' but he tries to get by without resorting to violence – which is difficult for any screen tough guy as there is always someone wanting to pick a fight with them in a bar or some public place. As Eastwood told *Playboy* when asked if he got into many fights, 'No, not too many. I don't provoke a lot of them. You know, there's a lot of actors who claim they're always being harassed. But I'm never harassed. People leave me alone.'

But it seems that is not always the case, for, as he told journalist Vernon Scott in 1973, he had been involved in brawls. 'People seem to expect that I'm a whole lot like the characters I play in movies. In a way that helps because not too many guys want to pick fights with me. Once in a while I run into a guy who is antagonistic and I try to be as friendly as possible.

'I think I've only been in three brawls since I became a so-called celebrity – and I tried to avoid violence, all three times.'

He expanded a little more on the subject in 1970 for Graham Peters of the *Mirror Magazine*. 'If he is just a drunk I try to talk him out of it. I try to tell him it is just a silly idea and why don't you run away somewhere and enjoy yourself because that's what life is all about.

'Once there was a guy who I couldn't talk out of it, so I just hit him.'

He also said, 'I get violent over stupidity – my own.' The fact that he is rarely seen to lose his temper does not mean that he is always the cool, calm person he appears to be. 'I may not be as cool as my exterior. Or maybe I'm the type who doesn't show it. I can't really be objective about it. But sure, some things bug me.'

As for the critics who slammed *Hang 'Em High* as well as the *Dollars* films, he said, 'The worst thing you can do is just impress the critics. I'm not overly affected by them. I figure everybody's entitled to his opinion, and reviewers are employed by publications to express these opinions. I've even seen unfavourable reviews of my pictures that I agreed with. I've always felt, though, that it's easier to write an unfavourable review than a favourable one, because it takes more knowledge to write a good review. Anybody can do a pan, but to say what really works – that's tough.'

Unshaken by the critics, Eastwood immediately went back to work, determined to capitalize on his own popularity, in *Coogan's Bluff*. Yet even before that film was in the can he was signed to co-star with Lee Marvin in the Western musical *Paint Your Wagon* for $750,000 plus a piece of the profits.

As with *Hang 'Em High*, Eastwood worked closely on the development of *Coogan's Bluff* as this was to be another Malpaso picture. To complete the unfinished screenplay, Eastwood had Dean Riesner, one of the *Rawhide* writers, come in to give the script its final touches. Finding all the previous rewrites unsatisfactory, they went back to one of the earliest drafts which they found a more effective basis to work from. Eastwood worked closely with Riesner, developing, in particular, the kind of cryptic dialogue that would become a hallmark of his movies.

During this development period, it became apparent that Eastwood and director Alex Segal had differing ideas on the storyline and so Segal departed the project entirely. Jennings Lang tried to secure Mark Rydell to direct, but he had other commitments and recommended Don Siegel who was under contract to Universal, which meant that securing his services would be relatively easy. But he was not a 'major' director. That was soon to change; for Siegel and Eastwood would each play a vital role in the other's career at this crucial time for both.

Born in Chicago on 26 October 1913, Siegel, the son of a mandolin virtuoso, was educated at public schools in New York and, as his parents travelled extensively, at Cambridge University in England. For a brief period he studied at the Beaux Arts in Paris, but after his father's fortunes dwindled, Siegel, at the age of twenty, took off on his own, hoping to work his way to the Orient aboard ships. He ended up broke in Los Angeles where an uncle arranged for him to meet film producer Hal Wallis who gave him a job as a film librarian. In time he became a film editor and directed inserts, graduating to the post of head of Warner Brothers' montage department. There he began working as a second unit director, developing an action style that would serve him well in later years.

After directing a number of shorts, he made his first full length feature film, *The Verdict*, in 1946. Soon after, Howard Hughes called him in to salvage *Vendetta*, but Siegel turned Hughes down on the premise that the film was beyond help. Impressed by his forthright attitude, Hughes hired him to direct Robert Mitchum in *The Big Steal*.

During the fifties he directed a number of films that led European film critics Godard, Truffaut and Rohmer (all of whom would become directors) to crown him a gifted *auteur* with a consistent style and point of view. The French film industry publication, *Cashiers du Cinema,* had been applauding Siegel since the early sixties, but somehow Hollywood hadn't caught on. During the early sixties Universal mainly gave him only TV movies and small – budget pictures like *The Lineup* and *Riot in Cell Block 11*; films which established him as a director with a spare, lean style with the emphasis on action and swift violence. His screen heroes were usually anti-heroes, men who create their own morality, often in direct contrast to society; Eastwood's films had so far presented him in similar form.

Siegel's 1964 thriller, *The Killers*, was superior to most other TV movies and liberally sprinkled with violence that was considered too strong for the small screen, and so Universal released it theatrically. It proved successful.

In 1967 Universal gave him a larger budget for *Madigan*, a tough New York-based cop thriller. The studio were looking for another similar vehicle for Siegel when Clint Eastwood considered him for *Coogan's Bluff*.

'Siegel's work wasn't staid and stiff like some of the older directors,' said Eastwood. 'Yet he wasn't a focus nut like some of these young guys who like to show they're behind the camera by popping the focus back and forth. Then I looked at *The Killers* and said, "Ask him if he's interested".'

Lang thought it a wise move as Siegel was 'warm' in France whereas Eastwood was 'warm' throughout the rest of Europe as well as Japan. So Lang made an approach to Siegel who showed interest.

Siegel told me, 'He invited me to his house for a weekend, and said "Here, have a brew," and tossed a can of beer at me. After we drank a few of those I felt we had a mutual admiration and an agreeable concept for *Coogan's Bluff*. So I said I'd direct the film but only if I could be producer as well. Well, I mean, I was dealing with a man who had his own company and here was my chance to take a big step up the ladder. And Clint said, "Why not?" '

This was not a Western, but began with a Western flavour, as Arizona deputy Coogan captures an outlaw Indian out in the desert, and then heads for New York to extradite a criminal, Ringerman. However, red tape gets in his way and things are further complicated when Ringerman lands himself in hospital after a drugs overdose. Legally powerless to touch him, Coogan bluffs Ringerman out of his hospital bed but loses him in the city. He continues to pursue his quarry, despite having been relieved of his duties by the local Police Chief, and finally captures him after a frantic motorcycle chase. As the police turn up on the scene, Coogan states, 'I'm making a citizen's arrest.'

As with *Hang 'Em High*, there were to be no other major stars – costs would make it prohibitive and this was to be a Clint Eastwood star vehicle – so, as subsequently became the pattern, Eastwood surrounded himself with good character actors, most notably on this occasion Lee J Cobb as the harassed Police Chief. For the role of Ringerman, Don Siegel recommended thirty-year-old Don Stroud who had made his film debut in Siegel's *Madigan* a year earlier. Siegel also brought *Madigan*'s leading lady, Susan Clark, to the cast. Unlike the majority of Eastwood's leading ladies who were blonde, Susan Clark was a brunette. She found Eastwood to be something of an enigma. 'I don't think anyone ever knows what he's really thinking,' she said.

Few scenes were shot in the studio as Siegel and Eastwood made full use of real locations and buildings to cut costs. Most of the film was shot in New York, except for the opening scene filmed in the desert of Arizona. Eastwood's work on the screenplay had ensured that this was a totally visual scene, and not a word of dialogue was spoken for several minutes. It was an effective opening, followed by an engaging encounter for Coogan with a female friend in her desert home where the Marshal turns up to discover Coogan in his friend's bath. There Coogan receives orders to head for the big city to bring back a prisoner, and the film is suddenly transformed as a helicopter delivers Coogan to New York.

For the aerial shots, Siegel wanted to forgo the usual 'back projection' studio-bound set and took Eastwood, the extras and his camera and sound man up in a real helicopter, care of New York Airways. Pan Am allowed the film unit to film the landing (and the eventual take-off at the end of the film) from their helipad atop their skyscraper.

The Eastwood–Siegel partnership ran smoothly from the very beginning. Said Siegel, 'I found Clint very knowledgeable about *making* movies. He's very good at knowing what to do with the camera. I also found that he's inclined to underestimate his range as an actor. We started out on *Coogan's Bluff* with a casual mutual admiration. Then he started to come up with ideas for camera set-ups, which I would call *Clintus* shots. We never tried to win points with each other. He didn't try to impress me that he's a big movie star, and I didn't try to impress him I'm a big director.'

The film's climactic scene allowed Eastwood to indulge in one of his favourite pastimes – riding motorcycles at high speed. However, much of the actual motorcycling was performed by a stunt man, although Eastwood did do some of the riding himself. Motorbikes had become a passion for him.

'On a bike you control everything,' he has said. 'You're out there in the wind. The speed is nothing – it's that you're by yourself on a vehicle in the free air, and you manoeuvre it, lean with it. With a car, or a horse, you and the car are always separate; with a cycle sometimes you feel you're part of it.'

He was insistent about doing his own stunts, and this even led to the kind of temperamental behaviour rarely displayed by Eastwood. Said Don Siegel, 'Once, when I told him he couldn't do a certain stunt, he stormed off the set in a rage. He's insane and childish about doing his own stunt work. I think he's actually very lucky never to have been hurt. Maybe he thinks he needs to prove to himself he's not frightened. Well, I can tell you he's *not*. He doesn't need to prove it.'

After *Coogan's Bluff* wrapped, Eastwood went back to Maggie – and a little peace and quiet. 'When I finish a film I drift back to my own little area where I can be with people I want to, and ten minutes later, with no one.'

With his Carmel home under construction, it wasn't unusual for him to take off to spend time there, for as he said, 'I'm really Carmel, off-in-the-backwoods stuff. If I get really uptight I go up alone, or my wife will go up ahead of me. Depends on how we both feel. Most of the time I'm off with a flick.'

When Eastwood did take off, it was usually on his motorbike. 'He's an outdoors person,' said Maggie, 'but he's not all that wild about horses. He rides motorcycles instead, but he's bashful about it being known too much because it's Steve McQueen's thing. At the moment [1970] Clint has a Norton, a Triumph and a Honda. He parks them alongside his Ferrari, his Chevy pick-up truck and my Cadillac. He loves tracking down on Big Sur on his bike and rides one into San Francisco if the mood takes him.

'Often I ride pillion with him because he's a careful rider who loves the power of the bike, and sometimes we ride off into the sunset on one of them just like a fade-out scene in an old movie.'

Eastwood was home only for a month and then off again, early in 1968, to board a plane bound for England where he was due to co-star with Richard Burton in MGM's expensive and very noisy war epic, *Where Eagles Dare*. Malpaso had no hand in the making of this film. It was produced by Elliott Kastner and directed by Brian G Hutton. Kastner had signed Eastwood to the film during the making of *Coogan's Bluff* for $800,000 – Eastwood was insurance for MGM who were pouring a great deal of money into this project and were not convinced that Burton, who had top billing and reputedly received $1,200,000, would pull in the crowds. In fact, after so many screen flops, *Where Eagles Dare* was designed to put Burton back on top. Kastner, an agent-turned-producer, had gone to novelist Alistair MacLean and said, 'Look, Richard Burton is keen to make a film along the lines of *Guns of Navarone*. Can you write an original screenplay for him?' MacLean said he could, and set to writing *Where Eagles Dare* as an original screenplay.

Kastner then went to Burton and said, 'Alistair MacLean is anxious to write a screenplay for you along the lines of *Guns of Navarone*. Are you interested?' Burton said he was.

Where Eagles Dare was set purely in the realms of fantasy. An important American officer has been captured by the Germans and is being held in an impregnable castle in the Alps. Burton and Eastwood head a team to infiltrate the castle and rescue the officer. With much derring-do Burton and Eastwood not only rescue the officer, but reveal Patrick Wymark as a traitor after various confusing twists and turns in the story. As Eastwood tells Burton at a point when the plots and counter-plots become convoluted, 'I'm about as confused as I ever hope to be.'

Arriving at Heathrow Airport alone – Maggie, pregnant, remained at home – bringing with him just two bags, he headed for customs and discovered a commotion up ahead that was causing delays. Eastwood asked a policeman, 'What's the commotion?'

'It's Richard Burton and Elizabeth Taylor,' said the policeman. 'They've just flown in from Geneva in their private jet.'

Dozens of cases and numerous personnel on Burton's payroll as well as the famous couple themselves and a horde of photographers and reporters had virtually brought Heathrow to a standstill. Nobody noticed Clint Eastwood – he wouldn't have wanted it any other way. After the Burton-Taylor entourage had moved on, he passed through customs alone and with no fuss.

Filming began at MGM's studios at Borehamwood where Elizabeth Taylor, who was not in the film, spent a great deal of time watching her husband at work. Eastwood got on well with Burton, and he made quite a friend of Liz Taylor too. She had been offered a film, *Two Mules for Sister Sara,* which she seemed keen to do; it would be her first Western, playing a prostitute disguised as a nun. There was a great part for Eastwood, she told him, as a mercenary. He read the script and liked it immediately, although he knew that much of the dialogue had to be cut to fit his own special screen persona. He called Irving Leonard and asked him to set up a deal with Universal.

Working with the likes of Burton, Donald Houston, Michael Hordern, Patrick Wymark, Peter Barkworth and Mary Ure – all people with a traditional classic theatre background – was a new experience for Eastwood. 'I just stood around trying to figure out the espionage tricks, or firing my machine gun, while Burton handled the dialogue,' he said. But, even if he didn't know it, Richard Burton was as much in awe of him.

'Within three minutes of shooting time,' said Burton, 'we all realized we were in the presence of a very remarkable man.' He compared Eastwood to the likes of Spencer Tracy, James Stewart and Robert Mitchum, actors who 'appear to do nothing and they do everything.'

Said Burton, 'We make a great pair – he with his lanky frame and me with my stocky Welsh body. He's a fine actor and will become one of the big stars of the future.'

Eastwood felt good about this film. It was fun to make and he could sense it was going to turn out well. 'This part is a real beaut,' he said, 'plenty of action, and with Richard Burton in it I don't suppose it can fail.' Obviously he had not seen Burton's recent films. *Where Eagles Dare* was designed to give Burton a box office success after so many turkeys.

Clint enjoyed working with Burton so much that he was prepared to overlook Burton's drinking habits which resulted in late arrivals. This attitude of Eastwood seemed to impress the contingent of British actors. Peter Barkworth told me, 'Clint was extraordinarily unpretentious. He didn't keep a high profile. Richard Burton did. And when this resulted in very late arrivals on the set, or an inability to cope with a scene – drink played a big part in all this – Clint just resigned himself to it, as the rest of us had to, and didn't complain.

'Clint was immensely liked and respected. While we were in a gästhaus on location in Austria, we talked – and he initiated the conversation – about house and garden; what our domestic lives were like at home.'

Barkworth recalled an incident which demonstrated the good humour expressed between Eastwood and Burton, as well as Clint's knowledge of film-making. 'The group, including Clint, was being filmed climbing a hill in the snow. "Clint," said the director, Brian G Hutton, after the first take, "don't keep your head down. I want to see your face."

'"Sorry," said Clint. Take 2. "That's better Clint. Okay, that's a wrap."

'Clint said to me afterwards, "I did that deliberately. If you keep your head down you'll get another take. I was just giggling a bit about something that Richard had muttered to me, and I knew the take would be no good." '

Away from the set, during his free time, Eastwood took to his rented motorcycle to tour London, visiting all the pubs he had discovered during his *Fistful of Dollars* tour. He also lifted weights and did press-ups in the London apartment he'd rented. At the studio, between takes, he was often seen jogging round the studio grounds.

As well as forming a friendship with Burton, Eastwood became firm friends with one of the two leading ladies, Ingrid Pitt (the other being the late Mary Ure). Polish-born Ingrid, famous for a number of horror films during the early seventies and now a successful writer, was a stunt woman prior to *Where Eagles Dare* and won her role opposite Eastwood and Burton with the help of Yakima Canutt, the film's second unit director who was responsible for large-scale action sequences in films like *Ben-Hur, El Cid* and *The Fall of the Roman Empire*. She came to the set with a sense of fun and enthusiasm that appealed to Eastwood who must have found her a refreshing change from other actresses who were reluctant to tarnish their glamorous image by letting a little on-screen action ruffle their hair. Ingrid could handle action scenes as well as he could. What's more, she was beautiful and they flirted outrageously with each other without overstepping the mark. With them it was always, 'Shall we?' – 'No!' – 'Okay.'

With Ingrid, Clint was able to enjoy a racy kind of friendship full of suggestive remarks and spirited fun. She told me, 'I used to hear him leave his dressing room. He would bang his door shut and then he would make as much noise as possible going down the corridor, so that I could hear bang! bang! bang! It was only later that he said to me, "I hope I didn't disturb you with all that banging. You see, Richard and I had a bet as to who could *bang* Miss Pitt first!" '

Ingrid spent a great deal of time waiting around on her own and said, 'I should have learned to play golf. That was Clint's favourite sport when he wasn't called. I *wish* I could have played it as well. But he did take me for rides on the back of his motorbike. One day he took me to Brand's Hatch. We were speeding around the track when all of a sudden we saw Elliott Kastner standing just off the track, waving us down. He was furious because the insurance wouldn't cover us for this kind of thing.

'Richard was very naughty and Clint enjoyed his sense of humour. Elizabeth would phone him at the studio and he would tell her that I was sitting on his lap which would make Elizabeth furious. On our way home from the studio we would stop at all the pubs. Always there would be someone who would come up to Richard and say, "Aren't you . . . ?" and he would say in a gruff voice, "No, mate." And they would say, "I didn't think you were." But everyone knew Clint immediately. There was no way they would mistake him.'

With all the studio work complete, the unit moved to the Bavarian Alps for the location shooting. There, high on a mountain, was a magnificent impregnable Nazi castle. Its only access was by cable car running from the village of Ebensee; this was not a film for any actor with vertigo to want to be in. Actors, crew and equipment were ferried from village to castle by cable car; this mode of transport was to provide some of the film's most thrilling highlights as Burton and Eastwood fight the enemy thousands of feet above the ground; well, not actually Burton and Eastwood but their stunt doubles. The stars had filmed their contributions to the cable car fight scene in the safety of a studio mock up against a blue screen so that dizzying shots taken from the actual cable car could be matted in after and edited with the authentic location footage.

Filming the hair-raising stunt scenes fell to Yakima Canutt. With a team of parachutists and stunt men he captured the film's most exciting moments on film while Brian Hutton, working with the principal actors, provided the film's nail-biting suspense.

Not that the film was all comfort and luxury for the stars. They were often filming in deep snow, such as the scene in which Burton and his team parachute behind enemy lines, filmed near and above Ebensee. Canutt's team of parachutists did the actual drop, but Burton, Eastwood and the other actors had to wade around in freezing snow. Filming up in the castle was also a cold experience although fortunately the interior scenes had been shot on sound stages at Borehamwood.

After the film was finished Eastwood joined Burton for a private screening of the film. Afterwards Clint declared, 'They gave this film the wrong title. It should have been called *Where Doubles Dare*.' Much later, Eastwood joked, 'Richard and I shared all the hazards and I guess that brought us closer together. Seriously, though, he was great to work with and I thoroughly enjoyed making the picture.' Clint Eastwood and Richard Burton seemed unlikely friends, and went years not seeing each other, but to the end of Burton's life they were good ol' barroom buddies.

8

The Last Masculine Frontier

On 15 May 1968 Maggie Eastwood gave birth to a son, Kyle. Eastwood was still filming *Where Eagles Dare* and received the news by phone. He was bitterly disappointed not to be there. Ingrid Pitt recalled the day Clint celebrated the birth of his son. 'There were two celebrations going on on the set. One was for the huge diamond Richard had bought for Elizabeth and the champagne was flowing. But Clint was celebrating the birth of his first and only son. It's interesting to see the different priorities they had.'

Four days later he completed his work on the film and flew home to meet his son. But again he was home only for a month before starting work on another film on yet another distant location, although not as far as the Bavarian Alps; Oregon for *Paint Your Wagon*.

Since the success of *My Fair Lady* all the major studios were pouring millions of dollars into large-scale musicals; *The Sound of Music* at 20th Century-Fox, *Oliver* at Columbia, *Camelot* at Warner Bros, *Thoroughly Modern Millie* at Universal (not at MGM though, where they were struggling through hard times kept at bay only by *Where Eagles Dare* and reissues of *Gone With the Wind* and *Ben-Hur*), while Paramount opted for *two* epic musicals, *Darling Lili* and *Paint Your Wagon*.

Paint Your Wagon was a multi-million dollar musical stage production by Alan Jay Lerner and Frederick Loewe, adapted for the screen by Paddy Chayefsky and directed by Joshua Logan whose previous screen musicals *South Pacific* and *Camelot* made him seemingly the perfect choice for this musical horse opera. But it would seem that from the very early stages, *Paint Your Wagon* was in for a rough ride. The budget was originally set at eight to ten million dollars; a big enough sum in 1968 but one which nobody at the studio balked at during a time of big budget musicals.

Logan wanted Julie Andrews to play the Mormon woman who winds up with two husbands, but she preferred to be in *Darling Lili* for husband Blake Edwards, also at Paramount. So Logan settled for beautiful Jean Seberg who was popular in Europe if not in America. Therefore two major stars were needed to play the men who would become her husbands. Lee Marvin, then at the height of his success and popularity, was wooed and won by Alan Jay Lerner, who was also producing. Lee Marvin told me, 'I *had* to make the film because Lerner said, "Look, Lee, if you don't play this part we can't make the film." If I hadn't made it, nobody at Paramount would have talked to me again. Come to think of it, nobody at Paramount did talk to me again, anyway!' He received a reputed $1,000,000 plus a percentage *plus* $20,000 a day or $100,000 a week overtime to play Ben Rumson who was born under a wanderin' star.

To fill the big muddy boots of Pardner (who talked to the trees because nobody else would listen to him!) they persuaded Clint Eastwood for $750,000 plus a piece of the box office action and soundtrack sales. The fact that Eastwood had to sing didn't faze him since he had warbled a bit previously, though none too successfully, back in his *Rawhide* days. Alan Jay Lerner told me, 'I had learned by experience that it was better to start with an actor who could sing rather than a singer who could act and Clint had a pleasant singing voice. He sang without any recording tricks and he wasn't as paranoid about it as Lee was.' Apparently, Lee preferred to be put in the recording studio on his lonesome to record his songs, most notably *Wanderin' Star*.

What appealed to Eastwood about the role was its change of pace from his previous roles. He said, 'Marvin's character is a wild one, Ben Rumson, a gold-seeking drifter, hard fighting and drinking. I'm much more naive as Pardner, a farmer from the Mid-West raised with sort of a purist background. My brother is killed and while burying him, Ben discovers gold in the grave, and stakes the claim for both of us. It's really an off-beat relationship when we end up marrying the same girl because of the shortage of women in California during that period.

'It opens things up for me. It gets me back out of all the anti-heroics, opens everything up because of the wider range to it, if you know what I mean. I sing in it and play a lot of light comedy, too. The range is almost farce to a deep and tender poignancy. It is also a very romantic role.'

He was hugely enthusiastic going in. But there were already some behind the scenes disagreements brewing. Logan wanted to make the entire film on the backlot of Paramount where he would have more control and keep the costs down. Alan Jay Lerner, however, wanted authenticity and felt the only way to get it was to film on location. This meant building an entire gold rush city, No Name City (appropriate name for an Eastwood location), up in Oregon, as well as Tent City. These were constructed at great cost at East Eagle Creek, near the 9,000ft Boulder Peak in the Wallowa-Whitman National Forest.

The logistics of building No Name City might not have been any more than they were to build any frontier town, but Lerner told his production designer, John Prescott, 'Build me the city solid enough but which will completely collapse on cue.' The film's climax would have the whole city fall apart, a little like the production itself.

Truscott and his team of construction engineers discovered that there was a labyrinth of underground rivers directly under the site where the city was to be constructed. The entire area had to be filled in with tons of earth to make the ground solid enough. The US Forestry Service pitched in with two hundred construction men to fill in the tunnels and build the city.

Of the 150 buildings, more than half were individually rigged to collapse on cue. Many of them, as well as the trees, were rigged so that they would start a chain reaction. The front of the Grizzly Bear Saloon (for which some $20,000 was spent on the sculpturing of female figures) was rigged to fall forward into the street while the entire rear had to fall into the river behind it. The undertaker's establishment was designed to sink slowly into the ground.

Trees were specially imported from Hollywood. Horses were driven in from Nevada and water oxen transported from New England. Eight 40ft vans made a round trip each week between Los Angeles and Baker, hauling in the materials and merchandise needed to stock the saloons, hotels and stores.

The cast were lodged a two-hour drive away from the set. Access to the location was by a 46-mile dirt road that had to be maintained now and again at $10,000 a mile.

Joshua Logan and his wife rented a house, bringing their own servants. Jean Seberg brought her Spanish maid. Clint Eastwood brought only his motorbike and his golf clubs to the farm house he rented with a forty-acre spread. 'They had a nine-hole golf course,' he noted with glee, 'so I played golf for kicks.' As the problems that ensued grew worse, golf would help him to keep his sanity.

Lee Marvin didn't care where he lived just so long as there was plenty of booze available!

Josh Logan began to wonder if they'd made a mistake about Lee Marvin. The director had been warned about Marvin's heavy drinking that had marred previous productions, although Ken Hyman, producer of *The Dirty Dozen*, had told Logan, 'The fact that Lee gets drunk and stops the picture for a day or two is not important because he'll make it up to you in so many other ways.'

Logan was shooting a scene in which Jean Seberg had to gaze into East Eagle Creek where the cool clear water bubbled over the rocks. As the cameras rolled, Marvin, from behind a tree, suddenly roared, '*Stop*!'

Jean leapt back. 'What's wrong?' she cried.

Marvin staggered forward. 'What's *wrong*?' he repeated in mock indignation. 'Don't you realize the fish are fucking in there?'

Seberg burst into laughter. But Logan groaned under his large-brimmed straw hat and hoped that things wouldn't get any worse than this. Marvin, meanwhile, was hoping the same thing about Logan. An earlier choice for the film had been Don Siegel with whom Marvin had made *The Killers*, and Lee would have preferred to have Siegel direct this film. Logan was predominantly a stage director, and Marvin was nervous of the fact. And the more nervous he became, the more drunk he got. Clint Eastwood began to wonder what he'd got himself into.

One day in the middle of a scene, Marvin said, 'I don't see any point in wasting money here. I'm going fishing.'

Don Siegel came up to the location to visit Clint and Lee Marvin. He told me, 'When I arrived I found that the whole picture had closed down because Lee Marvin was somewhat...unavailable – incapacitated. Everyone was unhappy and I was rushing around telling everyone that everything would be okay, that I'd worked with Lee a lot and that he'd pull himself together and get back to work. Nobody believed me, not surprisingly. But I did prove to be right eventually. Anyway, I went up to Lee's to have breakfast – breakfast with me is something of a sacred ritual. I got there and found he had no food in his house except for one wrinkled old avocado.

'Clint came over to pick me up and Lee started talking gibberish; just sounding off, making no sense at all. I said to Clint, "Do you understand anything he's saying?" Well, Clint couldn't make it out at all. I said, "Look, I came here for breakfast but there's nothing to eat except this wrinkled avocado. I've had four beers but I need something to eat." Lee just sat there grinning, and I got mad at him so I picked up the avocado and squashed it on his head. Lee burst into laughter, and I began laughing, but Clint thought we'd both gone crazy. As I told Clint, there are moments when one act can be more expressive than dialogue with Lee Marvin.'

The problems got worse. Drunk or sober, Marvin kept holding up filming. His problem, he told me, was his lack of confidence in Logan as a *movie* director.

'Josh Logan has wanted to make the film in the studio and I figured he thought a sound stage was like a theatre stage because that's where he felt comfortable and in control. But he was out there in the middle of Oregon with real people and real wagons and real guns. And there was just a whole buncha crap going on up there. They had Clint Eastwood singing – I mean this big tough guy who usually killed ninety-seven people in each of his films, and he's sitting there playing a guitar and being Elvis Presley and they didn't know what to do with him. And they had all these buildings falling down and it was just *lunacy*. Or at least, that's how I saw it. Well it was crazy. I got along just fine with Josh in the end but we could have used Richard Brooks [who directed Lee in *The Professionals*] or Don Siegel.'

Tom Shaw, the associate producer, phoned Richard Brooks. 'We're in a helluva mess up here,' Shaw told him. 'Nobody's talking to anybody. If you're not doing anything could you come up and finish the picture?'

Brooks was nonplussed, especially when Shaw said, 'They asked me to ask you because they're afraid to call you.'

'What the hell's happening up there?'

'Lee's in trouble again and nobody can handle him. It's deeper even than that. Guys are running around with other people's wives or girlfriends – a lot of things are going on. Clint Eastwood is not talking to Lee or Lee is not talking to Clint Eastwood. Whatever it is, it's not working. There's a lot of money up here. The film's got a chance. It's a good show.'

Brooks told him, 'Forget it.' He had no intention of replacing a respected colleague. But the pressure wasn't off him yet. Alan Jay Lerner caught a plane to Hollywood to personally visit Brooks in the hope of persuading him to take over the picture.

'Come up and do the picture,' pressed Lerner. 'Whenever Lee shows up he causes trouble.'

'You mean he's been drinking?' asked Brooks.

'Yeah, but even when he's sober we got problems.'

'That doesn't sound like Lee,' Brooks told him. 'There must be something else wrong because he's movie-wise.'

Lerner flew back to the location having failed his mission. Finally Lee Marvin himself called Brooks. 'Come here and do something,' he pleaded.

Brooks made it plain to Marvin. 'It won't work. It's shameful for Logan. What would you do if anybody did that to you?'

'I'd knock the hell out of him.'

'Then why do you expect me to do it to Logan?'

'You're right,' said Marvin.

By this time the story had been leaked and the secret approaches to Brooks made public. Joyce Haber wrote in the *Los Angeles Times*, 'Logan is in so much trouble on Lerner's and Paramount's big budget musical that they're saying from Hollywood to Baker, Oregon, that he's about to be replaced. Likeliest candidate for Logan's job, Richard Brooks.'

Logan felt crushed. Eastwood, who'd kept quiet all this time, joined the controversy. He sent his agent to Paramount to tell them that if they wanted to change the director they had better see him first or there would be plenty of trouble. Said Logan, 'Clint Eastwood stood by me. It was a strong thing to do and I admired it.'

Lee Marvin took some advice from Richard Brooks and one night asked Logan to drive him home from the location. It was a two-hour drive and they got to talking about theatre and acting and found they actually had a lot of common ground. 'From that moment on,' said Logan, 'I had his confidence to the degree where I think he would have lain down and rolled over if I'd asked him.'

Maggie and Kyle came to visit Clint for a while. But location filming lasted almost four months and Eastwood grew bored and frustrated. To kill time he 'slopped the hogs for the guy who owned the farm.'

Then the rumour spread that he and Jean Seberg were more than just good friends. It was the kind of story that Hollywood gossip columnists were as likely to invent as much as report. There was certainly a close friendship between her and Clint. She bought him a pair of olive 'Sneaky Pete' sneakers, and they turned up together at the wedding of a couple of the film's extras; Logan, his wife and Lee Marvin were also among the guests. Again, like Inger Stevens, she was a tragic leading lady for Eastwood.

More than a year after making *Paint Your Wagon* Seberg became pregnant and the *Los Angeles Times* published an item that claimed the father was a member of the Black Panther Party. Previously the FBI had been investigating Seberg's alleged support of the Black Panther Party, and the FBI were instrumental in publicizing her pregnancy. But the baby died at birth. Distraught, Seberg transported the dead baby to her hometown in Iowa where the corpse was exhibited in a glass coffin so that everyone could see that it was white. 'After that,' said her first husband, novelist Romain Gary, 'on the anniversary of the stillbirth, she tried to kill herself.' Not long after, her lover, actor Hakim Jamal, was murdered. In 1979 she took a large fatal dose of barbiturates. Her decomposed body was found about a week later wrapped in a blanket in the back seat of her car. Gary claimed that the FBI was directly responsible for her death. The following year Gary killed himself.

Eastwood said, 'She was fine to work with – a sweet gal.'

The *Paint Your Wagon* unit finally moved back to Hollywood to film interiors at the Paramount studio for a further month and a half. When it was all over, Eastwood was cautiously optimistic about the outcome.

'I haven't seen it yet,' he told Tony Toon by trans-Atlantic phone call, 'but it has good material and I guess that potentially it's a great picture. It's taken from a show which was on Broadway fifteen years ago but I should say that the screenplay is better than the original.'

When asked if he expected to appear in other musicals, he said, 'I'd like to see *Paint Your Wagon* first.'

After he saw it, Lerner decided to recut it to match *his* vision. The studio didn't like it much, but then they didn't like Logan's original cut, so they made two more versions. 'The director's version, the first one,' said Eastwood, 'was actually the best one but that wasn't the one that got released.'

Eastwood judged the final outcome himself by seeing all four versions. A good many stars go nowhere near a theatre showing one of their films. But Eastwood makes a point of watching himself on the screen. 'So many of my colleagues claim they don't go to see their finished product,' he said. 'If they're telling the truth, I still think it's nonsense. How else would you know for certain unless you saw the finished product whether or not you did what you set out to do?

'So much of film-making is shot out of continuity you can't really be objective about it and be sure that it worked. Sometimes it does and sometimes it doesn't. But when you go to the theatre you learn about yourself as an actor and grow within yourself. You know what you're made of and what worked and what didn't, and you'll correct next time what didn't.'

Watching *Paint Your Wagon* in its final re-edited version – the version that the public saw – Eastwood was convinced it would never work for an audience. In fact, he felt that in retrospect, it was doomed as soon as the budget began to rise. '*Paint Your Wagon* was a mistake. At $8,000,000, the original budget, it would have been a bargain. But at $20,000,000 it was a disaster. The company was terribly jaded, demoralized, and not even a tight director like Don Siegel could have saved it from suicide.'

It was true that the film's budget had soared by the end of production, although the final figure is something no one can quite agree on. Lee Marvin was convinced it came to $16,500,000. Paramount settled on a figure of $22,000,000. Logan simply observed, 'I've never known any subject that's as full of holes as how much a picture cost or made. Whatever they tell you is not true.' Whatever the final cost, the film didn't earn enough to make a profit. Domestically, it grossed $14,500,000, which would have been a very healthy figure if the original budget had been stuck to.

On behalf of the critics, Pauline Kael summed it up, saying it was 'one of those big movies in which the themes are undersized and the elements are juggled around until nothing fits together right and even the good bits of the original show you started out with are shot to hell.'

This experience made Eastwood determined that he would only make films for his own company in future, with the exception of *Kelly's Heroes* which he had already signed to do for MGM and director Brian G Hutton.

'I had this great urge to show the industry that it needs to be streamlined so it can make more films with smaller crews,' he said. 'The crews will be employed more, so there'll be just as much work. What's the point of spending so much money producing a movie that you can't break even on? So at Malpaso we don't have a staff of 26 and a fancy office. I've got a six-pack of beer under my arm, and a few pieces of paper, and a couple of pencils, and I'm in business.'

He now expanded Malpaso which had its offices in a bungalow at Universal Studios where he had negotiated for a further three films. Part of this expansion was due to the demise of Malpaso's president, Irving Leonard. Clint's old friend Bob Daley took over the running of the company in January 1970. Other old friends came on the Malpaso bank roll. Sonia Chernus left CBS to become Eastwood's script editor, her task being to read all the screenplays and screen treatments offered to him. At first Eastwood insisted on reading all the scripts himself but came to trust Sonia Chernus's judgement (I should know; I tried submitting some scripts and had them all rejected by Miss Chernus – unread!).

'I used to have to say "Well, I'll give it a look myself," ' he said. 'Never could take advantage of that old saying, "You don't have to drink the ocean to find out it's salty." I'd read scripts from beginning to end, even if the first fifty pages were just awful.' He used to figure that if a script was *that* bad, he had to stick it out to find out if it got any better. He'd sit up late each night, reading these awful scripts, finally throwing them to one side and asking himself, 'What the hell have I wasted the last two hours on that for? I could have been sleeping or out walking the dog!'

'It takes an awful lot of reading to find the right material,' he said. 'You have to wade through miles to get one inch. I've been easing up though. Sonia and Bob are doing some of the reading and I'm taking their word on more things.'

Fritz Maines also joined the company as, among other things, Malpaso's own unit publicist.

The future looked healthy. After *Two Mules For Sister Sara* Eastwood was set to do *Kelly's Heroes*, and then he hoped to do a modern-day story about a gambler in Chicago, *Cully, the Arm*. That film never came to fruition but it reflected very much how Eastwood regarded himself at that time. 'The character's probably closer to me than any I've done so far,' he said. 'Not a superstar; just a guy who has a lucky streak, has a certain talent for his profession.' He had planned even beyond that. 'Then I'll hit some cool clean water. Want to do some Westerns up in the timberlands. When I get really jaded in the business, I'll pick scripts for location.' His plans to make 'some Westerns' would be delayed, but he would very soon, before becoming jaded, choose only films that offered attractive and accessible locations.

Universal had happily contracted with Eastwood to make *Two Mules For Sister Sara* because they figured that the partnership of Elizabeth Taylor and Clint Eastwood would be a winning combination. He had interested Don Siegel in directing and they planned to film in Mexico, with a Mexican cameraman, Gabriel Figueroa. Eastwood began growing his stubble for the film and, in the spring of 1969, took his gunbelt from his previous Westerns and headed for Mexico with Don Siegel.

Siegel told me, 'We were all virtually set to begin filming except for Liz Taylor. She suddenly and unexpectedly backed off and Malpaso and we were left with a film all ready to roll and no leading lady. We began a hurried search for Taylor's replacement and we came up with Shirley MacLaine. She understandably wanted her part rewritten to suit her own style of comedy. Clint had already cut out two-thirds of *his* dialogue.'

Said Eastwood, 'I try to give the audience the idea without saying, "Why does the character do this at this time?" You don't have to say it all.' He had no qualms about tailoring somebody else's work to suit his own style. It was exactly what the likes of John Wayne had done.

He arrived at Cocoyoc in Mexico, an hour's drive from Mexico City, and found to his consternation that Universal were having trouble getting his motorcycle into the country. He was at a loss. Said Don Siegel, 'Clint may look as though he was born on a horse but he prefers his iron horse.' Eastwood was relieved when his bike finally arrived.

For a Malpaso film, this was an ambitious project with a three-month shooting schedule, requiring some large-scale action sequences, including the blowing up of a train and a battle between French soldiers and Mexican revolutionaries, portrayed by hundreds of Mexican extras. To co-ordinate the spectacular action sequences, Buddy Van Horn was hired as stunt director. It was the first of many films Van Horn made with Eastwood.

During filming, MGM flew Eastwood out from Mexico City to Las

Vegas as part of the publicity junket for *Where Eagles Dare*. Maggie went with him, and MGM put them up in the Riviera Hotel where columnists from all over the world came to interview Hollywood's new superstar. Eastwood had just come fifth in the box office ratings for 1968, just one notch below John Wayne but outdrawing Dean Martin, Steve McQueen, Jack Lemmon, Lee Marvin and Elizabeth Taylor.

He was quite flushed by his success. 'It's all pretty amazing,' he said. 'It's a better time for actors now. They used to be owned by companies, be assigned to pictures. Directors were tops. Now actors choose their own scripts. I'm in control. '68 was a good year – fifth top box office, second action star – Marvin was first – and I got the Laurel Award for being the most promising newcomer. Funny!'

In between interviews, Eastwood, typically dressed in T-shirt, slacks and sneakers (the pair given to him by Jean Seberg), mingled with silk-suited MGM executives. 'Have to go and talk about employment,' he explained to columnist Earl Wilson. 'I spent a year on the unemployment line. Now that it's rolling along, I don't want it to stop.' He loomed over them all, looking down on men who normally looked big. He rarely spoke, just listened, then drifted on to the next interview.

Ingrid Pitt was also there, and as the press closed in on both her and Eastwood, Clint, possibly in an attempt to protect her, suddenly fell into the swimming pool. Some newspapers suggested that Ingrid had pushed him in, but she told me that this was untrue. They remained good friends for many years and she told me, 'Clint will always be one of my very favourite people.'

The junket over, MGM flew Eastwood back to Cocoyoc to resume filming his latest Western. 'I really love *Two Mules*,' he said. 'I identify with this story – the ironic cowboy, selfish, but with a tinge of compassion.'

He was playing once again a mercenary, not unlike the Man With No Name, but this time *with* a name, Hogan. He happens upon the rape of a woman by a gang and proceeds to wipe them out. Having rescued her, he intends to continue on his way, having been hired by Mexican rebels. But when he discovers that she is a nun, he finds himself compelled, albeit reluctantly, to help her en route. Along the way she saves his life when he is pierced by an arrow from an Indian, cutting it out and healing his wound. They finally reach their destination after numerous adventures where he leads an attack on the French garrison and then discovers that Sister Sara is actually a whore working under cover for the rebels.

The Western is a genre he clearly enthused about. 'Westerns – a period gone by, the pioneer, the loner operating by himself, without benefit of society. It usually has something to do with some sort of vengeance; he takes care of the vengeance himself, doesn't call the police. Like Robin Hood. It's the last masculine frontier. Romantic myth, I guess, though it's hard to think of anything romantic today. In a Western you can think, Jesus, there was a time when a man was alone, on horseback, out there where man hasn't spoiled the land yet.'

He was pleased too that this was a Western with a major role for a woman. He said, 'It's the only Western I know that has a great part for a woman – not a dance hall, ballsy broad, but a *woman*. The average Western isn't written for the female. The *cliché* broad says, "Don't do it, Charley!" and Charley answers, "I've got to do what I've got to do!" Besides, it's an outdoors show; it's hard to work with women – make-up, wardrobe, all of it – while the guy, well, you just stick him in some smelly outfit.'

By now Don Siegel had arrived at a way of knowing how to get what he wanted without compromising what Eastwood wanted. 'You must be very honest with Clint,' said Siegel. 'He is very opinionated – certainly not to be pushed around.'

Later Eastwood was to say, 'Don pretended to let me do what I liked, but he never actually let me get away with anything. In fact, I learned a huge amount from just watching him work. He knew exactly what he was doing at all times.'

Not everyone involved with Eastwood at that time was as impressed by him as was Siegel. A press agent said, 'He doesn't effuse intellect. The only things he can readily talk about are things he's immediately concerned with – his part, his image, his acting, or his hotel room. He expresses no interest in anybody else.'

Eastwood himself readily admitted, 'I hate to break things down to their smallest parts. I work on more of an animal level, on a feeling level. I don't do a lot of philosophizing and intellectualizing.'

He does however possess a dry sense of humour, as he displayed for columnist Deedee Moore when he brought a tray of drinks to the table while she was interviewing him. 'I'm probably the highest paid waiter around,' he said softly.

He went off into the desert with assistant director Joe Cavalier and a crew to shoot the opening credit shots, filming various animals in the foreground with Eastwood riding by in the background. Said Siegel, 'I told Joe what I wanted and it took him two weeks to get it, but it was worth it because it established a feeling for the kind of animalistic man who was our hero.'

During the filming, Eastwood came across a novel, *The Beguiled*. Its screen rights were owned by Universal. He persuaded Don Siegel to read it, and then they agreed to join forces in an attempt to bring it to the screen.

He was also engaged in trying to get another property to the screen during the filming of *Two Mules*. He had already bought the option on a story of a disc jockey by Cheryl 'Jo' Heims, *Play Misty for Me*. He tried to interest Jennings Lang in it, but he responded with, 'Jesus Christ, who in the hell wants to see Clint Eastwood play a disc jockey?' Eastwood didn't give up.

For two weeks, Maggie was on the *Two Mules* location with him. 'Usually I try to visit him on location for five or six weeks at a time and take the boy with me,' she explained. 'It relieves the monotony of some of the tough locations he has had recently.'

'She usually comes on every location *after* I'm situated,' said Eastwood, 'visits awhile, then leaves.'

While with him in Mexico she carried a pillbox full of vitamins which they tucked into daily. For lunch they ate little but drank Sunshine Valley Garden Treat Tea. By this time they were both heavily into health foods, a fad that began, according to Eastwood, when he walked into a health-food store with a friend who was looking for some special kind of bread. 'There was a little old lady in there,' recalled Eastwood, 'talking about pesticides and things, and I thought that what she said made sense.' From then on he and Maggie began eating organic food. As for the Treat Tea, Eastwood said, 'It has a peppermint taste and no tannic acid – one of my wife's hangups. I don't drink coffee or tea usually. Value my nerves too much. People who drink coffee, smoke – they shake not with their hands or face; they shake with their eyes.'

He did, however, drink Olympia beer, his favourite brand. When asked if Olympia was organically brewed or not, he wryly replied, 'I don't know how organically brewed Olympia or any beer is, but there are certain things you just *can't* sacrifice.'

*

Maggie by now had resumed her picture painting. 'I had to leave it alone for a while when Kyle came along because a baby disorientates your thinking and takes up a great deal of your time,' she said. 'A child needs constant attention. But I have gone back to painting now. I don't do it for a living, although people have offered to buy some of the things I've done.'

While in Mexico she was constantly on the lookout for inspiration for her pictures, preferring to paint pictures that create mood and feelings rather than just do landscapes or portraits. 'For example, when I was in Mexico with Clint, I saw a little old lady coming down the street all in black, and I liked the picture it made – all dead black against the stark white of the adobe buildings in the sun.'

Unable to stay for the three months' duration, Maggie flew back to their gradually progressing house in Carmel which she called 'our forever house.' Their plans were that Kyle would grow up there and go to school, a long way from the fast and tempting life of Hollywood. Whenever Maggie saw brickwork, or a door, or a wall she thought Clint might like for the house, she took a photograph of it with the expensive Japanese camera he bought her, and sent the picture to him for his approval. 'He's looking forward to the new home,' she said, 'to healthy foods like fish, beef and poultry with baked potatoes and salads.'

Although a dutiful and loyal wife, friends made it clear that she was no mere 'little lady at home,' as Deedee Moore noted. Said one, 'Maggie's no mop – she's got more balls than a Christmas tree. Clint talks to her about *everything*. It's just that Clint likes things done the way he wants them, and Maggie does them – that way.' Said another, 'Clint doesn't make a move without Maggie. She reads all the scripts – sometimes two or three a day, deals closely with Clint's agent, manager and press agent. And she's clever enough to give Clint all the credit for choosing the script.' She had, it was said, perfected his signature so she could sign autographs for his publicity pictures.

During the early days of filming, Eastwood, often a star to shrug off the trappings of stardom, ate lunch with the crew. But when he realized that Shirley MacLaine ate lunch in her trailer, he began eating *his* lunch in his trailer.

As with all established stars, offers arrived daily for films, commercials, opening stores. A phone call came through to him at Cocoyoc from a man offering him a hundred thousand dollars to do a hair spray commercial. 'You got the kind of hair style we think is good for our image.'

'What do I have to do?' asked Eastwood.

'Nothing. Just be the man in our commercial.'

Eastwood shook his head in amazement. 'Where were you when I needed you, buddy,' he said, and promptly turned down the hundred grand.

One of the film's more interesting locations was an old sugarcane factory plantation bombed by Zapata and virtually untouched since the Mexican Revolution. Arriving early in the morning on the set, he was dressed half in costume – saggy jeans, cowboy boots, a bowie knife – and half his casual gear – white T-shirt, Jean Seberg's sneakers, sunglasses. Disappearing into his trailer, he turned on a cassette of Wes Montgomery's *California Dreaming*, whistled along with it and studied his script. For breakfast he drank orange juice and ate sunflower seeds.

'Okay, Clint,' called the assistant director, 'we're ready for you.' Eastwood put on the rest of his Western garb and strode onto the set. Shirley MacLaine was dressed in a nun's habit. The script called for them to hide among the ruins from French troops. When threatened by a rattlesnake, Eastwood kills it.

A real rattler was used, and Eastwood admitted to *Playboy* that he did in fact kill the snake himself. 'I ended up killing the rattlesnake,' he said, 'but I didn't want to.' Apparently the Mexican authorities didn't want a rattlesnake loose after filming, so Eastwood, in the guise of Hogan, killed it for the cameras. 'It wasn't the happiest thing I ever did. I cut the snake's head off and handed the body to Shirley MacLaine.'

Killing the snake went strongly against his principles. He refuses even to hunt, although he enjoys fishing. 'I guess I have too much of a reverence for living creatures. There's so much beauty in them.'

He proved his point one night when, during the shooting of a night time scene, a large moth flew onto the set, dazzled by the arc lamps. A member of the crew immediately chased after it, trying to swat it and stamp on it. Eastwood flew into a rage.

'Leave it alone,' he yelled at the startled moth hunter. 'They need killers like you in Vietnam,' Eastwood told him, and then, gently cupping his hands around the moth, guided it to safety.

During the filming of the attack on the garrison, Shirley MacLaine noticed how much Eastwood worked out his anger and violence through performing.

'You should have been there for the garrison scene,' she told reporters later in New York. 'He gets those guns in his hands and really gets going.' She hunched down, hands at her hips as though she was about to draw imaginary six-guns. 'He's in there banging away after the camera stops! Really, the rest of us in the scene are doing all the work, and *we're* satisfied with the take. But *he* wants to do another. You should have seen the look in his eyes!'

As was becoming usual on an Eastwood picture, rumours of romantic flings ignited and then died; a girl was flown in to Cocoyoc from the Bahamas; Susan St James, whom he met in Acapulco, was transported to the location – those were two of the stories the gossip columnists reported. What was certain was that each day he picked up the phone and called Maggie without fail.

It's also true that throughout his career he has proved magnetic to women. As one female friend told columnist Deedee Moore, 'I've seen the most aggressive women slipping him notes in restaurants. It's amazing to watch.' However, not all women have been flattering about him. One unswooning Hollywood lady said, 'I've never seen a man trying so hard to prove his masculinity – except maybe Warren Beatty. But at least Beatty shows intelligence and makes an effort to be charming. I get the idea that in bed Eastwood would be computer sex – push the right buttons. A giver he's not. He's more a personality than an actor. Pleasant and...? but under the surface – interested only in himself. After you look at him, what's left? He's kind of narcissistic. His closest relative is the mirror.'

As filming progressed, MacLaine, and most of the American contingent, were struck by Montezuma's Revenge. Even Eastwood lost a lot of weight although he evaded the terrible sickness that MacLaine suffered and which held up filming for a while. She came back to work, still unwell but desperate just to 'finish the picture and get the hell back to humanity and civilization.'

Clint joked, 'I lost all this weight waiting for my meals to arrive.'

The picture was finally finished. It had been a long, hot and sometimes gruelling location. Eastwood did not look forward to the prospect of spending several more months away when he began filming *Kelly's Heroes* in Yugoslavia. Don Siegel retired to the cutting room with his film editor to assemble *Sister Sara* and there the great flaw in the film became evident. There was no chemistry between Eastwood and MacLaine. Eastwood, it was becoming clear, worked best on screen as a loner, without a partner who was equal or, as in this case, somewhat superior. As Eastwood came to realize, 'The woman has the best part, something I'm sure Shirley noticed.'

Universal became unsure how to handle the release of the film. It was impossible to promote it as a 'Clint Eastwood Film' because Shirley MacLaine had top billing. But before the film was ready for distribution Eastwood would be finished on his most unhappy film, *Kelly's Heroes*.

9

New Directions

Clint Eastwood thought *Kelly's Heroes* was going to be one of the best war films ever. 'It should have been,' he said. 'It had the best script, a good cast, a subtle anti-war message.'

He had high hopes for it, as did Brian G Hutton, his director from *Where Eagles Dare* who once again had the backing of MGM and a cast that included Telly Savalas, Donald Sutherland, Carroll O'Connor and Don Rickles. Originally called *The Warriors*, it was fashioned somewhat on *The Dirty Dozen* as a group of oddball GIs advance the war effort for their own gains; their aim is to secure millions of dollars' worth of gold held by the Germans. It had elements of loud action and comedy, all put together with a multi-million dollar budget. Today Eastwood would probably argue that had they cut the budget, forcing them to film closer to home and reducing the number of extras and the amount of hardware, they might have come closer to ending up with the kind of film they had all envisaged.

But MGM were desperate for a successor to *Where Eagles Dare* and that meant pouring money into this production and sending the cast and crew off to Yugoslavia for five months. Eastwood arrived at the location travelling, typically, light; one suit, a couple of pairs of jeans and a spare pair of tennis shoes. He drove out each morning to the set on his motorcycle, usually an hour early, and then sat around playing cards with the technicians.

Filming was tough from the very beginning. Special effects supervisor Karli Baumgartner, a German, used real dynamite instead of the usual mixure of cork and black powder. Eastwood had to drive a jeep through a series of such explosions, all timed to perfection so that Baumgartner fired off each explosion just as Eastwood drove past them. 'Maybe he was getting even for World War Two,' Eastwood joked.

In an opening scene, Savalas and Eastwood had to run from a barn that exploded behind them. Savalas told Hutton, 'That barn's going to blow up and we'll be killed.'

Hutton asked Eastwood what he thought. 'Let's ask Karli what he thinks,' said Clint.

Baumgartner told them, 'I don't recommend you doing this stunt.'

That settled it. Two stunt men doubled for Eastwood and Savalas. The cameras rolled and Baumgartner blew the barn to pieces. The stunt doubles were unhurt but they couldn't hear properly for the next few days.

For the first time since the *Dollars* films, Clint had no leading lady. The film was completely free of women, although the original script included one. She was to be played by Ingrid Pitt, from *Where Eagles Dare*. 'I was virtually climbing on board the plane bound for Yugoslavia when word came through that my part had been cut,' she said.

Despite the size of the cast and number of egos involved, there was generally good humour throughout. But there were plenty of other set-backs. Donald Sutherland fell seriously ill and almost died mid-way through production. Comedy actor Don Rickles came on the receiving end of Eastwood's humour when he injured his leg slightly and became convinced he would bleed to death. While other members of the cast consoled him and assured him he wouldn't die, Eastwood dryly uttered, 'Better get Shecky Greene into costume.'

Rickles retaliated by sending up Eastwood's image of the laconic guy little given to showing too much expression in his face. 'Clint is the only man in the world who can talk with flies on his lips,' he said. 'Now Clint is my friend and the star of the movie; you know, Mr Big. But what can you do with a guy that doesn't even know what air conditioning is? Give him an army cot and a nail to hang his clothes on and he's happy.

'How can Telly and I go to the producer and demand better treatment when Clint's happy with a room in one building, a toilet in another and the ocean to shower in?'

Telly Savalas likened Eastwood to the great Hollywood stars of the Golden Era. At the time the media – or just the PR men – were calling

Eastwood's rise to TV stardom came in the late fifties and early sixties opposite Eric Fleming in *Rawhide*. *(CBS TV)*

Eastwood found profit in death as the Man With No Name in *A Fistful of Dollars*. *(Jolly Films/United Artists)*

In *For a Few Dollars More*, Eastwood joined forces with Lee Van Cleef (left) to capture bandit Gian Maria Volonte (right). *(PEA/United Artists)*

Noted stage star Eli Wallach stole much of the attention and glory from Eastwood in *The Good, the Bad and the Ugly*. *(PEA/United Artists)*

Eastwood and Lee Marvin played singin' pardners stakin' their claim on Jean Seberg in *Paint Your Wagon*. *(Paramount)*

In between scenes of *Where Eagles Dare*, Ingrid Pitt often rode pillion with Eastwood. *(Ingrid Pitt)*

Eastwood became the object of desire for Geraldine Page (left) and Jo Ann Harris (right) in *The Beguiled*. *(Universal/Malpaso)*

him the new Gary Cooper. Said Savalas, 'Gary Cooper was more of a man of instinct. But Eastwood and Cooper both project one thing beautifully – pure Americanism. In that sense, Clint belongs to the great tradition of American stars – Cooper, John Wayne, Gregory Peck, Henry Fonda, James Stewart, Spencer Tracy, Clark Gable, etc.'

Eastwood was keen not to be compared to Cooper, or anyone else. 'I'm just a tall, lanky American who came on the scene at the right time. I don't see myself as Gary Cooper's heir, but I am flattered at the comparison.'

Hutton felt that Eastwood was a return to the old style of a man's man of the silver screen. He said, 'On the screen Clint Eastwood is a man who knows where he's going. He knows what he's after, and he knows how to get it. In an age of uncertainty in the arts, politics, and everything else, people enjoy watching a man like this in action. They don't want to see the anguish of a Brando or a James Dean anymore. They want to escape into something more positive.

'I think we went twenty years of film, from 1947, when Brando hit, until 1967, when Clint hit, with actors who, for the most part, played characters who were confused, not sure of themselves, unable to cope. Clint's character has always been a guy who knows who he is, knows what he wants and goes out and does it. Regardless if he's good or bad, he's at least certain.

'Clint, aside from his talents, is all-American – in the way he feels, does things, the way he looks. Clint Eastwood may not be considered by some to be a great actor, but I don't think anyone can deny he's right there.'

At a time when America was divided over the Vietnam War – half said to get the hell out, the other half said to stay the hell in – Eastwood, who in *Kelly's Heroes* was depicting something of the futility of war (at least in its uncut version), gave his own views. 'When I was in the Army I was against the Korean War, and I'm against the war in Vietnam. But I'm not among the people who say let's stop Vietnam, zap! If you're going to stop it, I'd like to say, "Here's a constructive way." '

One view of his was to send all the men who killed for fun – including hunters – out to Vietnam and bring back the boys who didn't want to be there. But he wasn't impressed by those who said that Vietnam was a different kind of war. 'People have been making out that Vietnam is something different. Hell, we've been fighting wars for a thousand years, and will a thousand more. Competition inspires great things. But you sure as hell can have competition without war.'

Perhaps it's not too surprising that after *Kelly's Heroes*, he made no more war films (unless one includes *Heartbreak Ridge*). His abhorrence of war, and the mess that *Kelly's Heroes* ended up, kept him virtually firmly in the more comfortable cops and cowboys roles.

At the end of filming, Eastwood stopped off in London to promote *Paint Your Wagon*. It had been premiered in America and Eastwood, Maggie, Lee Marvin and his lady Michelle had attended the charity opening at the Pacific Cinerama Dome Theatre. Its presentation in 70mm, spread across the giant curved Cinerama screen, enhanced the film for its spectacular elements, and so Paramount negotiated to open the film in London at the Astoria where a Cinerama screen and single-lens projector system had been installed. Despite his disappointment with the version of the film that was being shown to the public, Eastwood happily fulfilled his obligations to Paramount to promote the film. He was only in London for a few hours to do a couple of interviews. Reporters noted that Eastwood looked as nervous as the Paramount personnel who were overseeing the interviews. 'I'm looking forward to being home again,' Eastwood said, 'particularly as I have only managed to spend four weeks in the last year there.'

The British reporters discovered him to be soft-spoken and, still being unused to and uncomfortable with interviews, apt to trip over words but quick to correct himself when his tongue slipped. He drank weak tea without milk and was 'not much to look at, a bit shy, taciturn and dresses off screen in casual clothes that wouldn't raise an eyebrow at a village fête.'

Back in America, Eastwood prepared to do battle with MGM when he learned that they were going to cut some essential scenes from *Kelly's Heroes*. He begged them not to cut the film. He even called Jim Aubrey, the studio's head, and said, 'For God's sake, don't run that picture for the critics until Brian has had a chance to do some more work on it. You're going to cut off maybe millions of dollars in box-office receipts.'

'Look, Clint, leave it with me and I'll think over what you've said,' replied Aubrey.

Aubrey thought it over and decided to release the film as it was. The critics were no kinder to this than most of Eastwood's previous films. Judith Crist, who never liked anything he did, believed it was 'made for no possible reason other than a chance to use the Yugoslav army at cut rates.' The more serious-minded *Monthly Film Bulletin* described it as 'over two hours of consistently devastating explosions, pyrotechnics and demolition.'

Eastwood considered it a box-office failure, although according to the book *The MGM Story* it was a hit in the USA and an outright smash in the UK and other countries in 1970. It certainly couldn't have done too badly as Eastwood came in at No 2 at the box office that year, and his standing couldn't have been attributed very much to *Two Mules for Sister Sara* which did poorly in 1970. In regard to *Paint Your Wagon* and *Kelly's Heroes* specifically, he said, 'They should have been better. It's awful when a concept is lost and the focus is altered. The trouble is compounded when performances are changed by too much meddling and by too many people working at cross purposes.'

As for *Two Mules for Sister Sara*, part of the problem seems to have been due to the formation of CIC, a distribution set-up between Universal and Paramount. In the UK, CIC, not knowing quite what to do with the film, expanded the 35mm negative up to a grainy 70mm print and opened it at the Casino Cinerama Theatre in London. The home of Cinerama films was too prestigious a theatre for a film that needed the same audience that came to see *The Good, the Bad and the Ugly* at the New Victoria Theatre, and audiences stayed away. As CIC was getting itself into gear, they seemed to forget to put the film on a full general release, as they also forgot with certain other films such as *Silent Running*. As far as the UK was concerned, this was probably due to contractual problems over Universal distributing its films through the Rank Cinema circuit, while Paramount released its films through the ABC Cinema chain. Ultimately the ABC (soon after called EMI) circuit had the monopoly on CIC's films, but in the interim a number of movies were neglected, and Eastwood's fans wondered why their hero's latest Western didn't turn up at the local cinema.

Miserable at the way his recent films had fared, both in production and on release, Eastwood put his maxim about careful choosing of locations into effect with his next picture, *The Beguiled*. He maintained that the formation of his own company was to give him this kind of control, thereby 'ruling out long locations. We spent four months in Oregon on *Paint Your Wagon*, four months in Mexico on *Two Mules for Sister Sara* and five months on *Kelly's Heroes* in

Yugoslavia. After three weeks, you get awful restless to know what home is like.'

For *The Beguiled*, Louisiana was chosen; not exactly on the back doorstep perhaps, but this was to be a relatively short location. Once again, Don Siegel was to produce and direct, and Jennings Lang was once more overseeing the production on behalf of Universal. The setting was the American Civil War, and no doubt Universal felt they had another exciting Eastwood Western on their hands. If they did, they were in for a shock.

Clint played a wounded Union soldier who takes refuge in the claustrophobic confines of a small girls' school in the South, run by Geraldine Page (one of Eastwood's co-stars from *Rawhide*). His overtly physical presence arouses passions in the head teacher as well as the girls and they vie for his attentions. Finally, when she realizes she cannot have him for herself, Page cuts off one of his legs. Then the youngest of the girls, in retaliation for the death of her turtle, feeds him poisonous and deadly mushrooms.

This was a film with little action but a feeling of growing mystery and ultimate horror; a sort of gothic Western. For the first time in an Eastwood film, the cast was predominantly female, and he remarked, 'Shirley [MacLaine] was fun, but in *Beguiled* I worked with *eight* leading actresses, and they were all fun too.' Actually, there were *nine* actresses – Geraldine Page, Elizabeth Hartman, Jo Ann Harris, Darleen Carr, Mae Mercer, Pamelyn Ferdin, Melody Thomas, Peggy Drier and Pattye Mattick.

Supervising the few stunts was Buddy Van Horn, making this his second outing with Eastwood. He also played a small part in the film and was billed in the cast list as Wayne 'Buddy' Van Horn. He became a member of Malpaso's regular ensemble and occasionally did a little acting too. Eastwood would later elevate him to director. Making his debut as a director of photography on this film was Bruce Surtees, son of multi-award winning cinematographer Robert Surtees. Bruce Surtees had served an eight-year apprenticeship as a camera operator, mostly working on Eastwood's American films. He brought to *The Beguiled* a soberly brooding quality that photographically united the dripping Louisiana locations with the shadowy interiors of the seminar conceived by art director Alexander Golitzen, another Malpaso regular.

As location shooting continued, Robert Daley, at the Malpaso offices at Universal Studios, was setting up Eastwood's next film with the studio, *Play Misty for Me*. It was important that future projects were continually developed, and Daley's and Sonia Chernus's jobs were to do exactly that.

As filming *The Beguiled* quickly progressed, somebody came up with the idea of a TV programme about Don Siegel, and Eastwood immediately seized upon the opportunity of directing it. It was subsequently shown on TV.

An interesting aspect of the film was its use of original Civil War photographs for the credit title sequence. However, not all the photographs were authentic. Some of them were still frames from Universal's Civil War drama *Shenandoah*. They even managed to superimpose the face of Eastwood over one of the authentic pictures.

This was a film which called for a different kind of performance from Eastwood in which he had to deliver twice as much dialogue as usual as well as varying emotions. Surprisingly he said, 'My role in *The Beguiled* was easier to play than the lone Westerner was. In those Leone films, I had to establish an image for the audience while saying very little, showing very little. In *Beguiled* I was dealing with straight, normal, emotions from my own standpoint, which were simply those of survival.'

Despite his own control over every aspect of production, he had made one enormous mistake. When *The Beguiled* was released in 1971 it could find no audience. As he admitted, 'It probably would have been a more successful film if I hadn't been in it.' Eastwood fans didn't want to see him play a character who ends up getting his leg cut off and emasculated by a bunch of women. 'They wanted a character who could control everything around him,' he conceded.

Those who thought Eastwood was merely an action film star stayed away, especially when Universal designed an advertising poster that put a gun in Eastwood's hand and a cigar in his mouth, making it look like a typical Eastwood actioner. He was furious with the campaign. 'I was terribly disappointed by the way *The Beguiled* was sold,' he said. 'I told the studio before I made it that it was a completely different kind of story, a psychological gothic horror film. Then they sold it as just another Clint Eastwood picture, me with a cheroot cigar and stubble beard, which was awfully unfair to both my regular audience and those who wanted something different. That sort of thing can kill you in the business.

'But it was good for me in a career sense,' he said on a more positive note, 'because it did give the few people who saw it a different look at me as a performer.' Most reviews of the film were moderately favourable, although Judith Crist said it was 'a must for sadists and woman-haters.'

Eastwood was nonplussed by Crist's immovable loathing of his work. 'Judith Crist, for some reason, hasn't been knocked out over everything I've done – or *anything* I've done, as a matter of fact. I think she liked *The Devil in Miss Jones* (a porn film), but she thought *The Beguiled* was obscene!' Today *The Beguiled* is regarded as a classic.

One lesson it taught Eastwood was a sense of what kind of roles were right for him (although he occasionally strayed from the path, often effectively in films like *Honky Tonk Man* and *White Hunter, Black Heart*).

'You have to cast yourself in things you do well,' he said in 1974. 'John Wayne has been the success he has been over the years because he does what he does better than anybody else can. A lot of people have said he doesn't really act. Just let them try to act like he does and they'll find they can't do it. You'll never go to any acting school in the world where people stand around trying to be the lone, enigmatic stranger, either. But at the same time, a lot of actors who play Henry the Fifth can't play my characters. They'd be ludicrous. To me, an actor's success comes not only from the magnetism of his personality but more from his ability to select material that would be commercial with him in it.'

With those thoughts in mind, his choice of films from then right up to the end of the seventies resulted in not one single failure, and established him as the number one star of that decade.

In the summer of 1970, the house in Carmel was ready for the Eastwoods to move in lock, stock and barrel. Clint began to settle into his idyllic life. 'He is something of a loner who prefers the rustic scene to city life and doesn't care too much about clothes,' said Maggie. 'Ninety per cent of them are casual.'

The couple shared certain interests; she liked to ride with him on his bike occasionally, they both played tennis and they both went to a shooting club. They also watched movies, and not at home; they went to cinemas where Eastwood watched his own and other people's films, gauging what the audiences enjoyed. To avoid being recognized, he went disguised in glasses, a false moustache and a hat. 'It makes me look quite different,' he said. 'By the time I get a hat on, and the moustache and glasses, it drops my IQ by about fifty points, which makes it about five!'

They also entertained at home, but never large gatherings. 'He doesn't like parties,' said Maggie, 'and enjoys himself most with small groups of people who he knows and likes to be with.' The couple often enjoyed dinner with two or three other couples, but guests were never made up of Hollywood mogul types. The only full-scale social event they became involved in was the annual Clint Eastwood Invitational Celebrity Tennis Tournament at Pebble Beach, the proceeds of which went to local charities. It all began in 1970 when Don Hamilton, the pro at the Pebble Beach Tennis Club where they had been staging a small celebrity tennis tournament, said to Eastwood, 'What we want to do is hold a big event each year for charity.'

'Perhaps you'd better get a better tennis player,' joked Eastwood.

'Better still,' said Hamilton, 'why don't *you* sponsor it?' Eastwood did, and it became a success. In 1972 the event raised nearly $50,000.

Although he was earning something like a million dollars a film now, neither he nor Maggie could forget that little more than ten years ago they were struggling to survive. Consequently, despite their immense wealth, they maintained simple values, although they still spent lavishly on their home if not on their own clothes and personal belongings. When asked what difference money had made to them, Maggie said, 'It brings some problems but not the big problems of not having enough. I'd sooner have it than struggle to make ends meet. I suppose it offers an opportunity to bring up the boy in the real countryside. And we can afford a housekeeper [a Mexican woman called Ophelia Rodriguez who had seven children of her own]. It's also enabled us to do a lot of travelling which we hadn't done before. Freedom of choice and movement is wonderful, although it becomes more complicated now that Clint films on an international scale.'

The Eastwoods were coming increasingly under public scrutiny. Maggie was becoming as well known as any other Hollywood wife, and as the public's, and the media's, interest increased, so Clint began to draw more of a veil around himself and his family. Interviews became less frequent, and eventually to get an interview with him at all was a coup. He became ever more a recluse; 'I'm not too thrilled with the idea of talking about myself.' He felt he'd reached a stage in his life where he had done too many chat shows, many of which he regretted 'because of the sheer boredom of it all. I find myself kind of on the defensive about interviews, because the thing everybody seems to like is shock. I've always admired guys that can do that. Like Lee Marvin. If I could talk like Lee, my interviews might be more exciting to read.'

Part of his reclusive nature was his need to protect the freedom he – and Maggie – enjoyed in their marriage. 'There's always a certain respect for the individual in our relationship,' he said, 'we're not one person. She's an individual, I'm an individual, and we're friends. We're a lot of things – lovers, friends, the whole conglomerate – but at the same time I'm not shooting orders to her on where she's supposed to be every five minutes, and I don't expect her to shoot them at me.'

He needed his time alone, not just so he could take off to satisfy his loner's soul, but to make the occasional visit to Roxanne and daughter Kimber, then six.

'From the beginning I always called him Daddy,' said Kimber, 'and he would buy me cuddly toys. We didn't see him very often, but my mother remained faithful to him all those years.'

Roxanne never knew exactly when he would show up and usually he visited them about four times a year. Said Kimber, 'He would normally phone just before he showed up and my mom would cook him his favourite spaghetti with aubergine or an Italian casserole. He would usually stay one night and then he would be gone again.'

In retrospect, Kimber said, 'I would not put up with what Mom did. I need to feel more secure.' But for Clint, it was a difficult balancing act, trying to maintain his marriage, his public image, his private life and his secret life.

But he did try to find opportunities to give Kimber a feeling of family life. When he went skiing in Vail, Colorado, with ex-President Gerald Ford, he took Roxanne and Kimber with him, booking them into a hotel suite of their own. 'It was one of the few times that I felt like we were a real family,' said Kimber, although he was never able to introduce her as his daughter, no matter how much he might have wanted to.

From time to time columnists asked him questions about his marriage – questions that became more difficult to answer. He always gave Maggie the credit for the survival of their marriage. When Deedee Moore asked him if he was happy with Maggie, he replied,

'Either happy or extremely loyal.' And, he added, 'It's going to be old doorways if my marriage doesn't work out. I don't believe in duplicating mistakes, though I'm older now.'

Back on the film front, he was deep in preparation for *Play Misty for Me*. It was a very different kind of film for him; a contemporary thriller in which he played a disc jockey, not a tough hero, who spoke softly over the air waves of a radio station, each night, saying, 'This is Dave Garner with a little verse, a little talk and five hours of music to be very, very nice to each other by.'

Dave takes phone calls on the air. 'Hello,' says a woman's voice.

'Hi, what'll it be?' asks Dave.

'Play *Misty* for me.' She is a regular caller and always asks for the same tune. He meets up with her in his local bar, discovers her name is Evelyn Draper, and after a couple of dates with her she proves to be insanely jealous and possessive. Meanwhile he tries to patch up his relationship with the girl he really loves, Tobie, but Evelyn continues to plague him, to the point of becoming psychotic. She uses Tobie to lure him into a trap in which she attacks him with a kitchen knife. He fights her off, while she slashes at him, and she finally falls to her death from his clifftop house.

To him the film would be 'strictly a comment on an available guy who's somewhat of a celebrity in a small town. And this kookie girl becomes intrigued by him; she sees herself in a romantic situation and they have an affair. To him, it's just an affair; he's in love with somebody else and he tries to level with her, telling her he's involved elsewhere.' The film was, he said, 'a suspense sort of psychodrama, with an added element; it looked at that whole problem of commitment, that misinterpretation of commitment between a man and a woman.'

It was an idea that intrigued him, if not the executives at Universal. 'Who wants to see Clint Eastwood play a disc jockey?' they asked.

'Who wants to see him play *anything*?' asked Eastwood. He knew very well that what they really wanted was to have him make another Western. He had taken the project to CBS and United Artists and both had turned it down. Even Universal had rejected during Eastwood's early attempts to hawk it.

He was No 2 at the box office, second only to Paul Newman. Million-dollar offers were coming in from all over town, but he knew now that all he wanted to do was make his own films. No other star prior to him or since would prove to be so independent, except perhaps John Wayne who, with his Batjack Company, produced virtually all his films since the fifties, usually with his son Michael as producer. Kirk Douglas came close to such independence during the fifties with his own company, Bryna, but often found himself in grief with his directors. Eastwood came up with the perfect solution; to direct himself in *Play Misty for Me*. As one studio executive noted in 1970, 'He's become so serious this year. Like he knows he's a corporation. And I don't mean an institution; he's been that since the spaghetti Westerns. He's a multi-million dollar conglomerate.'

According to the rules of the Director's Guild, anyone wanting to become a director can do so provided someone gave them a job. Being head of Malpaso, he told himself, 'Kid, you got the job.'

He went to Lew Wasserman, the head of Universal, and said, 'I can make it cheap, all on natural sets.'

'Okay,' said Wasserman. 'Take it and run with it.' He voiced his only reservation. 'Why would you want to do a film where the woman is the best part in the film?'

No doubt Wasserman was only curious, for he was happy to let Eastwood make a film for them for no upfront salary but simply a percentage of the profits. Eastwood went away, knowing he could make his film but suspecting that the studio was really thinking, 'We'll let the kid fool around with this film and then he'll probably do a couple of Westerns for us, or some other adventure film that'll seem more commercial.'

When he told them he was going to direct it himself, they were thunderstruck. Few film stars had directed themselves successfully, and they had no reason to believe that he could do it any better. But he was determined to make his film, and make it his way, and if they didn't let him direct the film, he'd find some other studio which would. They gave in, but only after getting him to agree to act in the film for no fee, and take only a percentage.

He'd virtually already made his most important decisions regarding the film. It would be filmed completely on location in and around Carmel, right on his doorstep. 'It was a small story and lent itself perfectly to being shot on natural sets,' he said. 'Working in authentic and realistic backgrounds in Europe during my years there as an actor had taught me the value of utilizing such locations.'

He added, 'If I know the Carmel area like my own backyard, it is largely because my own back yard *is* there.'

For the scenes showing Eastwood at work as a disc jockey, he filmed at Carmel's own radio station, KRML. Other local landmarks that Eastwood found use for in the film included Cannery Row, The Sardine Factory, The Windjammer and the residential areas in Carmel Highlands and Carmel Point.

He had no doubt in his mind that directing is 'an instinctive thing. The instinct to hire the right person – the right cameraman to go with the right director, and the right actors to go with the other actors, and so on, so the ensemble fits.'

That was his key to movie-making – working as an ensemble. His choice of the right cameraman was Bruce Surtees from *The Beguiled*. Robert Daley was elevated to the position of producer. The task of polishing up Jo Heim's original script went to Dean Riesner. On the set, Eastwood limited his crew to just 25, helping to keep costs low and efficiency at a premium. Most of them had worked previously with Don Siegel and Eastwood had the distinct impression that they were all waiting for him to prove himself. He said that it lasted just one day and that by the second morning they were all working together as a totally involved and compatible unit.

For the role of Evelyn Draper, he needed a special kind of leading lady, one who could convey a psychotic personality yet display sexual magnetism. He'd worked with too few actresses to find one among his former leading ladies, but came up with Jessica Walter. The studio were not happy with his choice and tried to persuade him to change his mind. None of her previous films had been particularly successful, such as *Pro* with Charlton Heston and *The Group*. Eastwood wasn't interested in how many successful films she'd been in; he wanted her for her talent, not her track record. Against the wishes of the studio he cast her. For the role of his girlfriend, he picked pretty blonde Donna Mills. She probably hoped the film would project her into a bigger league, but she didn't become a star until she landed a leading role in the glossy TV soap *Knots Landing*.

His most unconventional piece of casting was convincing Don Siegel to appear as a barman. 'I couldn't turn Clint down,' said Siegel. 'First of all, we're close friends. Even more important, I had to give him my support in his first directorial effort. I had always encouraged him in his desire to direct, and if he insisted on turning me into an actor, I simply had to roll with it.'

The scene Eastwood shot first was one involving Siegel who had never acted in his life. He was nervous, afraid of letting Eastwood down and kept insisting, 'You're making a big mistake. You shouldn't be doing this; you should get a good character actor.'

'Don't worry about it,' Eastwood told him. 'If I screw up as a director, I've got a good director on the set.'

In fact, Siegel was so nervous that he couldn't remember his lines so he had them written on bits of paper which were stuck all over the set. Unfortunately, he kept mixing them up, and Clint claimed that after that time Siegel was more tolerant in his treatment of actors.

The veteran director felt that he was able to give a reasonable performance because Eastwood gave him such confidence.

Siegel had previously warned Eastwood that he would neglect his own performance if he wasn't careful, and that proved true when he realized he was concentrating most of his directing efforts on Jessica Walter who proved impressive right from the beginning of filming. As an aid to directing, he used a then revolutionary method, Video West, a video system linked to the movie camera, allowing Eastwood to immediately view each take on the set on a TV monitor. This way he was able to make on-the-spot corrections, and it eliminated unnecessary retakes. Consequently, he brought the film in ahead of the five-week schedule by four days and $50,000 under its original $950,000 budget.

He came away highly satisfied. But there were still some who remained cynical. 'Everybody asked the same question,' he said, ' "How does it feel to direct a movie?" In the beginning I would smile and say it was great. But most of them wanted to go deeper than that and they would make a flat statement like, "It's tough to wear two hats." If I agreed, they wanted to know why. And when I'd try to explain about separating actor from director in the thought processes, when I'd try to point the difficulty in retaining complete objectivity, they'd lose interest before I was through.

'On the other hand, if I said it wasn't too difficult keeping the two jobs separate, it would lead to a headache. One story came out with the headline "Clint Eastwood Says Directing Is A Snap".'

Critics were split over his ability to direct. Andrew Sarris of the *Village Voice* felt the film 'marks a surprisingly auspicious directorial debut for Clint Eastwood as director. It is one of the most effectively scary movies of this or any year.' Roger Greenspun, in the *New York Times*, disagreed. 'It is sad that this film with its locale and some of its moods out of *Vertigo*, and its central obsessional action almost an inversion of Preminger's wonderful *Laura*, should echo so briefly in the imagination.'

Other critics likened it, favourably and unfavourably, to Hitchcock's *Psycho*. When asked if he was trying to emulate the Hitchcock chiller, he said, 'No, I certainly wasn't trying to duplicate *Psycho* in any way. I never saw it that way myself, other than the attacks. Those attacks could be sprung upon the audience with the same kind of suspense and energy as Hitchcock used, I thought. But other than that, I saw it as a story of constriction, the blanket thrown over one, the bound-in feelings, the frustration of trying to solve it and not being able to; of having to sit down and calm the person you want to escape from. No exposition after that is necessary.'

Shortly after completing *Misty*, Eastwood took Maggie with him to Italy where he had been invited to speak to students about his work. He was also there to attend the première in Milan of *The Beguiled* which the Italians took readily to their hearts. When he and Maggie arrived in Milan they were met by crowds caught up in a wave of Eastwoodmania. To the Italians he was their greatest screen hero and they presented him with an award. But the hysteria he met with and the constant adulation heaped upon him at every opportunity was something he was unfamiliar and uncomfortable with. He told Iain Johnstone that he doubted if he could ever find the courage to return to Italy and risk facing it all again. This would have proven a great disappointment to Sergio Leone who harboured the hope that he might work with Eastwood again, a fact that the star might have remained unaware of. In 1973, in reply to a question of whether he would work with Leone again, Eastwood said, 'You mean if Sergio Leone came back and said, "We've got a new place to take you?" I'd make any kind of film if I liked the script. But I'd have to see the thing. I don't know. I doubt it at the moment.'

In 1977 Italian star Franco Nero, who was made famous as *Django*, told me, 'Sergio Leone has told me that he wants to make another Western and he wants Clint Eastwood, Terence Hill and me all together.' Leone never got to make another Western after *Duck, You Sucker*! (aka *A Fistful of Dynamite*) in 1970. His time between then and 1984 was spent setting up and making his gangster epic *Once Upon a Time in America*, and then spent his time preparing other non-Western projects until his death in 1989. But it is doubtful that Eastwood, once he became firmly established as a totally independent film-maker, would have worked for Leone or any other big-time director apart from Don Siegel.

During the weeks that passed following the completion of *Misty*, Eastwood sorted out his feelings about directing and concluded that while 'directing is much tougher than acting in many respects, it is also much easier in other ways. One required a different thought pattern from the other. Both are tremendously challenging and gratifying to me, and I intend to continue doing both in the future.' Then added, a little impetuously, 'but not at the same time.'

10

Harry and the Drifter

A story, *Dead Right*, written by Harry Julian Fink and his wife Rita M Fink, had been bought by Warner Brothers and offered to Frank Sinatra who chose to do the film as his celluloid swan song. He was going to play Detective Inspector Harry Callahan, a New York cop whose job is to find a psychopath who calls himself Scorpio.

Prior to filming, Sinatra injured his hand and had to pull out. Paul Newman read the script, liked the main character, but didn't like the way Callahan was depicted as an unkempt, scruffy character. He suggested to Warners that Clint Eastwood might make a more acceptable dirty Harry Callahan. Eastwood rather liked the ring to it – Dirty Harry. But he felt the character needed tidying up and that the only reason he should be considered 'dirty' was because he got all the dirty jobs. The film became *Dirty Harry*. The script went through a number of revisions – there were five versions; in the original draft the killer was supposed to be killed by a police marksman as he boarded a plane. Eastwood had it changed so that Callahan himself takes out the killer in what would be a classic ending.

He told Warners he was interested provided the picture was made under the Malpaso banner. They agreed. He also told them he wanted Don Siegel to direct. Siegel was now a director in demand and was at this time being called upon for speaking engagements at the film departments of leading universities, including Dartmouth, Loyola, USC and UCLA. Boston University were asking him for memorabilia. Warners offered the job to Siegel who accepted because he found the script a refreshing change from all the other scripts he'd read recently in which the cops were the sadists and perverts. He now wanted to function only on the highest creative level of film-making, and insisted he also serve as the film's producer with Robert Daley as executive producer.

The story begins on a rooftop where a girl takes a swim in her sundeck pool. From a nearby building a sniper shoots her dead, and thereafter makes his demand for $100,000 from the police or more deaths will follow. He signs himself 'Scorpio.' Harry Callahan, of the San Francisco Police, is advised by Lt Bressler and the Mayor that they are going to pay off the killer. Callahan's new partner, the young, bright and eager Chico, is amazed by what appears to be Harry's surly, negative attitude toward everybody and everything. Following another death, Harry, on a hunch that the killer's ego will bring him back to the same district, stakes out a rooftop with Chico, but although Harry proves correct, they lose 'Scorpio' following a gun fight. The killer next kidnaps a 14-year-old girl and buries her alive, demanding $200,000. Harry is given the job of delivering the money, receiving messages from 'Scorpio' at various telephone booths until he finds himself in Mount Davidson Park. There the killer bushwhacks Harry and informs him that the girl will die. Chico emerges from the bushes, opens fire and is wounded by 'Scorpio' but as the killer tries to make his attack, Harry drives a knife into his leg. Later, following a clue from a hospital where the wounded killer has been treated, Harry traces 'Scorpio' to Kezar Stadium where he shoots the sniper and then tortures him. Consequently, because Harry denied him his rights, 'Scorpio' is set free by the DA, even though the kidnapped girl is found to have died. The killer walks free and later hijacks a school bus, demanding more money. Harry, who has been ordered to keep away from him, takes matters into his own hands and trails 'Scorpio' to a quarry and, with his powerful .44 Magnum hand gun, kills the killer. Then Harry takes his police star and throws it away.

Some thought Eastwood was making a mistake with this film. They told him that police films were out. He recalled that they said the same thing about Westerns when he went off to Europe to make *A Fistful of Dollars*. 'All you can do,' he said, 'is just do your own thing, follow your instincts. If the project is right, people will go for all kinds of pictures.'

Don Siegel told me, 'Clint knew how he wanted to play this character and it wasn't really in the original draft that the Finks wrote, so he brought in Dean Riesner to spruce up the script. This isn't anything new or innovational or radical in Hollywood. John Wayne, who functioned within the business very much the way Clint does, used to bring in screenwriter James Edward Grant to fashion his scripts to suit his own persona, and that's what Clint does. We also changed the film's location from New York to San Francisco, so Clint could film close to home.'

As was now usual for an Eastwood star vehicle, there were no other big name stars in co-starring roles; just good supporting character actors. Regarding this, Siegel told me, 'A Clint Eastwood film is exactly that. Well, I hope when I'm directing, it's a Clint Eastwood-Don Siegel film, but really the American public go to see a film with Clint Eastwood because *he's* the star, so there is no need to bring in other star names.'

When I asked him if it was because Eastwood didn't want competition on screen, Siegel replied, 'I don't think that's strictly true. In the last film I directed Clint in [*Escape From Alcatraz*], we had Patrick McGoohan, a superb actor.'

But McGoohan was not, I pointed out, a major Hollywood star. 'Well, no, but actors like McGoohan, or any of the other actors who've worked with Clint, are strong actors,' he said. 'When I've directed his films, we've always chosen the cast very carefully, finding the best actors for the part. In *Dirty Harry*, for instance, we had Harry Guardino to play Bressler and he's been working constantly since the fifties in films, TV and on the stage.'

I pressed my point that there were still no major Hollywood *names* partnering Eastwood, (and indeed this remained the case until *City Heat* in which he was teamed with Burt Reynolds). Siegel responded, 'That's really because Clint is, off and on screen, a loner. He's a man who can take care of the situation on his own. When, in *Dirty Harry*, they give him a partner to work with, he's unhappy about it. He doesn't want or need anyone else. So there are no roles to offer to Paul Newman or Burt Reynolds or someone like that. Besides, what Clint was doing in his films, with or without me, was to stream-line the whole process of making films so that they were made more economically, and to bring in another major star would mean to add maybe another million dollars to the budget.'

There is also the point that there are no other temperaments to have to cope with, as there were on *Paint Your Wagon*. But mostly, it would seem to me, that what Eastwood came to realize quickly was that it was his name above the title that brought people in to theatres all over the world, and on the occasions he had to share the billing, or even take second billing, the films were less successful. It is something he has tried not to analyse but prefers to leave to his own instinct, because he's afraid that if he did, he might lose his way. 'What you represent to an audience is best left to them to decide,' he said. 'It could upset your instincts. You might seize up, start acting to your own idea of yourself.'

Making his film debut in *Dirty Harry* was Andy Robinson as 'Scorpio.' 'Clint and I found Andy Robinson in an off-Broadway production of *Subject to Fits*, which was a long-running hit in which Robinson played the epileptic hero,' Siegel told me. 'Every night on stage he had to fall down a flight of stairs, and he was absolutely covered in bruises, all up and down his arms, over his hips and across his behind. I figured that was a mark, or *marks*, of dedication, and thinking he might be right for the role of the killer, we gave him a test. He was absolutely marvellous in the film. A strong actor, right for the part, but, as you said, not a star name.'

Having accepted the role of the villain in *Dirty Harry*, Robinson spent the first few days watching his bruises disappear, only to have even more hideous bruises and cuts inflicted on him, care of the make-up department when the character he played had himself beaten to a pulp in order to frame Harry. Siegel's own 18-year-old son, Kristoffer Tabori, flew in from New York to play a cameo bit as a hippie.

The whole film was shot entirely on location. For the opening scene Siegel and cameraman Bruce Surtees took their cameras to the top of a high rise apartment block with a swimming pool on the roof. From a neighbouring, higher building Andy Robinson, armed with a telescopic sight rifle, claimed his first victim, a pretty young girl swimming high above the streets of San Francisco. 'It was not a film for anyone with vertigo,' said Siegel, 'but fortunately Clint loves heights. We were up there, high above the city where Bruce Surtees captured a breath-taking panoramic shot of the city, panning the camera around on top of the building as Clint walked around the edge. As I said, it wasn't a film for people with vertigo and anyone in the crew who couldn't take it stayed down on the ground!'

Avoiding studio sets altogether, Siegel managed to borrow the offices of Mayor Alioto during the three-day Memorial Day weekend for the first confrontation between Callahan and the fictional screen Mayor (played by John Vernon). In this scene Harry's attitude to police work is quickly established when the Mayor announces that his policy is not to have any more trouble following an incident when Harry shot a suspect.

Harry replies, 'When an adult male is chasing an adult female with intent to rape, I shoot the bastard. That's *my* policy.'

'Intent?' queries the Mayor. 'How did you establish that?'

'When a naked man is chasing a woman through an alley with a butcher knife and a hard-on,' replied Harry, 'I figure he isn't out collecting for the Red Cross.'

Harry leaves as the Mayor muses, 'I think he's got a point.'

This leaves no one in doubt about the kind of cop Harry is. In the scene that follows, in which Eastwood thwarts a bank hold-up by blasting away the hoods with his Magnum gun, he delivers what remains a classic piece of dialogue. Standing over the surviving robber, who has notions of picking up his gun and making a fight of it, Harry stares down his pistol at him and says, 'I know what you're thinking. Did he fire six shots or only five? To tell you the truth, in all the excitement I kinda lost track myself. But being that this is a .44 Magnum, the most powerful hand gun in the world and would blow your head clean off, you got to ask yourself one question; do I feel lucky? Well, do you, punk?' It was a piece of cryptic dialogue that would remain memorable, and in all future films Eastwood would try to find other such cryptic and memorable lines.

Siegel took advantage of real locations that were available to him. For a short scene in which Harry takes himself off to hospital with an injured leg, Siegel moved his unit and cast into the casualty department at the General Hospital. Where real locations were unavailable, art director Dale Hennessy improvised. He turned the seventh floor of the Pacific Gas & Electric Building into a functioning police department. Hennessy also had a 40-foot revolving 'Jesus Saves' sign erected on the Blue Shield Building, acting as a centrepiece for a shoot-out between Harry and 'Scorpio' on the rooftops.

While *Dirty Harry* was still in production, The Hollywood Foreign Press Association concluded that Eastwood was now the world's top movie star and presented him with a Golden Globe award. *Life* magazine put out their 23 July 1971 issue with Eastwood on the cover and proclaiming, 'The world's favourite movie star is – no kidding – Clint Eastwood.' They somehow couldn't believe their own proclamation, and inside they asked, 'Who can stand 32,580 seconds of Clint Eastwood?' It answered its own question with 'Just about everyone.' In America alone he was the second top favourite movie star behind Paul Newman. At this stage, he had not in fact enjoyed complete success with all his films since his return to America. *Hang 'Em High* was, surprisingly, his most successful film domestically. *Coogan's Bluff* had done well, as had *Where Eagles Dare* but his other American films had been disappointing at the box office. The reason for his continuing popularity in 1971 was certainly the constantly reissued *Dollars* films. They had each been re-released fifteen times up to 1971 and all-night screenings of all three films in one programme were packing them in.

Siegel fell ill midway through production of *Dirty Harry* so Eastwood took over the filming of the sequence in which Harry disuades a would-be-suicide from jumping from the top floor of a building. A week had been set aside for this scene. Eastwood opted for the use of hand-held cameras to give the scene a semi-documentary feeling. And he didn't think twice about stepping aboard a fireman's crane and being hoisted high above the streets for the dramatic rescue. He felt he had to be clearly seen as the man on the roof makes a grab for him and then struggles as Harry pulls him onto the crane. The man being rescued was played by stunt man Buddy Van Horn who worked closely with Clint on how to execute the scene without the two of them plummeting to the ground. Under Eastwood's direction, the scene was completed in one night.

A more dangerous stunt performed by Eastwood was when he jumped from a bridge onto a bus as it sped along a freeway. Siegel set the camera up on the bus (which actually moved at a much slower pace than it appeared to), and Eastwood made the leap successfully. He felt once more it was important for the audience to be able to see that it was actually *him* and not a stunt double since the camera was positioned on the bus, and his face would be clearly visible. It added to the myth that the on-screen Eastwood was some sort of super hero.

Regarding the confusion about the on-screen Eastwood and the real Eastwood, when he was asked if, while in a liquor store to pick up a six-pack, he would react like Dirty Harry if a hold-up took place, he said, 'I'm sure that if somebody were pointing a gun at me and I were standing there with a six-pack, I'd say, "Care for one?" '

But what, he was asked, would happen if someone broke into his house? 'He'd risk getting shot,' replied Clint who has kept loaded guns in his house for many years, as do many Americans.

One of the most dramatic locations for the film was Mount Davidson Park by night in which Robinson beats up Harry at the foot of a giant concrete cross. Siegel also filmed by night in the Kezar Stadium for the moment when Harry catches up with his man and brings him down with his gun. Putting his camera on a helicopter, Siegel's last shot in the stadium begins with a close-up of Robinson crying in agony on the ground as Harry treads heavily on his wounded leg, and swiftly tracks up and away into a dramatic high long shot, showing Eastwood alone with his victim in a vast, darkened stadium. It was the scene that contributed to the controversy that later surrounded the film in its depiction of a cop who denied the criminal his rights. Pauline Kael, in her review of the film for the *New Yorker*, described the film as 'deeply immoral.' She added '*Dirty Harry* is obviously just a genre movie but this particular genre has always had a fascist potential and it has finally surfaced.'

The 'fascist' label stuck and a storm was kicked up. Critics contended that the appeal of the film was evidence that the United States yearned for someone to come along and solve social problems through violent authoritarianism. What Wayne was to the forties and fifties, Eastwood was to the seventies. There were, they felt, political overtones in *Dirty Harry*.

Eastwood bitterly refuted such political assessments. 'I don't think *Dirty Harry* was a fascist picture at all. It's just the story of one frustrated police officer in a frustrating situation on one particular case. I think that's why police officers were attracted to the film. Most of the films coming out at that time were extremely anti-cop. They were about the cop on the take. And this was a film that showed the frustrations of the job, but at the same time, it wasn't a glorification of police work.'

He considered himself a political 'moderate' but his views on social disorder tended to support Dirty Harry's insistence on the need for a firm hand in cleaning up American society. But Harry was probably closer to the Lone Ranger than the Secret Police. He was, in fact, both protecting the law while opposing the flaws in the system; a paradox which Eastwood found central to the role.

'I think the appeal of the Dirty Harry type character is that he's basically for good, and he's got a morality that's higher than society's morality. He hates bureaucracy and he thinks that the law is often wrong. If that's being called fascistic, they're full of it. We convicted people in Nuremberg for not adhering to a high morality and going along with the system as it was.

'I assume the audience is *identifying* with my character who has always fought against the criminal system. Unless they're identifying with 'Scorpio', I think the audience is rooting for me to kill that character, snuff him out. It's a vicarious, cathartic kind of violence.' (In 1974, following the Zebra killings, somebody wrote on a wall in San Francisco, 'Dirty Harry, where are you when we need you?') 'The politicians have not caught up to the mood of the public as far as criminal justice is concerned. I think there should be a mandatory sentence for crimes committed with handguns. The law isn't tough enough. My name has been on some of those lists against gun control, but it's been done without my permission. People in those groups don't support prosecution hard enough. There's no way to outlaw handguns, because our society is so inundated with them; it would be impossible to stop criminals from getting them. But there shouldn't be any plea bargaining for crimes with handguns. Maybe it's too simple – maybe it's too conservative, too cut and dried – but it works in other countries. I like guns myself, but I'm not a hunter. I don't feel the urge to bring anything down.'

Siegel was equally defensive. 'You know, at that time I had script after script arriving on my desk that was about cops who were crooked, or perverted in some way, or sadistic,' he told me. 'Now I don't consider myself a promoter of the cop, or a cop lover, or whatever you want to call it, but I figure that the first person you call on when you're in need is a cop. I certainly don't condone cops who flout the law, but I certainly don't condone a psychopathic killer. It seemed to me that here was a chance for us to show that perhaps there is a case for calling a spade a spade. I think Clint thought so too. And we were called fascists for it.'

Real policemen, it would seem, liked *Dirty Harry*. Said Daley, 'Cops love him. It's pretty hard for him to get a traffic ticket.' Many policemen wrote to Eastwood asking him to speak to police groups and women police officers' organizations. He felt compelled to turn down the requests because, he said, 'I don't claim to be an expert on law enforcement.'

Politics asside, the film failed to endear itself to American critics. *Variety* said, 'You could drive a truck through the plot-holes in *Dirty Harry*, which wouldn't be so serious were the film not a specious, phoney glorification of police and criminal brutality. Clint Eastwood in the title role is a superhero whose antics become almost satiric. Strip away the philosophical garbage and all that's left is a well-made but shallow running and jumping mêlée.'

Wrote Roger Greenspun of the *New York Times*, 'The honourable and slightly anachronistic enterprise of the cops-and-crooks action movies over the last few years [*Madigan*, *Coogan's Bluff*] takes a sad and perhaps inevitable step downward in *Dirty Harry*. . . . It is not the hard-hat sentiment that I find so disturbing in all this, so much as the dull-eyed insensitivity. *Dirty Harry* fails in simple credibility so often and on so many levels that it cannot even succeed (as I think it wants to succeed) in perversely complementary psychoses.'

Eastwood responded, 'Most important critics are aged between 40 and 50. Most of the people who go to the movies are between 18 and 25.'

His response was correct. Released in December 1971, *Dirty Harry* was a huge success and went immediately into profit. Eastwood had taken a look at the character of Harry Callahan and figured that this was someone the public, if not the critics, would go for. 'What I liked about playing that character was that he becomes obsessed; he's got to take this killer off the street. I think that appealed to the public. They say, "Yeah, this guy has to be put out of circulation, even if some police chief says 'Lay off'." The general public isn't worried about the rights of the killer; they're just saying "Get him off the street, don't let him kidnap my child, don't let him kill my daughter".'

The film reached the UK and the rest of Europe in 1972 by which time Eastwood was already well into his next film. In between finishing *Dirty Harry* and starting the next movie, Maggie fell pregnant again. The baby was due in the spring of 1972, by which time Eastwood would expect to have finished filming. This time he was not going to make the mistake of not being able to be at the birth of this child.

Daley had been busily engaged in setting up no fewer than three films before *Dirty Harry* was in the can; *The Hostiles*, *Sinola* and *The Dance*. The first of these, *The Hostiles*, did not come to fruition, but *Sinola* went into production in New Mexico, but by the time it was in front of the cameras its title had been changed to *Joe Kidd*.

Although it was a Malpaso film, Sidney Beckerman produced.

Choice of director was John Sturges, the man behind such classic Westerns as *Last Train From Gun Hill*, *The Gunfight at the OK Corral* and *The Magnificent Seven*. Eastwood may well have expected him to be able to turn out another classic. But things didn't bode well from the start. The whole concept of the film had a sense of irony about it since it was essentially a remake of an Italian Western; Sergio Corbucci's visually impressive snow-bound *The Big Silence*. Reputedly, Eastwood had seen the film and was so impressed with the idea of making a sort of 'Arctic Western' (*The Big Silence* was virtually all set in snowlands) and by the peculiar gun featured in the film, that he bought the rights to the film and ensured that it was never released in America. Screenwriter Elmore Leonard's task was to take certain elements of *The Big Silence* and turn it into an exciting Eastwood vehicle. Suddenly here was Hollywood imitating the Italians as never before.

Sturges was not a director Eastwood was able to either control or collaborate with, in the way he had with Siegel. Unfortunately, Sturges had already passed his prime as a director and was unable to inject much style into the film. His editor of twelve years, Ferris Webster, recognized that the director was in fact going through a 'period of awful pictures – what I call dogs.'

Shot entirely on location in the High Sierras, including Inyo National Forest, the film benefited from Bruce Surtees's superb grim and gritty photography, producing a quality that would blend perfectly with Eastwood's own directorial efforts in later Westerns.

The title role, as personified by Eastwood, was an enigmatic loner hired by a powerful landowner (Robert Duvall) who leads a company of gunmen against rebel (John Saxon) a Spanish-American out to save the original Spanish land grants of his oppressed people. Joe Kidd eventually changes sides and, in a climactic finale, drives a locomotive off its tracks and into a saloon in which Duvall's gunmen are congregated. The fine cast included Don Stroud, from *Coogan's Bluff*, as a member of Duvall's band of gunmen who becomes Eastwood's violent foil.

In its October 1979 magazine – and later in its spring 1989 edition – the Clint Eastwood Appreciation Society offered a fascinating theory regarding the origin of Joe Kidd as a character. Although Eastwood had, as usual, kept exposition in the script to a minimum, we do learn that he used to hunt meat for the army and that before that he hunt-ed men 'anybody with a price on his head,' as Duvall notes. 'That was a long time ago,' replied Joe Kidd. Since the character in *A Fistful of Dollars* was originally called Joe, as he was in *The Good, the Bad and the Ugly*, was Joe Kidd, asked the CEAS, perhaps the same bounty hunter in the Leone films?

Lalo Schifrin as choice of composer was a big plus; he'd worked previously on *Coogan's Bluff*, *Kelly's Heroes*, *The Beguiled* and *Dirty Harry*. He came up with a score that was as close to an Italian Western score as any American composer had yet produced. But it also had a style of its own as Schifrin injected it with just a hint of jazz.

As president of Malpaso, Eastwood had approval of the final cut and worked with editor Ferris Webster to produce a film that certainly had its highlights. Webster, who had been under contract to Sturges, went on to become editor on most of Eastwood's later films. Another of Sturges's staff who, through this film, became a member of the Malpaso ensemble, was assistant director Jim Fargo.

Despite its flaws, *Joe Kidd* was a better film than *Hang 'Em High* and works surprisingly well on TV since, despite Surtees's excellent Panavision photography, it comes across more as a superior TV movie. He must have thought it would have been more the film he envisioned had he directed it. But he had no future plans to direct and act at the same time. After *Play Misty for Me* he had said, 'It was a great experience all the way around and I intend to do it again. But I'm not going to try to both act and direct in the next one. I'd have to be insane to do both again.' Following the débâcle of *Joe Kidd*, he was certainly mad enough, if not exactly insane, to decide that he would direct himself in his next Western.

He had intended to make *The Dance* but it was put aside in favour of a Western which he hoped would be everything he wanted it to be, unlike *Joe Kidd*. It was called *High Plains Drifter*, from an original screenplay by Ernest Tidyman. Eastwood had commissioned the script after he read about a case in which a girl, Kitty Genovese, was murdered while 38 witnesses looked on and did nothing about it. It reminded him of *High Noon*, and that gave him the idea of making a new Western – taking the theme of *High Noon* but with elements of the Kitty Genovese case. *High Plains Drifter* would, in essence, be about a town in which the townsfolk stand by and watch their Marshal whipped to death. It was, perhaps, a look at what might have happened had Gary Cooper, in *High Noon*, not survived.

'Gary Cooper [in *High Noon*] asked for support from the town that he had served so well, and they ended up crapping on him,' he said. 'The community [in *High Plains Drifter*] didn't want to get involved either. They weren't totally evil, they were just complacent, and they just sat back and let their Marshal get whipped to death. It's a sort of comment on the thing that's very current, of not wanting to get involved. Like the Kitty Genovese case a few years back.'

When asked to assess his own potential to act in such a similar situation, Eastwood said, 'I would hope that I would, at a minimum, raise the telephone and notify the police. At a maximum, wipe the guy out. I mean, people are capable of heroic action in life, but nobody knows what he'd do before the occasion arises. I'm sure that prior to World War Two, Audie Murphy never thought of himself as a war hero.'

It may have seemed like just another Western, but this one was different from anything else. It had supernatural overtones, as the Marshal returns from the dead like an avenging angel to wreak vengeance upon the town and his killers.

The film begins with the ghostly apparition of Eastwood appearing out of the haze and riding into the town of Lago. A group of local toughs, unimpressed by him, try to kill him while he is in the barber's chair; naturally, he wipes them out first. Seeing that here is a man who can take care of himself, and expecting a gang of outlaws soon to return to town to cause havoc, they try to hire his services to protect them. He agrees to help, but only after they agree to his terms, which basically puts the town, its people and its facilities completely at his disposal.

The final stage of preparation, before the outlaws return, is to paint the town red; a sardonic joke played by Eastwood that is lost on the townsfolk. Then, to their horror, he rides out, leaving them at the hands of the approaching outlaws – men who had once whipped the towns Marshal to death. As they set about painting the town even more red, Eastwood returns and, using a whip, kills the outlaws one by one. His mission accomplished, he rides out of town, half of which has been destroyed in a fire, and disappears into the haze.

Eastwood ensured he held all the reins for this production, directing the picture while his close friend and associate, Robert Daley, produced. Early in 1972 Daley and Eastwood, along with art director Henry Bumstead, went off in search of a location, scouting lake areas in the Sierra Nevada mountains for several weeks. But they could find no background that would blend with the austere mood created in Ernest Tidyman's screenplay. Finally they explored California's Mono County foothills and found the ideal canvas at Mono Lake, just east of Yosemite; this was to prove to be one of Eastwood's favourite locations. He envisaged *High Plains Drifter* as being something very different from any other Western, and Mono Lake provided a bleak desolation with its surrounding high plains, the distant peaks of the Sierras and the stillness of the lake itself.

On 23 May 1972 Maggie gave birth to a daughter. They named her Allison. Clint had some time to spend with his growing family before filming began on the new film in July. During his time in between films he steered well clear of Hollywood. He'd arranged his life so that he only went to Hollywood for wardrobe and casting meetings. There was still some work on the house to do. Over the past three years there had been delays due to architectural plans and bad weather. 'I love the country up the coast right along the ocean. One of the reasons I like it up north is that very few people know or care that I'm an actor. My wife and children aren't bothered either.'

Once when he was in Hollywood he told Vernon Scott, 'I've got to leave in a hurry. My lungs are crying out for some fresh, smog-free air. My new house has a projection room and facilities for editing films. Once it's completed I will hardly need to come to Hollywood at all. And that suits me fine.'

While Eastwood spent time at home, art directors Alexander Golitzen and Henry Bumstead supervised the construction of a full-scale frontier town; Lago. Such a feat would normally take around eight weeks. Golitzen and Bumstead had three and a half weeks to accomplish it.

A three and a half mile road was graded and rolled firm enough to withstand the weight of generator trucks, a Chapman crane and other bulky equipment. A crew of 46 skilled craftsmen and 10 labourers worked for 12 hours daily for 18 days constructing 14 complete buildings, including a two-storey hotel complete with exterior stairway and porch. Three additional days were spent painting and decorating the sets. Props and furniture for the general store, saloon and barber shops were transported to Mono Lake from Universal Studios' storehouse. Most of the film's key sequences would be shot in the town, and many of the buildings had to be more than just 'fronts' as filming interiors on location was required by Eastwood. There would be no phoney studio interiors. The town included a cemetery, and as a joke Eastwood had erected two tombstones, one with the name 'S Leone' and the other with the name 'Donald Siegel.'

Another location used in the film was the Winnemucca Dry Lake near Falcon in Nevada, where the flatlands meet the horizon; this served as the setting for the opening and closing scenes when Eastwood rides out of, and later back into, the haze.

He arrived on location, surrounding himself with technicians he knew well and trusted. Bruce Surtees was again his cinematographer, film editor Ferris Webster came out on location; also composer Dee Barton, who'd written the score for *Misty*, spent time in Lago; few film composers ever get the chance to spend time on the set, usually beginning their work after the film is complete.

When his cast members – Verna Bloom, Marianna Hill, Mitchell Ryan, Jack Ging, Billy Curtis (*Play Misty for Me*, *Hang 'Em High*), Paul Brinegar (Wishbone in *Rawhide*), Geoffrey Lewis (who would become a regular member of the Eastwood acting ensemble) – arrived, none of them failed to be impressed by the extraordinary town erected by the side of a huge lake. The only sounds were the waves gently lapping on the shore and the cry of sea-gulls; when Eastwood rides into town in the opening sequence the soundtrack is filled with the noise of sea-gulls and the heavy patter of horses' hooves.

Eastwood shot his film in continuity, partly because the town had to be partially destroyed at the end, but also so he and Ferris Webster could work on editing a rough assembly of the film on location. To enable himself and Webster to view the actual rushes as soon as they were available, he had a special small log cabin erected on the location. He had always found that most cutting rooms were 'abysmally depressing' and he found that everyone's efficiency and creativity was heightened if the cutting room had some pleasant atmosphere.

To keep the audience guessing about the mystery of the flashback scenes in which the Marshal is seen being whipped to death – Eastwood's Stranger is only identified as the Marshal at the end of the picture – Buddy Van Horn played the part. For these whipping sequences, Bruce Surtees donned heavy padding and, armed with a hand-held Arriflex camera, became the Marshal's eyes as the stunt men laid into him with whips.

Once again Eastwood, as director, used the Video West system, and after each scene was completed he and Surtees watched it replayed in the Video West truck that was always nearby.

During filming, Eastwood was appointed by President Nixon to the National Council on Arts, to serve with Rosalind Russell on the eight-member council as a representative of the motion picture arts for a six-year term.

For the scene in which the Stranger orders the people to literally paint the town red, 380 gallons of paint were used. Then, finally, explosives experts Jack McMasters and Harry Stewart blew up some of the buildings and burned them down. With Lago largely in cinders, the shooting was over and everyone went home. Eastwood was particularly tired. He wanted the seclusion of Carmel and the opportunity to take off on his motorbike, or in his old and dirty pick-up truck.

11

Cops 'n' Politicians

Following on from the success of *Play Misty for Me*, with so many of the elements that helped make that a pleasure to make – Jo Heims' script, the locations, the contemporary story – Eastwood planned to do another Heims scenario, *Breezy*. But this time it was a love story, something he'd not attempted before, and there were to be no .44 Magnums, no women leaping out of the dark with knives, none of the violence of the previous films in any shape or form. It was the story of Frank Harmon, a middle-aged real estate man – well-to-do, attractive, bitter about women since his divorce – and Breezy, a 17-year-old girl, vibrant and pretty, and something of a hippie. Frank and Breezy meet accidentally and find themselves the perfect example of the generation gap. But Breezy keeps bouncing back into Frank's life, and despite their age difference, he finds himself falling in love with her.

The part of Frank was obviously written by Heims especially for Eastwood, and this was a film he wanted to direct as well. 'There was a time when I put my faith in others, and things didn't always turn out right,' he said. 'Now I'd rather do it myself, with my own team. At least this way, if a picture doesn't turn out right, it's my own fault and not somebody else's.'

There were not the apprehensions expressed by Universal when he first said he was going to direct *Play Misty for Me*. It was now apparent that he was not just an actor playing at being a director, but a serious and gifted directing talent.

He saw *Breezy* as another chance to break out of the typical Eastwood mould. 'Now that I'm free to do films my way, I look for scripts that have an unusual quality to them, not the usual Clint Eastwood story where a guy grabs a gun, wipes out a few people and solves his problem.' If this was a contradiction to the realization he had had with *The Beguiled*, that such radical departures from his usual action-type films tended to result in commercial failures, he could argue that *Breezy* was a film which he believed, at that time, would succeed on its own merits. 'I depend a lot on my own instinct and how I personally feel about a script,' he explained concerning his reasons for selecting a script. 'First, I read a script for story value. Is it the type of thing I want to do? Is it something I myself would like to see? Does it have a message? Then I read it again and study the overall picture. Where do I fit in? What's the general appeal? Will it play to full houses, and so forth?'

Clearly he thought *Breezy* answered all these questions positively. Never having handled such a sensitive subject before, he decided he needed all his concentration *behind* the camera. So for the first time he chose not to act. It's probable that he also thought it would do better without him in it. He still recognized that *The Beguiled* would have done better if it had starred somebody else.

The role of Frank went to William Holden, and the age of the character became, specifically, fifty. A search began to find Breezy. Among the actresses auditioning for the part was a blonde who had made her film debut a couple of years earlier in *Willard*. She was turned down; her name was Sondra Locke.

The part went to Kay Lenz, daughter of San Francisco disc jockey Ted Lenz. She had been in show business since the age of eight weeks, appearing on the *Hollywood on Television* show which was produced by her father. Prior to *Breezy*, she was best known for her work on TV in *The Monroes* when she was known professionally as Kay Ann Kemper.

She told me how she came by the part of Breezy. 'I was auditioning for a part in a Movie of The Week film called *The Weekend Nun*. It was a bit like a cattle auction with all these girls after the same part. I was quite desperate to get the role because I hadn't done much work in a long time, and I eventually got it. The editor of this film [Ferris Webster] was also working for Clint Eastwood, and he suggested to Robert Daley that he come along and see some of my scenes. Because my role was not the central character, they took a sequence and edited it so that I became the central figure, and showed it to Bob Daley. Then they re-edited it to its original form.

'Bob rang Clint and told him about me, and Clint said he'd like to see the same scene. So they had to re-edit it again, and when Clint had seen it they undid it again. I then had to do a screen test for *Breezy* and I was *terrible*. But someone must have liked something about me because my agent rang me and said, "Hello Breezy." I couldn't believe it. I said, "I got it? You're joking!"

'A lot of people told me to watch out for Clint because he could be tough, but I found him to be very gentle and kind. He treated me as though I'd been in movies for thirty years. William Holden did too. I'd like to work with Clint again, to be directed by him.'

Holden, who'd been acting in films long before Eastwood, was impressed with him as a director. He told me, 'Many actors who have tried directing have turned out ambitious home movies, all ego and of no value to any audience. Well, maybe that isn't true of *every* actor who's directed, but certainly Clint Eastwood knew what he was about. He could have played the part himself, I thought, but he chose to direct it instead. It was a most agreeable experience. And I can't say that about every film I've made. There was no crap with Clint. I'd like to work with him again.

'How did I find him on a personal level? He is something like me, in that he likes to keep his circle of friends rather tight. There are too many people trying to hustle in on your scene, and he handles that side of his life well. I feel glad to be one of his friends. You know, people say that you can't really get to know him, that he is a man of mystery. I don't think that at all. I think he is as you find him, quiet, charming, thoughtful, but laconic. And because he is laconic, he gives the impression that there is something he keeps hidden, something mysterious about him. That's his magic, I suppose, but that air of mystery is due more to his screen image. You *expect* there to be something else there. It isn't; *I* don't think there is.'

Making an appearance in a single scene was Holden's son, Scott, as a veterinarian who saves the life of an injured dog. The dog, called in the film Sir Love-a-Lot, was a German wire-haired pointer by the name of Earl. Holden told me, 'This was the dog's debut and he behaved a damned sight better than some actors I could mention!'

All scenes were filmed in Los Angeles. Director of Photography was, this time, Frank Stanley who had assisted on *Misty* and *The Beguiled*. Jim Fargo, from *High Plain's Drifter*, was again assistant director. All about him, Eastwood had men he knew would get the job done *his* way.

Companionable on the set and keen to create a feeling of involvement, enthusiasm and good will among his cast and unit, he reserved his company during his off duty hours only for his friends. Said Kay Lenz, 'I didn't see too much of Clint away from the set. He had his group of friends and I think he didn't want anyone to intrude into his own life. But when I did see him away from the set he treated me like his kid sister. I didn't see him again until we opened the film, and he hugged me and made me feel just like his younger sister.'

Few people break through into the Eastwood social circle. He preferred to keep his company limited to those friends he had had from the early years. 'These are the people I liked when the going was tough,' he said. 'Why change? These old friends don't. They like me for myself.'

When filming was over, Eastwood reflected on his first film as director only, and said, 'I learned that it's a great deal easier to direct a picture with other actors than one in which you appear yourself. An actor-director is always thinking about two things at once when he's in front of the camera.'

He even went so far as to say, 'Eventually I would love to give up acting and just direct. I think every actor should direct at least once. It gives you a tolerance, an understanding of the problems involved in making a film. Also, I think every director should act.'

To Eastwood's dismay, *Breezy* was R-rated in the States. 'I don't think it deserves to be R-rated at all,' he complained, 'but it is because twenty-some states in the Union have statutes that say showing the nipple on a woman's breast is obscene.'

He was outraged, and berated the American censorship system. 'I understand that in Texas there was a move to give *Paper Moon* an R instead of a PG because an under-aged girl is swearing and kind of pimping for a hotel clerk in one scene. You could argue that the local community has the right to set standards, but if you accept that, you could argue that the community has the right to impose segregation. That's the long-range implication of something like the Supreme Court decisions on obscenity.'

He proclaimed himself as being against censorship, saying that 'it can be dangerous. If the press had been censored, we'd never have found out about Watergate, which needed to be exposed. As far as films are concerned, I think adult human beings ought to be able to see what they want to. I'm too much of an individual to think otherwise.'

Despite his belief in artistic freedom, he was, however, not impressed by pornographic films such as *Deep Throat* . 'I don't see that ejaculating in a girl's face is more artistic. If that's beautiful sex, if that's socially relevant, you can keep it. What you want to do in your own bedroom is great, but that's not necessarily what I want to look at.'

He said that he was actually turned off sex by *Deep Throat* and was amazed that no women's group attacked the film; 'I mean, it's making a joke out of a woman's anatomy, that's the whole theme of the picture,' he said.

Universal were somewhat stumped as to how to promote *Breezy*. They shelved it for a while, waiting for Eastwood to make his next film, *Magnum Force*, and see that on release before allowing the audience access to *Breezy*. Eastwood was incensed at the way the studio was handling the film (and this may have had much to do with the fact that he eventually moved over completely to Warner Brothers). But what Eastwood failed to realize – or remember since he had said it himself – most of the people who were going to the cinema during the late sixties and early seventies were aged between 18 and 25, and a story of a fifty-year-old man having a love affair with a teenager was not appealing to them. It was more the sort of thing that turned up on TV as Movie Of The Week. The critics dismissed the film, and so did the public. In time, as they did with many of the films he directed, the critics came to admire *Breezy*.

However, the critics had not been kind to *High Plains Drifter* either, but that didn't affect the public's reaction. *Sight and Sound* felt its 'ritualized violence and plodding symbolism make for heavy going.' *Variety* found it 'a nervously humorous, self-conscious near-satire on the prototype Eastwood formula.' In Europe the film was met with a barrage of venomous attacks. *Le Revue du Cinéma* found it to be 'an apology for fascism,' while *L'Aurore* thought Eastwood to be 'the perfect Nazi hero.' 'A *Mein Kampf* for the West,' said *Postif*, and added, 'Back in 1950, not one scene, not a single shot of this film would have obtained Universal's stamp of approval.' *Témoignane Chrétien* described Eastwood as 'the handsome blond Aryan,' and the film was 'typical Nazi ideology.' Even Sergio Leone disliked the film. Nevertheless, it was a sensational hit and put Eastwood on top, making him the number one American box office star.

Around this time he put some of his considerable earnings into a new venture, a restaurant in Carmel which he set up in partnership with some friends – years later a rift between Clint and one of these friends would result in a one-way public feud as the friend accused Eastwood of womanizing.

Serving up organic food, the inn was imbued with the atmosphere of an English countryside restaurant, based on the places he had visited and loved so much in England. He came up with a name that was as crazy as the pubs he'd discovered – Hog's Breath Inn. 'It was the craziest name I could think up,' he said. 'Somebody raised the objection that that's a bad name for a restaurant. I said that if a customer doesn't have a sense of humour, we don't want him anyway!'

His sense of humour, and no doubt sense of marketing, had a menu that included such dishes as a Dirty Harry Hamburger and a Fistful of T-Bone. The inn went on to become a tremendous success and something of an institution in Carmel – but then, Clint himself became a Carmel institution.

Christmas 1972 in Carmel came and went. The new year was ushered in. America held its breath as scandal shot through the very heart of its government as the word 'Watergate' became a synonym for corruption. As material for a film Eastwood would dismiss the scandal as unsuitable. 'I wouldn't do it,' he said. 'I think Peter Sellers would.' In 1976 Hoffman and Redford did it, in the hugely successful *All the President's Men*. In 1973 Eastwood's main concern about Watergate was its effect on people, and how the ineptitude of the government's secret service was exposed. 'I do think this Watergate thing is making people cynical,' he said. 'I hate to see the public get so callous about it, not care anymore, because they should care so that things like Watergate won't happen again. If nothing else, Watergate was the dumbest-handled thing in the world. I'm glad it was exposed, for the sake of turning off what might have been a dangerous trend. I'd hate to think that our intelligence forces around the world were operating as clumsily as that group; leaving money in telephone booths. It was like a poor man's James Bond movie.

'I'm sure that right now a lot of people are asking why President Nixon didn't check further into former Vice-President Agnew's background, or why there are so many people around him who seem to be of questionable honour. You'd have to say that he's a very poor judge of character. And on the other side, a lot of people wondered why Senator McGovern didn't check out Senator Eagleton.'

He was, however, fascinated by some of the quandaries thrown up by Watergate, particularly John Ehrlichman's opinion that any action, such as burglarizing Ellberg's pyschiatrist's office, was justifiable if it was being done in the name of security and for the President of the United States. '*Magnum Force* is all about that, about what happens when the law decides it's *above* the law,' he said. 'Pretty soon *everybody's* burglarizing. If breaking and entering are considered legal under *any* circumstances, I think pretty soon we'll all just go breaking into a neighbour's house and lift whatever we happen to want or need. Maybe information, maybe his wallet.'

Magnum Force was the sequel to *Dirty Harry*. 'Maybe it sounds strange for me to be doing a sequel,' he said, 'and in a sense it is. I receive hundreds of scripts a month, but good ones are rare. I became intrigued with the ideas in *Magnum Force*, and I thought about public reaction to *Dirty Harry*.' Those ideas, such as Watergate and the Brazilian Police Death Squad he'd read about, prompted him to hire writer John Milius (later to become a successful director) to write an original story around Inspector Callahan and his discovery of a group of policemen who have set themselves up as a secret death squad. It would appear that the film was in some ways an appeasement to those who accused the original picture of being fascist since this time Harry was concerned with the rights of the criminals being murdered by the death squad.

'There's a reason for the rights of the accused,' he said, 'and I think it's very important and one of the things that make our system great.' Not forgetting Callahan's treatment of 'Scorpio' in *Dirty Harry*, he added, 'But there are also the rights of the victim. Most people who talk about the rights of the accused have never been victimized; most of them probably never got accosted in an alley. The symbol of justice is the scale, and yet the scale is never balanced. It falls to the left and then it swings too far back to the right. That's the whole basis of *Magnum Force*. These guys on the police force form their own élite, a tough inner group to combat what they see as opposition to law and order. It's remotely based on that Brazilian police death squad. It's frightening. And this was a film that showed the frustrations of the job, but at the same time it wasn't a glorification of police work.'

To expand Milius's story into a screenplay, Eastwood hired Michael Cimino who had previously only worked on one, *Silent Running*. Eastwood worked closely with Cimino on the script, inviting the writer up to Carmel. Despite the fact that, at the end of *Dirty Harry*,

Eastwood had taken his police badge and thrown it into a swamp, he returned in *Magnum Force* assigned to stake-out duties with robbery. (Eastwood has said that Harry must have had a strong piece of elastic on that badge!) Briggs, the current homicide Lieutenant, has given Callahan this assignment because, he says, he doesn't want the public crying 'Police brutality' every time Harry goes out on the streets and pulls his gun. Briggs tells Callahan that he has never had to use his gun in all his years on the force. Harry tells him, 'You're a good man, lieutenant, and a good man's got to know his limitations.'

A crime lord and his henchmen are murdered as they are leaving court after being acquitted on a technicality. As more criminals are murdered in San Francisco, it becomes apparent that it is the work of a vigilante group, although Briggs insists that the killings are a result of a pending gang war, and he arranges surveillance on several big-time hoods. Harry, who is reassigned to Homicide, believes the crime lords are more likely to be victims rather than the murderers.

At a police shooting tournament, Harry is forced into a final competition with a rookie cycle cop called Davis. Harry loses and asks Davis to try his gun. He collects one of the bullets from the gun and matches it to a bullet taken from a murder victim. Later Davis and his colleagues confront Harry and ask him to join them. He turns them down and later finds a bomb in his mail box. He calls his partner to try and warn him, but is too late as a bomb goes off. Harry calls for back-up from Briggs, only to discover that Briggs is behind the police death squad.

Harry is pursued by the cycle cops, resulting in a climactic motorcycle chase at San Francisco's harbour and on board a wrecked ship. When Harry has finally disposed of his pursuers, Briggs threatens to frame him for murder. But as Harry drives away, the bomb he took from his mail box is triggered, and Briggs is caught in the explosion. Harry repeats his line, 'A man's got to know his limitations.'

Warner Brothers were obviously keen to have a follow-up to *Dirty Harry* but Don Siegel was unavailable – or unwilling. Eastwood didn't want the responsibility of directing this one – he wanted a rest from directing after *Breezy* – but he needed someone he could work well with; someone who would bring his vision of the film to the screen. He chose Ted Post from *Rawhide* and *Hang 'Em High*. Post had gone from his last Eastwood outing to another sequel, *Beneath the Planet of the Apes*, but since then had virtually worked exclusively in television; in fact his TV movies had earned him Best Director of the Year Award from the Screen Directors Guild of America for three years running. His technique was based on the premise that 'A good director makes the camera conform to the actors, and not the reverse.'

In the role of Briggs was the master of the two-faced authoritarian, Hal Holbrook. The rest of the film's actors were much less well known, such as Felton Perry as Harry's partner, and David Soul as the young rookie, Davis. Shortly after, Soul found stardom on TV in *Starsky and Hutch*.

Again the film was shot entirely on location in San Francisco. On the first day of shooting, Eastwood introduced Ted Post to the shiny new .44 Magnum he was using for the film. 'Here,' Eastwood said handing the gun to Post, 'get the feel of it. She's got a real kick when you fire her.'

Post seemed awestruck by the weapon. He gasped 'Good Lord!' and handed back the gun so they could get on with filming.

As Post's employer, Eastwood often discussed scenes with the director; he wasn't about to lose his own vision of the film.

During the film's climactic chase, Eastwood had the chance to race around San Francisco on a motorbike. But for the shot in which Harry rides his bike 60 feet into San Francisco Bay, a stunt man doubled him. 'I wasn't about to do *that*,' said Eastwood who had by now learned the very thing that Harry says in *Magnum Force*, which was 'A man must learn his limitations.' 'I enjoy doing stuntwork,' said Eastwood. 'As you become more important to the film, though, you have problems with the insurance company.'

During filming he agreed to be interviewed by *Playboy*. In many respects it was to be his swan song interview, as though he determined that this would be the last time he would speak extensively to anyone. Now that he was at the zenith of his life and career, everybody wanted to know about Clint Eastwood. It just made him want to become more reclusive than ever. Still, he went ahead with the three sessions it took for Arthur Knight, film critic and University of Southern California cinema professor, to complete the interview. The first session very nearly didn't come off. Eastwood was due to meet Knight at a hotel in Sausalito at 4 pm. Eastwood arrived on time but when Knight tried to begin the interview, his tape recorder wouldn't work. Ordinarily this would have been enough to send any Hollywood star into a huff and probably refuse to continue. But not Eastwood. He told Knight that he thought he could borrow a tape recorder from a friend, and he disappeared for ten minutes, reappearing with a cassette recorder. Then it turned out that Knight was armed with only one tape, good for just a single hour's worth of conversation. He made frantic telephone calls, finally tracking down a shop in a town about ten miles away that promised to remain open until he could get there. Eastwood, seeing that Knight had no car, drove him there and back.

The second session took place in the offices that Eastwood maintained over the Hog's Breath Inn, and the third in the Malpaso offices at Universal Studios. In this office, among the posters and film stills, stood a three-foot-high, papier-mâché rabbit piggy bank. The rabbit wore a Sheriff's badge and from his mouth hung a cigarette. In his hand was a hat and protruding from beneath it was a gun. It was, Eastwood told Knight, a gift from a school teacher in New Jersey who had said that this was her idea of the real Clint Eastwood.

If any Eastwood film had an eager audience waiting, *Magnum Force* was it. Dirty Harry was a character audiences of the seventies relished. And Eastwood recognized this. 'The secret of the man I play is that he's a super hero, a dream character for most men. Every guy in the audience says he wants to handle it just the way he's doing it on the screen. In these days of national wishy-washiness in everything, in the loss of individualism, in a computerized world where everyone's a number, this is appealing. A guy sits in the audience. He's scared stiff about his life. He wants to be that self-sufficient legend he sees up there on the screen in my pictures. A superhuman character who has all the answers, is doubly cool, exists on his own without society, without anyone's help. Of course, it will never happen that way. Man is always dreaming of being an individual, but man is really a flock animal.'

If this was the thing about Dirty Harry that appealed to Eastwood, it was also the same thing that made anyone look appealing to him, even Senator McGovern for whom Clint had no great admiration. He said, 'When Senator McGovern told that jerk who was harassing him to "Kiss my ass," I started thinking, "This guy is all of a sudden sounding good to me." Not because he used profanity but because he had a human reaction: he was tired of being bugged. When Harry S Truman told off that critic who said his daughter couldn't sing, and called him a stupid son of a bitch or whatever the hell he called him, it was the natural reaction of a father expressing resentment at somebody attacking his daughter. I think that appealed to a lot of people.'

*

Magnum Force opened in 1973, rush-released by Warners, and it was a phenomenal success, took $6,871,011 in its first week and headed quickly towards a $40,000,000 gross. Eastwood was the undisputed top movie star in the world. Universal nervously put *Breezy* out on release at last, wishing they had Eastwood starring in the film as well as directing it. It was a resounding failure. It didn't open in London until 1974. It played for just three weeks at the Paramount Theatre, and closed.

Being a celebrity never came easily for Eastwood. It was something he carried like a soldier's backpack; it's a necessary burden. Columnist Vernon Scott was with him when he stepped out of the Universal Studios restaurant to be spotted by half a dozen tourists who immediately crowded round him. He smiled for their cameras and even put an arm around the plump girl who wanted her picture taken with the superstar. In fact, he has always hated giving out autographs but remains tolerant and gracious to fans whenever he finds himself besieged. Only if they become unbearably persistent will he shake off his tolerance. Not that too many fans see him in public. He avoided the 'in' spots of Hollywood; a big night out on the town for him was to spend it with a few friends in a bar with a jukebox that played jazz.

Occasionally his quick dry humour saves situations from getting too unpleasant. A girl once flew at him at Warner Brothers Studios, screaming, 'I've wanted to tell you this for a long time. You're a no good son of a bitch for always making Mexicans the bad guys in your films and then killing them.'

'Don't be angry,' he told her. 'I kill lots of other people too.'

But he doesn't always resolve situations with a sense of humour. He told Arthur Knight, 'Yesterday some guy, making a TV series, called and asked to use my dressing room as a set. So, being an economically minded person, I said, "Fine, why build a whole set? Just move in and shoot." Then I go back and find the dressing room looking like a a public toilet. I mean the place is an absolute shambles. I'm going to tell that producer just what I think of his group, as soon as my secretary nails him down.'

During his days on *Rawhide* he used to attend a lot of rodeos when they'd pay him to make a personal appearance. By 1973 he had stopped making personal appearances but still enjoyed the rodeo, so he went to one in Salinas under heavy disguise. No one recognized him.

His discomfort with his celebrity status was really put to the test in March 1973 when he and Maggie went to the Academy Awards show at the Dorothy Chandler Pavilion. They were there simply to enjoy the evening and be entertained. But he was taken by surprise when the show's producer, Howard Koch, approached him and said, 'Charlton Heston isn't here.'

'So what?' asked Eastwood.

'He's supposed to be emceeing this part of the show, so we need *you* to fill in for him.'

Surprise now turned to panic. 'Where's Gregory Peck?' he asked, wondering where all the more distinguished members of the Academy were. 'There must be somebody around who could come out here and lend a little class to the thing.'

Recalled Eastwood, 'Koch's eyes were kind of twitching, sweat was running down his forehead and the TV guys were doing their countdowns: "Ten . . . nine. . . eight . . . seven . . ." and I'm standing there listening to him.'

Maggie joined in, saying to her husband, 'Go ahead. Help him out.' Before he knew what was happening, he was being whisked backstage. As he stepped in front of the cameras, trying to read Heston's cue cards, he could hear Maggie roaring with laughter. He could also hear Burt Reynolds – 'they both have very distinctive laughs, the kind you can distinguish out of several thousand people, and they were in the front row cracking up.'

Somewhere outside was Charlton Heston. His car had got stuck on the freeway and he had to abandon it and begin running. He told me, 'It was really one of the outstanding humiliations of my entire life, running along the sidewalk and hearing the loudspeaker announcing "Charlton Heston is supposed to be emceeing this part of the show, but..." and they had Clint Eastwood up there who was doing his best with my cue cards. But as he said, "Why pick on a feller who has said only eight lines in his last three pictures?" I've never been late for work in my life, and I had to do it in front of eight million viewers.'

And Eastwood had to do what he did in front of eight million people. He winged through his announcements and then walked off, finding his way backstage to the pressroom. There he found a small refrigerator and to his total delight inside it was a six-pack of Olympia beer. 'It was like some angel had put it there,' he said. He drank four of them as a page came running in, looked at him, said nothing and then ran out again. After finishing his four beers, Eastwood went back into the auditorium and sat down next to Maggie. She told him, 'A page was just down here asking me how many beers you could drink before getting drunk.' He felt there was no need to worry; on that occasion he would have needed at least ten to get drunk! From his seat he sat back and watched the historic occasion when Marlon Brando refused to appear to accept his Oscar for *The Godfather* but sent on an Indian woman instead to read a message in which Brando said he refused to accept the Oscar because of the way Indians had been treated in films.

Eastwood said around that time that he never expected to win an Oscar himself. 'I'm not going to say I'd hate to win one,' he said. 'But I'm not terribly politically oriented. I don't know if I'd be able to campaign properly, even if I had a vehicle.' Although he was talking specifically about Academy Awards, this also gave an indication of his political ambitions of that time. His attitude would later change, but mostly he was, he said, 'a political nothing,' and certainly not an extremist. He found extremists, either right or left, 'boring, inflexible people.' If anything, he considered himself a moderate, depending on the issue. Regarding civil rights he was liberal, on Government spending he was conservative. As someone who had always believed that a person had to work hard for what they wanted, he disapproved of Government programmes which he felt 'encouraged freeloading. The Government has to help people, to some degree, but it should be encouraging people to make something of themselves.'

This was a philosophy he tried to instil in Roxanne. Kimber recalled that her mother often said, 'If we don't have this much money by the end of next month I am really going to start worrying.' Clint tried to encourage her to make ends meet by working hard. Kimber knew that her father had been 'very poor as a child and I don't think that has ever left him. Sometimes he was mean with money, or at least that's how it seemed to me. He would sit down at the table and say, "I have got where I am by working hard for myself." '

It was a very difficult and confusing childhood for Kimber. She began telling some of her friends that Clint Eastwood was her father. Nobody believed her. 'In the end I just stopped talking about it,' she said.

As far as his other children were concerned, Eastwood wanted them to have as normal a childhood as possible. 'One of the reasons I'm making my home away from Hollywood is to give my children a different set of values than most kids in that town have. I don't take

Kyle to movies, and I don't show my own pictures at home. The only time my son is aware his father is an actor is when one of my old movies is shown on television.'

Kyle was now five; an age when boys naturally like to play with guns. Eastwood, who always owned his own guns, said that 'with kids, one has to be very intelligent about where one places guns.' Kyle liked to play with toy guns. To make him aware from an early age that one kind of gun was for playing with while another was the real thing, he took Kyle out to the shooting range where the boy watched his father firing a real pistol. 'There's no use trying to tell him not to have anything to do with guns,' he said. 'You can be an idealist and not buy war toys, but a boy will still pick up a stick and play shoot-'em-up.'

Clint's next picture was perhaps his least interesting and least remembered, *Thunderbolt and Lightfoot*, filmed in 1973. It was his first 'buddy' film, teaming him with the much younger Jeff Bridges who at 23 was twenty years younger than Eastwood. For the first time Eastwood played a man who was an elder statesman, in this case, a veteran bank robber who, with his young partner (Bridges), plans a carbon copy raid carried out some years before on a bank.

In casting Jeff Bridges as the younger partner, Eastwood was, for the first time in one of his own films, featuring a male star of some prominence opposite him. In fact, Bridges had made eight previous films, one of them being *The Last Picture Show* for which he was nominated for an Oscar. Eastwood's gang also included George Kennedy, an Oscar winner for his supporting role in *Cool Hand Luke*, but who never managed to become a major star, and Geoffrey Lewis, a gifted comedy actor who had been in *High Plains Drifter* and went on to become part of Eastwood's growing ensemble of players.

Following his collaboration with Eastwood on the screenplay of *Magnum Force*, Michael Cimino wrote this original script and, at the age of 31, made his debut as a director, under Eastwood's close guidance, no doubt. Following this film, Cimino became one of Hollywood's most sought after directors when he made the 1978 classic *The Deer Hunter*. After that his career floundered dramatically when he wasted millions of dollars on the huge, empty Western *Heaven's Gate*. But under Eastwood's influence he was able to make *Thunderbolt and Lightfoot* an enjoyable if unmemorable caper movie. However, in writing the script especially for Eastwood, it is said that no other screenwriter ever better captured the actual style, warmth and dry wit of the real Clint Eastwood.

The film marked the film debut of Clint's son Kyle in the ice-cream van scene, although as Eastwood said to Dave Turner, who runs the British-based Clint Eastwood Appreciation Society, 'He was hard to spot in that one!'

With the completion of *Thunderbolt and Lightfoot* Eastwood finished off a twelve-month period in which he had made three films. He thought it might be time to take stock a little of what he'd achieved, what he now was, and what the future might hold.

'Hollywood is a strange place; everyone is looking for a formula,' he said. 'One year it's two guys on a bike, the next it's a girl dying of cancer, and they flood the market with imitations. For years I bummed around trying to get a job and it was always the same old story – my voice was too soft, my teeth needing capping, I squinted too much, I was too tall – all that constant tearing down of my ego was bound to turn me into a better person or a complete bastard. And I know that if I walked into a casting office right now and nobody knew I was Clint Eastwood, I'd get the same old story. Everything they said was wrong with me is still there, but now I'm *Clint Eastwood* and all the other tall guys who squint too much and talk too low are the ones cursing me. Tough to figure that out.

'It could all end – just like that. But while I'm on top I'm going to make the most of it. I've learned one big lesson in all these years; any actor in pictures has to have something special. That's what makes a star while a lot of damn good actors are passed by. The public goes to see the *stars*. I didn't invent the rules. That's just the way it is.'

He decided that his next film would be one which he would direct without acting in it. The project, a suspense film – as yet untitled – was, by the end of 1973, all set to go ahead with locations chosen in Los Angeles. But it didn't go ahead. Possibly Eastwood felt it was time for a break. There was also talk of another film with Siegel, co-starring Michael Caine. That didn't happen either. (Caine was to star in *The Black Windmill* for Siegel.) After *Thunderbolt and Lightfoot* he said, 'I'd like to take it easy for about six months, slow down my pace a little, spend some time with my family. I still don't get to do as much of that as I'd like, but I don't think anybody does. It's the nature of the business – *this* business anyway.'

12

The Blue-Eyed Blonde from Tennesssee

Eastwood did not get in front, or behind, a camera again until August 1974. But he wasn't totally inactive all that time. He was preparing to film *The Eiger Sanction*. But this time it involved a lot more than just the usual preproduction work. This was a story of espionage and mountaineering. The espionage part Eastwood could handle. The mountain climbing was something else. He would be filming high up on the north face of the Eiger in the Swiss Alps, initially just acting – he hoped Don Siegel would direct. Much of 1974 therefore was spent polishing up the script, trying to get a director and learning to climb mountains.

The screenplay was based on a novel by Travanian, a story of a rather mild art teacher who turns out to be a retired hit man for a CIA-type organization. He finds himself blackmailed into undertaking two more killings for them, one of which will take place during an expedition to conquer the Eiger – fortunately, the professor also happens to be a great mountain climber too. What Eastwood wanted was a 'Bondish sort' of picture, and it took three screenwriters to fashion the main character closer to Eastwood's persona.

Despite Siegel's respect and admiration for Eastwood, he told Clint that he was not the right director for him, or maybe that this film was not right for the director.

He told me, 'I didn't like it. I didn't think the story was any good. And I didn't see myself climbing 10,000 feet to direct Clint. So I told Clint, "Look, I'm ready to make another film with you, but what good am I going to be to you when I'm 3,000 feet up and you're

10,000 feet up and there's 7,000 feet in between us and I say "*Anytime you're ready, Clint?*" '

Disappointed, Eastwood began looking around for another director. Ideally he needed someone who had an interest in climbing. Not surprisingly he could find no one; at least no one he had confidence in. He felt he knew what he wanted and needed someone with the same vision. There were two possibilities: he could either drop the project, or he could direct it himself. He liked the story too much to give up on it, so he chose to direct it also.

As with all his films, he wanted to film it on location. Too many films in the past about mountaineering contained terrible process shots of actors in the studio against back projection. He was determined that this would be filmed on the Eiger itself. Had he realized just how dangerous, and ultimately tragic, this film would be to make, he would have probably dropped it like a hot potato.

He hired climber Mike Hoover and took off to Yosemite National Park for a three-week period of intensive training. Hoover taught him to do a Tyrolean traverse to the tip of Lost Arrow, a high finger of rock looming out of the ground.

With several British climbers, including Dougal Haston, Dave Knowles, Hamish MacInnes and John Cleare, he went off to the Alps to pick out and set up locations. The climbers would also serve as consultants on the technical climbing. In August the whole film unit and cast arrived to begin filming. On 13 August, with the climbers involved in many aspects of filming, Eastwood shot a scene in which a climber is hit by a falling rock and is hoisted up to a ledge on the west flank. The scene involved a rope of three, with Dave Knowles the middle man. He was no stranger to the Eiger, having climbed the Heckmain Route in 1971 with Allen Fyffe, Kenny Spence and Ian Nicholson. But not even his immense experience could provide against unexpected accidents. Just after the scene was completed, a large rock came bounding down the rock face, hitting and killing Knowles and injuring a member of the camera crew.

Long after the event Eastwood was still shaken as he reflected, 'On our second day on the Eiger a boulder crushed our cameraman and killed a British mountaineering consultant.'

Eastwood had seen the fatal accident and had been greatly moved by the courage of the mountaineers. 'I like to think that this film may, in its way, be a tribute to David and his fellow climbers,' he later said. 'They're a breed apart.'

August was the most popular month for climbing the Eiger, and filming *The Eiger Sanction* occasionally proved somewhat useful to other climbers. The day following Knowles's death, a thirty-year-old German-speaking Italian climber from the South Tyrol, Reinhold Messner, and a young Austrian climber, Peter Habeler, came to try the Eiger. They started out at two in the morning and by dawn they were passing the First Pillar, and then surmounted the Shattered Pillar. At the bottom of the Difficult Crack they stopped, preparing to rope up. Then they discovered that it had been thoroughly roped up by climbing experts for the camera crew of *The Eiger Sanction*, and the two climbers were able more swiftly to overcome the Difficult Crack.

Filming also provided climbers with moments of horror. Two Englishmen, Pete Allison and Dave Cuthbertson, reached the Swallow's Nest where, because of the heavily iced-up conditions, they decided to descend. They started down and were near the bottom of the wall when Cuthbertson was horrified to spot an arm with a gloved hand sticking out of the snow. They reached the spot and began to grimly dig away the snow, expecting to find a frozen corpse. They were soon laughing however when they uncovered a fully clothed and equipped dummy that had been used in the film. And because much of the equipment and clothing on the dummy was in perfect condition, the climbers quickly stripped it and then reburied the film mannequin.

This was a film that, more than any other, was filling Eastwood with all kinds of apprehensions. The physical side of making the film was enough to occupy his mind. In one scene he had to cut his climbing rope to take a 15-foot fall over 3,000 feet of nothing. He was belayed by a safety rope and made the cut, and the climbers involved all agreed that he displayed courage that equalled anything he had depicted in his screen performances. It was an object lesson to Eastwood. 'I found out a lot of things about myself. Like how much courage I had. And how much stamina. I've never ever tackled anything as physically demanding as climbing.'

But he did begin to wonder what he thought he was doing. 'A couple of times I had the feeling I was going to get into trouble, maybe have an accident, and I said to myself, "What am I doing up here, risking my life? I have a wife and two kids. Why do this?" Frankly I was petrified, but then there was a challenge – and when there is a challenge, I have to meet it.

'Even though I had practised for weeks, it was still terrifying. I don't see how you ever get used to dangling on the end of a rope thousands of feet above nothing, held up by a man you hardly know. And when a glacier moves with that terrible groan, man, that's terrifying. One of the British climbers on our team said, "Don't worry. You'll get used to it." But I never did.'

About three-quarters of the way through the film he also began to have doubts about the story. He had to tell himself, 'Three months ago you thought this story was fine and that's the way we have to go with it.' He had no choice but to 'stay with the blueprint.'

After the location work was over, Eastwood spent much of the rest of 1974 working on the post-production. The editing he could do at his home but the music scoring by John Williams and other essential post-production work had to be done at Universal. Every day he had to spend in Hollywood he worked in the Malpaso bungalow where the posters on the wall now had an addition, *The Eiger Sanction*. Typically, although its subject matter was obvious to all, the poster showed him holding a gun. Each day he waited until the 12,000 visitors who took the guided tour of the studios had gone home, and emerged from the bungalow to take his three-mile run across the brown hills behind Universal.

Despite the script's shortcomings, he felt he had a film that people would want to see. 'Bumming around for three years before I was an actor taught me what the man with a small income will spend his money on seeing,' he said. 'We have to face it – death, disaster and doom are what people want to see today. It's as simple as that. Look at any of the pictures which have made big money – *Earthquake*, *The Towering Inferno*, *The Poseidon Adventure*, *Jaws* – they are all about disaster.

'If we are honest with ourselves, we enjoy those sort of films. Look at the front page of any newspaper, if you can bear it. That's the world as it is, not as we would like it to be. Man is a very violent animal. What's wrong with showing it.'

He was right. The film did well in 1975 despite a pasting from the critics. 'Long and ponderously predictable...the film takes an unconscionable long time to reach its climax,' wrote the *Financial Times*. The *Sunday Times's* Dilys Powell said, 'The landscapes tend to obliterate the actors.' The *New Yorker* described Eastwood as 'the first truly stoned hero in the history of movies.'

The French critics were particularly venomous towards, not just the film, but Eastwood particularly. 'John Wayne has spawned millions of children,' wrote Michel Grisolia in *Le Nouvel Observateur*. 'A dozen of his very own, hundreds of thousands ready to start Vietnam all over again to have his virility and, in addition, an illegitimate son, the fruit of the comically monstrous marriage between the "spaghetti Western" and a fistful of dollars: Clint Eastwood. And he's one of the most dangerous offspring, since he's not stupid, as his adversaries will tell you. His clientele; the immense American Silent Majority. A slightly masochistic majority, it would seem, since, to face it, there's no one more antipathetic than Clint Eastwood.'

Michel Perez wrote in *Le Quotidien de Paris*, 'Convinced that he is pursuing the tradition of noble virility so dear to the Western and epic heroes of yesteryear, we watch Clint Eastwood create his own myth, film after film, with all the naïvety of a Boy Scout certain that his is the combat of the righteous, approved by God and by his country's Silent Majority.... Of all the actors who have recently stepped behind the camera, Clint Eastwood is assuredly the one least encumbered by modesty.'

'Clint Eastwood, this second-rate actor,' wrote Louis Marcorelles in *Le Monde*, 'has retained the mishmash of genres, a taste for pastiche and for violence at all costs, from his sojourn in the studios of Rome.... This spicy cocktail has its charm. It bears magnificent witness to the extent to which utter brainlessness has pervaded Western man today.'

But Eastwood, and the film, had admirers. Alain Garel, for *La Saison Cinématographique*, was thrilled by 'a masterly last half hour, shot without resorting to the rear projection, there, unprotected on the open slope of the Eiger.' In *Le Revue de Cinéma* Pascal Merigeau stated, 'Eastwood's major merit here, yet again, is to not be contemptuous of the script he has agreed to make, but to do his very best to deliver quality entertainment. In so doing he gives us proof of a humility which some of our young geniuses would do well to learn from.'

Eastwood summarily dismissed the reviews. 'I don't pay much attention to those critics. I trust my own judgement about what people want to see.' In fact, the film was successful at a time when cinema admissions were dropping drastically. Clint Eastwood was now one of the very few movie stars who guaranteed an audience. Charles Bronson had had his day; Newman was past his prime (only to re-emerge in the late eighties); Redford was just peaking and Burt Reynolds was not as popular outside of the US as he was in the US.

One of Eastwood's great disappointments about the film was that the music score, by John Williams, was passed over in favour of Williams's score for the more popular *Jaws*. 'It was really a much better score than *Jaws*,' he said. 'These things can be so political, really.' Because the Academy never nominated any of the outstanding craftsmen who worked with him, Eastwood declined all further invitations to appear on the Oscars show.

Despite the film's success, Eastwood was positive about one thing, 'I will never do anything like that again. Just too damn dangerous.'

Around this time Bob Daley was sent a copy of a book, *Gone to Texas* by Forrest Carter. The book was a limited edition of just seventy-five copies. Eastwood was given the definite impression that Carter was a half-Cherokee Indian with no formal education who became famous among the Cherokees for his poems and stories. When he was talked into writing a story, he came up with *Gone to Texas*, the tale of the outlaw Josey Wales. Daley loved it and persuaded Eastwood to take a look at it. He did and agreed with Daley that here was a Western with a 'soul' to it. They called Carter in Arkansas and bought the screen rights.

It would have seemed a clever marketing ploy by Forrest Carter. He was, it turned out, a cowboy called Asa Carter who had a talent for writing and worked on speeches for Governor Wallace in the sixties. In 1970 Carter had run against Wallace for Governor but lost.

Sonia Chernus, Eastwood's script editor, wanted a chance to write a screenplay herself, and she was given the task of turning *Gone to Texas* into *The Outlaw Josey Wales*, collaborating with Philip Kaufman, the established director who was going to direct the film. At first this seemed a good idea to Eastwood; Kaufman had directed and co-written *The Great Northfield Minnesota Raid* and seemed to Eastwood to have the right qualities for a traditional but authentic-looking Western.

The story begins during the civil war. Josey Wales has a farm which is attacked by a band of redlegs who kill Wales' wife and child. He thereafter joins a band of Confederate guerrillas to seek out the redlegs. The war ends, the South surrenders, but not Wales. His former leader, played by John Vernon, dispatches bounty hunters and soldiers to bring back Josey Wales, now a wanted outlaw. Meanwhile, Wales has met up with an Indian Chief, a squaw and, eventually a white girl and her mother whom he saves from renegades. The story sees Wales return to farming, but before the end he must face the very man who led the raid on his farm at the beginning of the story.

The two most important bits of casting in the film, Eastwood as Wales aside, was the Indian Chief and the girl Wales rescues. For the Chief, Eastwood found a real Indian Chief, Chief Dan George who had been nominated for an Oscar for *Little Big Man*. 'He had no real acting training,' said Eastwood, 'but he thinks naturally, he listens naturally; he does a lot of things that actors train for years to do well.' The Chief's only problem was that he couldn't remember lines too well, and Eastwood, without realizing it, would want so much for Dan George to remember his words that Clint would mouth the Chief's lines while in shot. Ferris Webster roared with laughter when he saw this happening in the rushes and had to ensure such takes were eliminated from the final cut.

Casting the girl was a turning point in Eastwood's life. When searching for someone to play the title role of *Breezy*, among the young hopefuls was young, slim, blonde Sondra Locke. She tried for the role of Laura, and got it. 'It was a script I loved,' she said. 'It had heart, it had power and visually it was quite beautiful.'

The Outlaw Josey Wales was the much wanted boost that Sondra needed for her ailing career. The Tennessee-born blue-eyed blonde had made her film debut in the 1963 film *The Heart is a Lonely Hunter* for which she was nominated for an Oscar as the year's best supporting actress. According to the publicity, there had been some two thousand contenders for her role in that film. The years following that seemed to be jinxed; a movie she made with Robert Forster and directed by Noel Black went untitled and unreleased. Her next film, *Willard* was a popular success, but then she co-starred with husband and wife team Robert Shaw and Mary Ure in the quickly forgotten *A Reflection of Fear*.

Her private life was much less publicized but had a sense of the bizarre about it. At the time of the release of *Josey Wales* in 1976 she had been married to sculptor Gordon Anderson for nine years. They had been childhood friends. Sondra Locke's father, Alfred, said

'Gordon was a very strange lad from the time he was eleven.' Her parents were alarmed by Anderson's penchant for being able to dress and make-up Sondra for plays he liked to put on. 'Gordon used to do her make-up with water colour paints when she was just a little girl,' said Sondra's mother Pauline. 'He would dress her up and re-do her hair.'

'We're simple country folk,' said her dad, 'and didn't really understand a boy who liked dresses and make-up so much.'

Mom and dad disapproved of these activities, but all Sondra wanted to do was become an actress and Gordon seemed determined to encourage and push her all the way. 'She was very headstrong,' said Pauline. 'Children just seem to do what they want to do. I'm afraid that was the beginning of all this mess.' Sondra began appearing in plays and, the Locke family claimed, Gordon became obsessed with turning Sondra into a big Hollywood star.

Sondra has said, 'Even as a child I always felt that I was not connected with my family, my parents, the town. I felt as if someone had played a joke on me and had dropped me in that spot and I had nothing to do with it. I have always felt that I had to be responsible for myself and take care of myself because of a lack of rapport with my parents.'

The relationship between the couple concerned the Locke family because they suspected Gordon was not interested in Sondra in a romantic way. They knew 'it was all a sham.' Then, at the age of 19, in 1967, Sondra and Gordon ran off to Alabama and got married. Neither set of parents knew anything about the wedding until it was all over. Her parents were heartbroken; they had always hoped for a traditional wedding for their daughter. The family concluded that she married Gordon to punish them; it was her way of striking back at their intentions for her. They figured that, since Sondra and Gordon would not be spending the wedding night in bed together, they would have been laughing at the folks back home.

Although she has never elaborated on her marriage to Anderson, she said, 'We're alike. We grew up together in a small town and so we're like family. We're best friends.' Shortly after the marriage, Sondra and Gordon moved to Hollywood.

By the time Sondra came to work with Eastwood, she and Gordon were living in a Spanish style house in Los Angeles where she worked more often on the garden than on film sets. Offers of work came her way, but she didn't want to be just decoration in films that offered nothing but the chance to work. 'Just to work is not important to me,' she said. 'It would be like going to a job you didn't like doing. I want to be involved in roles that have some excitement. And I like to do things that are different.' *The Outlaw Josey Wales* gave her that excitement.

Filming began under Kaufman's direction. But things weren't going well; Kaufman suddenly quit and Eastwood took over the direction himself. Keeping mum about the sudden departure of Kaufman, Eastwood displayed his usual dry humour to convey his delight at directing himself again. 'When I'm directing Eastwood, I listen to myself a lot!' he said.

Even before working with him, Sondra was an ardent admirer of Clint Eastwood, both as an actor and a director. 'I had admired Clint for quite some time, and I felt his screen presence was something unique, direct and strong,' she said. 'I'd admired his work as a director. I particularly liked *Play Misty for Me* and *Breezy* and, happily, working with him fulfilled my expectations.'

In the opening sequences of the film, Eastwood touched on the subject of the Civil War, something most American film-makers had avoided like the plague since John Huston's *The Red Badge of Courage* in 1951. These scenes involved the Kansas Red Legs, a guerrilla force sanctioned by the State of Missouri, and Eastwood hoped the film would be something more than just a fictional episode from the civil war. 'There are in this film,' he said, 'a lot of thoughts about war and the victims of war.'

For the part of his young son in the opening scene, he naturally enough cast Kyle, making this his second screen appearance. Even at this young age, Kyle reminded Clint very much of himself when he was a boy. 'I notice traits in my son that were once mine,' he said. 'He can entertain himself, make up characters and play by himself all day long. Keep himself happy. I don't want to ask him about his characters because I don't want him to feel self-conscious when I'm around. "Uh, oh, dad's here, I'd better act normal!" If you've got secrets, they don't belong to anybody else...unless you want to tell.'

Where Eastwood succeeded so beautifully with this film was in bridging the gap between his more mythical type of Westerns, where the hero is a superhuman loner, and an authentic-looking Western with a historical and epic feel to it.

'*Josey Wales* is a saga,' explained Clint, 'a little like *The Good, the Bad and the Ugly*, except that in the Leone film the only character you got to know – somewhat – is the Eli Wallach character. In other words, Josey Wales is a hero, and you see how he gets to where he is – rather than just having a mysterious hero appear on the plains and become involved with other people's plight.'

John Wayne considered that Eastwood was 'the best cowboy in movies today,' and no doubt the Duke, who made his last film that year, *The Shootist* (ironically with Don Siegel), felt that Clint was his successor. But Eastwood had avoided becoming the 'new Gary Cooper' and he knew he could never be 'another John Wayne.'

'I do everything that John Wayne would never do,' he said. 'I play the hero but I can shoot a guy in the back. I react according to the circumstances at the time.'

While not as grandiose as, say *How the West Was Won*, *Josey Wales* looked a lot more expensive than its budget of just $3,700,000 suggested and had a real epic feel about it. In the UK the film found favour among most critics and is today regarded by many as Eastwood's finest Western – some would say *the* finest Western, although that is, arguably, overrating it. American critics were less kind. But as far as audiences were concerned, the picture was something of an event and it grossed $13,500,000 in America alone according to *Variety's* 1983 list of All-time Rental Champs, making it the twelfth most successful Western of all time.

Interestingly, Joel Findler and David Pirie, in 1981, compiled an inflation-adjusted list of the most successful Westerns for *Anatomy of the Movies*, in which *Josey Wales* was shown to come in at 39; virtually all of the films above it were classic Westerns of the thirties, forties and fifties, proving that in the scheme of things Eastwood's 1976 Western was not only *his* most successful Western (outdrawing even *Hang 'Em High* which came in at 48), but was bested only by the best of the genre.

Roxanne was still waiting in the wings for Clint. She was said to 'worship the ground he walked on.' Kimber, now eleven, was proud of her father and conscious of the fact that he was a rich and famous man on TV and in the movies. She looked forward to his visits; he always brought her a present and spent time playing with her. He'd ask her how she was doing at school, whether she had a boyfriend, whether she needed anything.

But Roxanne's patience had run out. Presumably she hoped that the day would come when he would walk out on Maggie and move in with her. In 1975 she finally gave him an ultimatum to leave his wife. He refused, and Roxanne told him it was all over between them. This may not have been completely unwelcome news to Eastwood, especially when she went to Europe to study to become a teacher of transcendental meditation. When she returned to America, Eastwood bought her a house in Denver.

It was now time for Eastwood to make a new move – if only as far as the Malpaso offices were concerned. Warner Brothers, Malpaso's partner in *Josey Wales*, was keen to have Eastwood over on its lot and working exclusively with them. So Eastwood and his employees packed their things in their Universal bungalow and moved over to Burbank. He was partly coaxed by the studio's guarantee that he could make films for them with no studio interference at all. Few of even the biggest directors get that kind of treatment. But there was a price to pay: Warners wanted another Dirty Harry film. Eastwood said he agreed to do it because 'I hate to see grown men cry.'

The posters for the third Harry film declared 'Clint Eastwood *is* Dirty Harry in *The Enforcer*.'

Reasons for Callahan's further exploits were publicized as being due to 'public demand.' Announced Bob Daley, 'We feel we know what the Eastwood fans want and expect. His character is a man in control of his environment. He represents the freedoms that are being lost in the age of big governments and bureaucrats. He plays the man who is going to win out.

The screenplay was by Stirling Silliphant and Dean Riesner. In a sense it was written to a formula, allowing Harry to tell the authorities to go to hell but to still fight the good fight, and this time without depriving the villain of his rights. After ending a hostage situation by driving a car straight into a shop where the victims are held, Callahan is transferred to the personnel division where he puts aspiring detectives to the test. Among them is Kate who turns out to be his new partner. He is not thrilled with the choice. 'Do not concern yourself,' she assures him. However, she has trouble keeping up with him as he goes off in pursuit of a man he suspects has planted a bomb.

Harry and Kate are assigned to investigating a series of incidents involving terrorists – or, as they prefer to call themselves, revolutionaries. Captain McKay, out to impress the mayor, makes an arrest and attributes the bust to Harry and Kate for PR purposes. Not only did they have nothing to do with it, but Harry knows they have arrested the wrong people. He is proven correct when the terrorists kidnap the mayor and hold him hostage on Alcatraz. McKay is all for paying the ransom but Harry goes after the kidnappers, and he is aided by Kate for whom he now has a new respect. In the resulting shoot-out on the island of Alcatraz, Kate is fatally wounded while saving the mayor's life.

The film took an interesting look at a new aspect of policework; the rising number of women detectives. It predated TV's *Cagney and Lacey* in highlighting the pitfalls and problems a woman faced in her determination to take a step up from being a uniformed policewoman. Interestingly, the actress chosen to depict these dilemmas as Harry's first female sidekick was Tyne Daly who became famous in *Cagney and Lacey* on the small screen.

By the time Daly met Eastwood to discuss the part, Eastwood had abandoned the necessity for actors to audition by reading from the script. 'Too often great readers turn out to be bad actors,' he said. 'Usually when I ask someone to come in to talk about a role, I've already seen their work in a theatre or on film, sometimes without their knowing I'd done so. That's how it worked with Tyne in *The Enforcer*. I wanted to cast her very much. To me she looked like a cop, not like a starlet popping in to give a "performance." I felt she'd be so good I was willing to rearrange the shooting schedule so that she could finish up with the play she was working in.'

Daly was really breaking new ground in *The Enforcer* and said, 'I was determined that real policewomen should not snigger at the part I play in the film. The difficult thing for the woman is becoming a part of the cop society. A lot of old friends pull away from her, and she really has to prove herself.'

Like most of Harry's partners, she ended up dead in the film, but her screen death made her famous, and as she said, 'I've been earning big, fat money ever since.'

Harry Guardino returned to play Bressler, the character the created in *Dirty Harry*, and Callahan's superior was played by the superb character actor Bradford Dillman. John Mitchum was brilliantly psychotic as the terrorist DiGeorgio.

With Siegel unable, or again unwilling, to direct, and with Eastwood wanting a break from directing following the rigours of

The Eiger Sanction, he gave the job to his assistant director James Fargo. But throughout, Eastwood was in charge. He deleted pages of script to keep the action going. During the filming of an early scene in which robbers hold people hostage in a liquor store, Eastwood reasoned with Fargo, 'Harry wants a car. So he should just take one and get on with it – like a mini-Entebbe raid.' Consequently, the script was revised on the spot.

When the filming was over, Fargo worked with Ferris Webster in the cutting room at Warner Brothers' Burbank studio, but for the final polishing Eastwood took over. He was fast becoming the consummate film-maker – and the most successful during the seventies. *The Enforcer* took $24,000,000 at the box office.

Back home again, daughter Allison, now four, would not let her father out of her sight. Even when TV cameras were allowed into his home for a special interview with Iain Johnstone, Allison insisted on climbing all over him. Everywhere he went, she went, and everywhere they went their basset hound Sidney went. Among the other pets claimed by Allison were two deer that had been deserted by their mother in a storm. He brought them home and, assisted by Allison, fed them milk from a baby's bottle.

Whenever he went to work out in his gym, Allison and Kyle followed. Kyle placed boxes on the floor so he could climb up and emulate his father jabbing at the punch bag. Allison was more concerned with setting up her dolls on the floor.

One day Joe Hyam, the studio's vice-president of publicity, came to the Malpaso office and told Eastwood, 'Barbra Streisand's got this great script. It's about a cop who brings a hooker back from Vegas to Phoenix to stand trial. Just think of the box-office combination if you did it – fantastic scenes between them.'

Eastwood was unimpressed. 'Really?' he said. 'Joe, I like Barbra a lot; she's a talented girl. But I'm nearly fifty years old and I don't think I could afford to spend six months of my life working with that woman.'

He was, however, interested in the story and managed to acquire the script from Streisand. It was called *The Gauntlet*. It was the tale of a Phoenix detective, Ben Shockley, who was unlike Dirty Harry as he didn't always get his man. He is sent to Nevada to bring back a hooker who is a valuable witness in a case that, unbeknown to Shockley, will pin-point corruption in his own police department.

Consequently, Shockley's superior has ordered that neither Shockley, nor the hooker, must return alive. As they are shot at and chased through the Nevada desert, he and the hooker fall for each other and finally arrive back at Phoenix in a bus which they have hijacked and which has to pass through the gauntlet of police officers firing thousands of rounds of ammunition into it.

Clint knew who he wanted to play the hooker; Sondra Locke. He had felt that in *Josey Wales* she had been 'terrific in a part that didn't call on all her considerable range.'

He said, 'When *The Gauntlet* came along I thought it would be interesting to cast physically against the way the part was written. Sondra is an outstanding actress. She's intuitive; you give her suggestions and she picks them up immediately, contributing her own ideas calmly and with no hang-ups. She's secure enough as a performer to allow herself to use her non-thinking instincts without over-intellectualizing, so she's very open to the possibilities of great things coming along naturally within the course of shaping the role.

'For the most part, I like to go for a first take without too much rehearsal. If it's working and everyone feels good about it, then why not go? The great thing about film is that you can always go back to the drawing board and do it again if your first attempt doesn't pay off the way you thought it would. With Sondra you can do that because she doesn't work by talking everything out in heavy detail. I think she will gain tremendous recognition for her performance in this film.'

He wanted to direct this one himself. Neither of his usual cinematographers – Frank Stanley and Bruce Surtees – was available for this film; each of them had become very much in demand. He tried out Rexford Metz – he too became an Eastwood regular. As for the cast, he had his leading lady – no other performer in this film would work so intensively with him as she – and he also brought in others he had worked with before: Pat Hingle (*Hang 'Em High*) and Bill McKinney (*The Outlaw Josey Wales*) among them. 'I subscribe to the theory,' said Eastwood, 'that casting is one of the most important parts of a director's job. By your casting choices you set yourself up for how you're going to work. I look for people with flexibility and I like to take chances with someone with less experience if I believe in their ability. I like to use people I've worked with before, who've done a good job.

'It's not that I'm looking to build a stock company *à la* John Ford, but when you know someone's ability and range, it's stimulating to continue working together to reach for more and more in them.'

Apart from the on-screen relationship of Sondra Locke and Eastwood, the main feature of the film was its explosive special effects. Of the $5.5 million budget, more than a fifth of it was to spend on the spectacular effects. 'The whole budget for the special effects,' explained Daley, 'is actually bigger than the whole budget spent on *Play Misty for Me*.' In one scene, fifty police officers open fire on a house, spending 8,000 rounds of ammunition. At the end of the onslaught, the house collapses. 'Rather than an ordinary explosion,' said Eastwood, 'I wanted the house to collapse to the ground as though it was being eaten away by a gigantic mass of termites.' The house was built at a cost of $250,000. It took a month to finish, complete with 7,000 drilled holes each filled with an explosive squib. 'Needless to say,' said Chuck Gasper who headed the special effects team, 'we only had one chance at the take.'

The scene was filmed in ninety-degree temperatures. Eastwood had gone over and over the sequence with Gasper and the camera crew before filming commenced. Because the film was shot on location, Eastwood and Sondra Locke had to take up their positions inside the house for the interior shots, as hundreds of squibs were fired off. The two were protected from flying fragments by a plexiglass screen. When the interior shots were complete, Eastwood and Locke left the building and Gasper proceeded to systematically detonate the remaining six thousand or so squibs, bringing the house literally crashing to the ground.

For the exciting desert chase in which Eastwood and Locke, on a motorbike, are pursued by a helicopter, an 85 foot high-tension tower was constructed in the Nevada desert. The helicopter, which finally crashed into the tower, was built expressly for the film, minus an engine. It was hooked onto the tension cables and rigged to explode on contact with the tower. The sequence cost $250,000. Filming was completed in Phoenix where a 13-ton bus, built at the Burbank Studios, was blasted by 8,000 squibs.

As an actress looking for a really good woman's role, Sondra Locke couldn't ignore the competition she shared with the special effects. 'This picture had all the excitement and special effects that most Eastwood movies have,' she noted, 'but there's also a dramatic relationship between the characters. It isn't often that you combine the dramatic element with the commercial aspects of a movie like this. But we provided both.'

Blonde she might be, but Sondra Locke was no bimbo. She was an intelligent woman, desperate to play a woman of strength, but she recognized that during the seventies there were fewer opportunities for actresses to portray such ladies. 'People associate strength with masculinity. In this age of action movies specializing in masculine virtues, it's very difficult for an actress to play a strong woman. In the old days, Joan Crawford and Bette Davis managed to be strong and feminine simultaneously. So did Irene Dunne. The best example of all, perhaps, was Vivien Leigh as Scarlett O'Hara.

'Those actresses dominated the screen – but not the leading man. Actually, a strong woman adds to the masculinity of the man she is playing opposite. Katharine Hepburn and Spencer Tracy played powerful characters to their mutual advantage. Claudette Colbert didn't dominate Clark Gable in *It Happened One Night*, yet she played a very strong woman.

'You need a strong and talented man to begin with if you hope to maintain your femininity. But I think a good many leading men confuse masculinity and strength. They're insecure about women's roles that accentuate strength.'

But what of Clint Eastwood? Was it true of him? She said, 'An actress never has to worry about bowling over an actor like Clint Eastwood. He's as secure in his masculinity as any man I've ever known.'

Just how much of an insight she was gaining into this, few knew at the time. But observers did notice that Eastwood and Locke were becoming particularly friendly on the set of *The Gauntlet*. As filming progressed, rumours of a romance between them circulated, although by now Clint was used to such tales. The rumours were duly refuted. *Photoplay* was surprisingly cynical of the reports and in June 1978 published an article titled, 'Clint & Sondra; Those Romance Rumours And Why She Laughs Them Off.' It reported how Sondra laughed at gossip items trying to link her romantically with Eastwood who, it pointed out, had been married to Maggie for 24 years while Sondra and her childhood sweetheart, artist Gordon Anderson, had the previous September celebrated their tenth wedding anniversary.

Eastwood, in an interview, referred to 'other women' and said, 'I guess Maggie understands those are the hazards of my business. I respect her and her opinions, although we don't always agree.' If Maggie was aware of other women, perhaps he assumed that she would turn a blind eye permanently. Or at least as long as the 'romance' remained just a rumour.

As far as their professional association was concerned, Sondra Locke talked happily about Clint. 'He's very generous with his actors,' she said, 'always cutting to the other person in a scene. Usually I get so immersed in a role I don't think about such things.'

She found that working with Eastwood for the second time was more difficult. 'My role in *Josey Wales* was easy and I thought of it as an adventure. The second time around I was truly nervous because of the responsibility I was given. Normally I do a scene to please myself because I'm self-critical. If I'm happy, I think others will be happy too.' But when she made *The Gauntlet* she found herself no longer just trying to please herself. 'In *The Gauntlet*, and for the first time in my career,' she said, 'I told myself "I've got to please *him*; Clint." '

It was hard to believe the stories circulating were just *rumours*.

13

Orang-Utans and Snake Charmers

The critics didn't take to *The Gauntlet* – Eastwood never expected them to. Although Andrew Sarris of the *Village Voice* noted, 'Gradually it begins to dawn on the audience that the Eastwood character is not nearly as bright as he thinks he is and that Eastwood, the director, is poking fun at Eastwood the macho legend.' Judith Crist thought it was 'the pits.'

Eastwood must have cried all the way to the bank in 1977, as did Warner Bros as they raked in the huge box office receipts. Eastwood was a walking gold mine; his films collectively had earned an estimated half-billion dollars. There were a few million dollars more to come. Robert Daley announced, 'We have three or four properties for the future, but nothing definite. We're kicking around a couple of comedy ideas, a period piece, and possibly a sequel to *Josey Wales*.' He added, as though somebody might have thought differently, 'One thing is certain. All of Malpaso's films will star Clint Eastwood and he will continue to direct which he prefers doing anyway.'

Agent William Morris announced, 'We understand Clint is looking for a script as a base for another movie in which Miss Locke will star. He will perhaps both direct and act opposite her in any new film.'

Suddenly it had become important to look for not just a Clint Eastwood vehicle, but an Eastwood-Locke vehicle. Never before had Eastwood become so involved in somebody else's career. It only added more fuel to the hot gossip.

Not everybody seemed aware of what was going on – or preferred to turn a blind eye. In 1978 I interviewed Doug McClure who told me,

'Clint Eastwood is a good buddy of mine. In fact he was my best man at my wedding. You know, people think of Clint as being like Dirty Harry or The Man With No Name – guns blazing, violence, blood! But he just hangs around in jeans, T-shirts, doesn't smoke and drinks only beer, and he runs up and down the beach every day; he meditates. And he's a real family man. He's got a wonderful wife, Maggie, and they're very happy, with their two kids. I guess Clint and I get along because we're both a couple of fugitives from television Westerns. It's true he doesn't like to be around too many people, has just a few friends, but he really centres his life around his home and family.'

The expected *Josey Wales* sequel featuring Eastwood never materialized – Michael Parks starred in and directed *The Return of Josey Wales*. It was awful. The 'period piece' announced by Robert Daley also disappeared. Clint was now intent on making a comedy, an ambition he'd had for some years. He was encouraged to finally take the plunge when Burt Reynolds forsook his tough-guy image to make *Smokey and the Bandit* which grossed around $100,000,000. Eastwood had a screenplay called *Every Which Way But Loose*, a perfect comedy vehicle for himself and Sondra Locke.

Clint would play Philo Beddoe, a goodnatured trucker with a working man's taste for cold beer and country music in California's parched and dusty San Fernando Valley. He has one special talent and consuming preoccupation: he's the best bar-room brawler that anyone can remember. He is in love with elusive singer Lynn Halsey-Taylor (Locke) who leads him across much of the great southwest in hot pursuit. Helping him in his romantic endeavour is his close buddy, Orville, his buddy's girlfriend, Echo, and an orang-utan called Clyde. While trying to track down Lynn Halsey-Taylor, the friends find themselves in turn being trailed by a disgruntled motorcycle gang, which has been fleeced by Philo, as well as a couple of disgruntled cops. And that was about all there was to it.

When Clint began to wonder if it was such a good idea, it had nothing to do with the story-line, or the fact that this would be his first comedy. 'I had a few misgivings about working with a 165-pound ape,' he explained. He and Bob Daley went to the MGM Grand in Las Vegas to see a show featuring an eleven-year-old orang-utan called Clyde. He had been disciplined to perform various stunts since the age of two. Although orang-utans are natural tree-dwellers and walk awkwardly on all fours, Clyde could walk on his hind legs. The

Berosinis insisted that Clyde was so intelligent and responsive that while they could claim responsibility for 70 per cent of Clyde's on-stage behaviour, the other 30 per cent came straight from Clyde as he improvised and reacted to people and situations.

Said Eastwood, 'After Bob Daley and I met with Bobby and Joan Berosini, the trainers, I thought, well, why not? It might be fun and I'd never done anything like that before, so we gave it a go.'

Before giving Clyde dispensation to co-star with Eastwood, the Berosinis wanted to ensure that filming would not affect Clyde's natural timidity. 'We've taken years to allow Clyde's personality to come out,' said Bobby Berosini. 'He's a lovable fellow, but he's also an endangered species from the forests of southeast Asia who clings when he's afraid and spooks at sudden movements. You have to be patient with him,' which is why Clint was so important to the filming.

'We wouldn't have done it except for Clint and his way with animals. The man could easily be a professional animal trainer if he wanted to be. He's very calm, and very secure, which puts an animal, particularly an intelligent, spontaneous animal like Clyde, at ease right away. We took a big chance with this film, but Clint made it simple, and we're very pleased with the results, although, again we would look to any future movies with the same doubts. Clint was the difference.'

Said Eastwood, 'Clyde was one of the most natural actors I ever worked with! But you had to get him on the first take because his boredom level was very limited.'

Filming in 1977 was under the direction of Jim Fargo with some extensive locations in Santa Fe and Taos in New Mexico, Denver in Colorado and the San Fernando Valley. Geoffrey Lewis, from *High Plains Drifter* and *Thunderbolt and Lightfoot*, played Orville while his girlfriend was played by Beverly D'Angelo. Veteran actress Ruth Gordon was comically watchable as Ma who really had no real function in the movie other than to berate Eastwood at every opportunity.

But the stars of the film were Eastwood and Sondra Locke. (Although in the end it was Clyde who stole the film.) For her role, Sondra Locke had to learn some basic guitar chords and sing in front of a live audience. 'It was a scary experience,' she said, 'but it was also very reassuring. I had a good time and it helped my confidence. I actually found myself looking forward to those scenes when I'd be able to perform as a musician.' The film gave her aspirations of being a singer.

To train for the numerous fighting sequences, Eastwood brought in

In his directorial debut, Eastwood captured a moment of pure terror as crazed Jessica Walter attempted to kill him in the climactic scene from *Play Misty For Me.* *(Universal/Malpaso)*

Eastwood, as *Dirty Harry,* cornered compulsive killer Andy Robinson, and subsequently spawned a new series of cop movies. *(Warner Bros/Malpaso)*

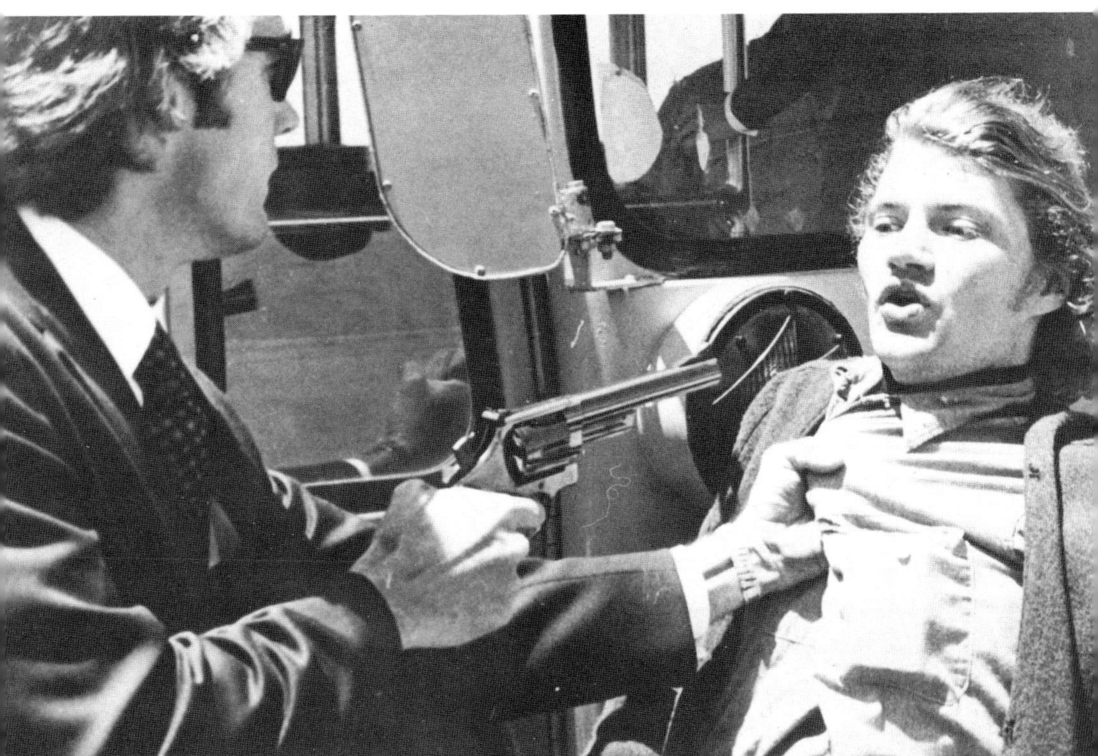

Behind the camera, directing *The Outlaw Josey Wales*. *(Warner Bros/Malpaso)*

Sondra Locke became Eastwood's regular leading lady, on and off screen, beginning their screen partnership in *The Outlaw Josey Wales*. *(Warner Bros/Malpaso)*

Eastwood with his most unusual co-star, Clyde, in *Every Which Way But Loose*. *(Warner Bros/Malpaso)*

As a mysterious, gently spoken, hard-hitting preacher, Eastwood helped miner Michael Moriarty and his lady, Carrie Snodgress, in *Pale Rider*. *(Warner Bros/Malpaso)*

Eastwood portrayed a hard-bitten veteran of the Vietnam War in *Heartbreak Ridge*. *(Warner Bros/Malpaso)*

His finest performance to date was as the John Huston-type film director in the superb *White Hunter, Black Heart*. *(Warner Bros/Malpaso)*

Al Silvani as assistant director and technical adviser. Silvani had had 42 years of experience training professional boxers and world boxing champions, including Rocky Graziano, Jake LaMotta, Nino Benvenuti, Floyd Patterson and Alexi Arguello. He had worked with Eastwood on numerous occasions as a trainer and adviser for action sequences, beginning with *Paint Your Wagon*. He had also worked with Sylvester Stallone in the *Rocky* films.

Silvani's job on *Every Which Way But Loose*, was to instil in Eastwood the attitude of a professional fighter. 'Even though the training methods I teach couldn't be imposed because of the obvious working schedule of the movie, I felt that Clint should know and understand what a professional fighter would be thinking and feeling,' said Silvani. 'Clint's an actor who's comfortable with a part because he gets into a guy he's playing. His personal interest in boxing made that mental commitment no problem at all.

'As far as the actual fighting is concerned, Clint is a natural upright boxer. He's a big guy with a great reach, which makes the jab an easy thing to teach. There really are only five punches in boxing; the jab, the right cross, the right uppercut, the left hook, and the left to the body. Clint is lanky, but he's got good power. What I had to show him was balance and movement, to get that power up from the legs and into the punch.

'Clint is dedicated and he's a real craftsman. He absorbs information and puts it into action through repetition and attention to details. The guy knows what he's doing and he's got a nice boxing style. When he puts together some of those combinations, well, it's something beautiful to see.'

The film was released around Christmas of 1978 when Warners opened the film in 1,246 cinemas across the States. In 1979 it proved to be the second most successful film of the year, pipped at the post by *Superman – The Movie*, also released by Warners. The peculiar thing was that this film attracted more than the die-hard Eastwood fans, and this had to be due more to the orang-utan than the pairing of Eastwood and Locke, or the awful script. Except for the expletives, it looked like a TV film; maybe an offshoot from TV's *The Dukes of Hazzard*. For once I had to agree with the critics. *Variety* observed, 'For Eastwood fans, the essential elements are there. Lots of people get beat up, Eastwood walks tall and looks nasty, lots of cars are smashed.' It added, 'This film is way off the mark. If people line up for this one, they'll line up for any Clint Eastwood picture.' (Actually, this prediction proved incorrect, as his next film proved.)

Frank Rich of *Time* magazine found it 'almost impossible to sit through.' Reported *Newsweek*, 'James Fargo directed every which way but well. One can forgive the orang-utan's participation – he couldn't read the script – but where is Eastwood's excuse?' However, the film took $48,000,000 domestic. Clint told *Newsweek* 'I'm not sure whether this is the end of an old career or the beginning of a new one.'

While audiences who came to see *Every Which Way But Loose* watched the on-screen romance blossom between Eastwood and Locke, the off-screen blossoming affair was being kept a tight secret from the outside world. However, speculation reached fever pitch in 1978 when Eastwood turned up at a screening of *First Love*, not with Maggie, but with Sondra Locke. They began to appear more often in public; throughout all this Maggie remained silent.

Publicly, all Eastwood and Locke would say was that they were 'just good friends.' The rumours were dismissed; he was still married to Maggie and Sondra was married to Gordon Anderson. Sondra Locke said, 'Everybody would love for us to say, "It's all true, we're madly in love." But people will believe whatever they want to believe. Even if it was true – which it isn't – I certainly would not talk about it.'

As though he'd been given a new lease of life at the age of 48, Clint took to what had fast been becoming Hollywood's favourite sport – racing cars. He bought himself a competition Ferrari for $100,000 and, along with Gene Hackman and James Brolin, took a five-day course under the tuition of veteran racer Bob Bondurant.

Every time he climbed into his Ferrari, executives at Warners broke into a cold sweat. *Every Which Way But Loose* had become their third highest grossing film ever, and they expected him to make a lot more money for them in the future. Said one, 'Eastwood sells theatre tickets no matter what the critics say. When you have someone like that working for you, you get nervous if they do juggling for laughs, let alone something dangerous.'

He began competing in celebrity races, and when he turned up at one such event with Sondra Locke, it became obvious to all that it was now only a matter of time before his marriage broke down completely. Still, he maintained that there was no problem in his marriage. And still Maggie remained silent. For a time it looked as though she would tolerate this mad fling of his and wait for it to pass. Maybe it was all something to do with Eastwood's credo that there should be freedom in their marriage without possession.

Distressed by all the speculation were Sondra Locke's parents. From their home in Wartrace, Tennessee, they wondered why she never contacted them. 'We don't know where she lives,' said Pauline Locke. 'I know it's somewhere in California because I have read it in the newspapers.' Alfred Locke reasoned, 'All the success must have gone to her head. Who wants to be associated with a couple of old hillbillies anyway.'

Sondra remained living with Gordon Anderson, but there was no jealousy involved. The Locke family considered the whole marriage was a 'sham' and each partner was free to live their own life.

During 1978 Eastwood was approached by Don Siegel for a film the director wanted to make, *Escape From Alcatraz*. It was to be something of a labour of love for Siegel, based on the true story of a convict who attempted a daring escape from the prison island of Alcatraz, and Siegel wanted Eastwood to star. That he should come to Eastwood was a measure of Eastwood's great success against Siegel's failure with his films since *Dirty Harry*. He had tried with Michael Caine in *The Black Windmill* and Charles Bronson in *Telefon* and had failed. Now he needed Eastwood for what they had hoped would be a sure-fire success.

Siegel had wanted to make this film since the sixties and had written a treatment called *The Rock*, based on a book by J Campbell Bruce, a journalist who, in 1963, had written an account of the escape. The project never got off the ground until writer Richard Tuggle made a visit to the prison and decided to try his hand at writing a script about the place. He approached Bruce with a deal to turn his earlier work into a screenplay, and they agreed to share the profits if Tuggle could sell the script. Bruce advised him that Don Siegel had once been interested in the idea, so Tuggle sent his screenplay to Siegel who bought the property immediately. Paramount expressed interest, especially when Siegel told them that he thought he could get Clint Eastwood involved.

Eastwood read the screenplay, and agreed to collaborate with Siegel for a fifth time. Eastwood was intrigued by this character, Frank Morris. 'He was very much a lone individual,' he said. 'In real life he was a man who was convicted of bank burglary and had escaped from jail on a number of occasions. When he gets into Alcatraz, which is supposed to be escape-proof, he finds a way to make an escape. With two other guys, he digs his way through the back of their cells, making papier mâché grilles to fit into the place of the real ones. He's very ingenious. He even made fake heads out of plaster and with hair stolen from the barber's shop so that it would seem like the prisoners were all sleeping in bed and their absence would not be noticed until the next day. They left the prison via a ventilator shaft on the roof and had a nine and a half hour start before anyone discovered they were missing.'

What really captured Eastwood's imagination was the question of Morris's fate. He said, 'We don't know if they made it. Nobody knows. We do know they made it off the island with some rafts that they made out of rubber raincoats and we know that the case is still open, 17 years after they made their escape in 1962. Nobody's heard from them in that time.

'The FBI thinks they're dead. They think they all died, drowned in the water. But that's just *their* opinion. Nobody really knows. They figure that out of the three convicts that got away, at least one of them would try to contact old friends or family; that's the nature of convicts, but nobody's ever heard from them.'

As was usual, the leading part had to be fashioned to suit Eastwood's persona. Siegel told me, 'Like in *Dirty Harry*, where we didn't know anything about him, whether or not he had a girlfriend or where he lived, we made Morris an enigma; gave very little exposition about him. We felt it gave him more of a mystique that seems to work well for Clint's audience.'

There was, by 1978, something of a difference in the relationship between Eastwood and Siegel, dictated by each man's recent track record. 'Clint owns an extremely successful film company, he's a powerful man and the wealthiest actor in the world,' said Siegel. 'He had control over the film, but I owned the script, which sometimes led to certain dissensions between us that I'd prefer not to go through. I don't like that kind of burden, but when you work with a top star like Clint you have to accept the fact that it's going to be that way. Clint always comes up with lots of ideas, and when they've been good I've welcomed them. But when I didn't agree with him, if I didn't think his idea was as good as mine, then I did it my way. You know, often, when his idea was no better than mine, it stimulated me into a new way of thinking; that's a pretty healthy way to work. And I've changed too. I'm a little feistier, more self-conscious of my position in the film industry, and since *Dirty Harry* Clint has become used to working with a different kind of director.

'But as he pointed out to me, he never really interfered when I was calling the shots and we do genuinely like each other and he's really very easy to work with. He was the boss, but *Escape From Alcatraz* is definitely a Siegel film.'

Much of it was actually shot at Paramount Studios, where a maze of prison cells was constructed because filming the whole film on Alcatraz was impractical; as much as possible was filmed on the island. To accommodate filming in the prison, now a tourist attraction, fifteen miles of cable had to be installed to bring electricity back to the dark island in San Francisco Bay. Windows were replaced and a temporary, peelable paint was used on the walls over the remains of graffiti from the 1968 Indian occupation of Alcatraz which had to be conserved as part of the island's history.

For the role of the Warden, Siegel cast Patrick McGoohan, a somewhat eccentric actor who became a cult figure through his TV series of the sixties, called *The Prisoner* – ironic since he was now the Warden. This was a role, he admitted during filming, that he wasn't enjoying much. 'One has to play heroes, villains or whatever, and that's all part of acting, so it's usually enjoyable,' he said. 'But having worked at the real place, Alcatraz, for a month brought to mind what actually happened up there. I don't find great satisfaction in playing this because it was such a terrible situation – the very fact that Alcatraz was allowed to exist in modern times. When I say I don't enjoy this part, it's just about the part because it makes me sick to see what happened in the penal system.'

The actual escape itself could only be filmed where it happened. And to Siegel's concern, Eastwood insisted they use no doubles. There was no storming off the set in a tantrum this time. Eastwood got his own way. With the two boys who follow him in the scene, he had to climb down the side of the prison and swim away from the island in a very strong current. 'I just don't think it was necessary to use stuntmen,' he said. 'This way we could actually see the real people doing everything. The other two actors with me were good stunt guys themselves so that was okay.'

Eastwood himself showed the other two actors how to climb without hurting themselves. 'They were very strong and eager, although not particularly big,' said Siegel. 'What was worrying was the knowledge that if they made a mistake in climbing down the building, it would mean death because we had nothing to protect them with. No nets or anything.'

Said Eastwood, 'Just to get out of the prison itself, we had to climb up three storeys, then get through a shaft on the roof and from there we had to slide three storeys down a drainpipe and then vault over some fences. Then we had to get into the water to swim off the island.

'It wasn't too bad and we didn't have to swim too far. We only swam out till we got into the current and then that took us around to the left out of sight of the cameras and a boat was waiting around the bend to pick us up. I guess it was a bit uncomfortable, especially with those strong currents, but nothing that was too tough to handle.'

Eastwood might not have been worried, but Siegel was. He told me, 'I got very nervous. I mean, twice I almost thought we'd lost him. He and the other two actors had a terrible time in the water, and when they reached a current it drove them towards the Golden Gate Bridge with tremendous force. It really was a tough fight for them to make it in the darkness; the boat was 400 feet away. I was in radio contact with Clint all the time while we filmed the scene, and when they disappeared into the darkness, I asked them how they were doing, and Clint said, "I can tell you right now that none of us could have made it if we were really escaping." I mean, Clint is a strong swimmer and won all sorts of trophies and so if he thought it was impossible to swim far from the island, then perhaps it's true that the real convicts drowned after all.'

The film didn't try to answer whether or not Morris actually escaped, but concerned itself more with the mental competition between Morris, a man who refuses to be imprisoned, with the Warden, a man who represents the escape-proof system. By its nature, the ending was ambiguous and anti-climactic, not helping the slow pace of the film. Although I now think it is a far better film than I assessed it to be when it was first released, it was not a picture that was ever going to become a classic. My own review of the film, in *Photoplay*, was not enthusiastic. 'The film plods along at a rather slow pace until Morris and three inmates put their escape plans into action.... The stark, almost documentary-look of the film in a colourless prison would have been better suited to black and white photography.'

Overall, the film received better reviews than was usual for an Eastwood film, and even those who had planned *Every Which Way But Loose* began to mellow to Eastwood's skills. Frank Rich in *Time* magazine found the film's 'cool, cinematic grace meshes ideally with the strengths of its star. Not a man to sell himself to the audience, Eastwood relies on a small assortment of steely glances and sardonic smiles. Thanks to his ever craggier face, the gestures pay off better than usual and so do the occasional throwaway laugh lines. At a time when Hollywood entertainments are more overblown than ever, Eastwood proves that less really can be more.'

Released in 1979, the film was a success, grossing $21,000,000 by the end of the year, but it was a lot less than the takings for *Every Which Way But Loose*, and Eastwood decided that he would return to the comedy genre once again with *Bronco Billy*. It was the somewhat gentle tale of a travelling Wild West show, run by Eastwood as Bronco Billy who operates his show on a shoestring. This time Eastwood had a beautifully humorous script to work from, complete with an assortment of oddball characters, including Two Gun Lefty LeBow (Bill McKenney) who has only one hand, and Chief Big Eagle (Dan Vadis), a snake dancer who keeps getting bitten by his rattlesnake. It's a simple life for all involved, until Eastwood becomes involved with a madcap New York heiress, played by Sondra Locke and her inept conman of a husband, Geoffrey Lewis. She runs away from her new husband, who only married her for her inheritance, and joins the Wild West Show. Because she seems to disappear off the face of the earth, her husband is accused of murdering her and ends up on the funny farm. There was a wonderful scene in which Eastwood leads his team in one last great train robbery, charging after an express train which has no trouble out-running them. It was Eastwood's best film for years in which he sent up his own image as a rough, tough, rootin' tootin' gunslinger.

'Naturally, the success of *Every Which Way* makes a film like *Bronco Billy* easier to make, decision-wise,' he said. 'A lot of people didn't like the script of *Every Which Way*, but I've always enjoyed movies that have a sense of fun. I liked the story of *Bronco Billy*. It has a special quality to it that attracted me to it right away, particularly the idea of a character rejecting all the modern cynicism around him with a positive attitude about his purpose, his life, his self-image as a traditional hero, and his sense of what is important and what isn't.'

He was so taken with the script that he decided to direct this one himself; presumably if he felt he was going to send himself up, he wanted it done under his own direction, and he certainly didn't hold back in poking fun at just about every Western – and Eastwood – cliché in the book.

While on location in New York he consented to a rare TV interview in which he was asked to define a Clint Eastwood picture. 'To me,' he began, 'what a Clint Eastwood picture is...is one that I'm in.'

Crucial to the film was the trick stunt riding performed by Eastwood, and these scenes were co-ordinated by Alan Cartwright, a 17-year veteran of trick riding. 'Clint's a very good rider,' he said, 'and in a film like this with stunts like we have, it helped us get around a lot of problems which could get dangerous.' It was Cartwright's first film assignment, and he said, 'The people were a pleasure to work with, particularly Clint who went out of his way to make everyone feel comfortable.'

It was, perhaps, the happiest film Eastwood ever worked on. Probably more than any of his films, this one was a true Eastwood-ensemble picture. It even featured Kyle and Allison, and in fact Kyle, at the age of eleven, was having aspirations of following his father's famous footsteps. Eastwood had no objections. He said, 'I feel that my children can go into any business they want, as long as they try to do it the best they can. That's the main thing. I don't care whether it's pharmaceuticals, engineering or the film industry. Pick what you want, but do the best possible.

'I don't think the film industry is too tough for them. I think they can handle it. And I think everybody should try to do whatever they want to do in life. Of course, my children have the advantage of having had a parent who was in the business and who's gone through it, so in many respects, that will help. For me, I had nobody, and therefore it was harder.

'But whether they'll go into the industry, I'm not really sure. We have talked about it lately. They go through different stages and sometimes they want to become actors and other times they decide on other professions. I suppose it's too early to tell.'

For Allison, *Bronco Billy* was a good film to make her debut in as it was one of her father's films that, at last, the critics on both sides of the Atlantic sat up and took notice of. In the States the *Village Voice* said, 'It's time to take Eastwood seriously as one of the most honest, influential film-makers in the world today.' The *New York Times* called it 'the best and funniest Clint Eastwood movie.'

In the UK, the critics were virtually unanimous in their praise; the *Monthly Film Bulletin*, not known for its admiration of Eastwood's work, said, 'Eastwood seems to have most enjoyed toying with some distinctly old-fashioned materials; a runaway heiress, a murder plot that isn't, some consequent punning on points of identity, and the most mischievously brittle set of greedy Eastern sophisticates since Frank Capra.'

Alexander Walker, in the *Evening Standard* wrote, '*Bronco Billy* is the kind of surprise this summer needs. A really likeable movie . . . Eastwood has wrapped the film in a nicely diluted patriotism, a nostalgic feel for Old Glory. His own lined and taut face now looks like some bedrock document of the Constitution preserved in a hall of Congress. He takes himself seriously but keeps giving us the merest twinkle of a wink.'

Only in France did the film meet with hostility from the press, although much of this seems to have been a touch of anti-Americanism. Giles Colpart in *La Saison Cinématographique* thought it to be 'the product of a vigilante America.' Jean de Baroncelli, of *Le Monde*, wondered whether the words aimed at the children in the film, in which Eastwood talks about honesty and patriotism, were really being spoken by Eastwood 'or a candidate named Reagan.'

Phillipe Garnier, of *Libération*, was one French ally, finding the film 'terrifically interesting, well directed, unfolds on many levels,' with a 'touch of Capra.'

If the film does smack of Americanism, then perhaps Eastwood is not entirely unlike John Wayne, for Eastwood later said, 'If ever I had a message to get across, you'll find it in *Bronco Billy*.'

But few people got the message. In America the public stayed away in droves. *Bronco Billy* was a box-office disaster, although it did better in Britain and in France. Suddenly Clint was not the great box-office draw he and everyone else had thought him to be. He was philosophical about the thought that his popularity might some day wane.

'It's inevitable that one day the public will stop wanting to see me,' he told Barbara Paskin, 'and when that day comes I expect to hang it all up. Not that I think about it too much, but I'm a realist and I know that such a day will come and hopefully by then I'll be able to either direct some films and still be involved with the business, or else just hang it up completely and do other things . . . like chase squirrels or pick up golf balls!'

14

A Multi-Million-Dollar Sea of Calm

In 1979 readers of *Film Review* in Britain voted Eastwood the most popular screen personality of 1978, and on behalf of the magazine Barbara Paskin presented the award to him at his Carmel home. During her visit, he worked out in his gym with lead weights 'that looked as if they could easily tip the scales at a couple of hundredweight.' Barbara Paskin was one of the few journalists he was giving interviews to at that time. 'I'm a bit of a private person,' he told her, 'and I like being left alone, and too often that doesn't happen.'

Although he was incommunicado to the press, all over the world newspapers and magazines were giving him more, though unwanted, space than ever before. While *Bronco Billy* was before the cameras in 1979, the relationship between Eastwood and Locke became more obvious to all around them. Sondra Locke gave a hint of their growing relationship when she said, 'I always saw something underneath those tough guy roles that made him interesting – a hint of vulnerability, a certain boyishness and humour within the superman image. And when we got to know each other, the boyishness became even more apparent. I've always been surprised that people didn't pick up on it right away; that, and Clint's great sense of humour.'

Still Eastwood refused to confirm that he and Miss Locke had become an item, and he tried to parry the stories alleging that his marriage was on the rocks. He even wrote to *People* magazine in a moment of anger when he read an article implying he was having an affair with Sondra.

'It's been very difficult for us,' he told Barbara Paskin. 'Marriages are tough to keep together anyway, in any business, far less the movie industry. So it's particularly rough on us with all the talk and stuff that's written. I try to keep our marriage private. Regardless of whether we're getting along or not getting along, it's nobody's business but our own.'

If it was tough on the Eastwood family, Clint really had no one else to blame but himself, since, as we now all know, he *was* romantically involved by then with Sondra Locke. Presumably, from what he had said, there were stormy scenes with Maggie, who still remained publicly silent.

The institution of marriage was something he no longer believed in, saying, 'The formality of matrimony is more important to the female of the species. If I were starting out now, at my present age and income – and this is totally hypothetical – perhaps I wouldn't get married at all. The only reason today is for the children. It makes their lives a little less complicated.'

How much more complicated he thought his lifestyle could make his children's lives is hard to conceive, although no one could have ever accused Clint Eastwood of being an uncaring and unloving father; he was just like any other dad – he didn't have all the answers and, in his own way, did his best for all his children under difficult circumstances. Kyle was now eleven and Allison seven. They knew that they had a famous father who was constantly in the public eye, although Eastwood thought that they had become immune to seeing him on the screen. 'I don't know whether they realize for sure that it's me up there or somebody else,' he said. 'I think perhaps they know it's me at first, and then they get wrapped up in it as they go along. Kids adapt to dramas very quickly.'

They were also having to adapt to the drama unfolding at home. After keeping quiet for so long, Maggie suddenly announced in December, 1979, that their marriage was over. The movie colony was stunned. The long enduring marriage had failed to endure, and Eastwood quietly moved out of their Carmel home, leaving behind his children. Bewildered, Maggie said, 'It was *my* decision to leave him, but now we both have a lot of decisions to make. I don't know what is going to happen, and that's why I don't know what to say.'

Divorce, for the moment, was out of the question, but the separation was official. Some reports said that Eastwood had seen lawyers in an effort to reach an out of court settlement with Maggie; she didn't want a long-drawn-out court battle, particularly over the children.

His children were now the most important people in his life and he returned to Carmel frequently to be with them. 'When I'm not working, I spend a lot of time with them. I pick them up every day and we do things. My whole life is devoted to them. I tell them my way of making a living is the same way someone else might be a plumber or whatever. I tell them "Forget what your old man is doing – it's only a job." All you can do with your children is give them some kind of values.'

Early in 1980 Clint and Sondra teamed up again for their fifth and worst outing, *Any Which Way You Can*, a sequel to *Every Which Way But Loose*. This time Eastwood's regular stunt arranger Buddy Van Horn was elevated to the position of director.

Clyde again stole the show, but this was in fact a different ape to the one used in the first film. Eastwood told Dave Turner, 'Well, the first Clyde – he's twice the size now and too big so we had to use another act.' *Variety* reported that the original Clyde was unavailable because he was making another film at the time, *Love Max*. For years Clint good-humouredly kept the notion of a *single* Clyde alive, and in 1991 told TV chat show host Terry Wogan, who asked if he kept in touch with Clyde, 'I haven't written to Clyde in some time. I think he's dating in Las Vegas.'

Daley Productions announced that the filming, taking place in northern California, wasn't hit by the strikes that held up other productions in Hollywood. The story saw the return of Philo Beddoe with his buddies Orville and Clyde. Ma was as cantankerous as ever and Lynn Halsey-Taylor came back into Philo's life. The Black Widow Motorcycle gang had regrouped and were back on the road in pursuit of Philo, as were men from the Sheriff's department. In fact, the story was hardly any different from its predecessor.

However, this time Philo has accepted $15,000 for the fight of his life against Wilson the Champ, but tries to back out. Unfortunately, the Mafia has become interested in the fight and sets out to ensure he goes ahead with the fight. Consequently all hell breaks loose as Philo dodges the Mafia, the Black Widows and the Sheriff's men. The only one unconcerned with all this is Clyde who has a hot romance going for him at the zoo.

Said *Variety*, 'This kind of thing is clearly beyond or beneath criticism.' That didn't matter; it took $39,000,000 in the States.

Several years later a report appeared in newspapers alleging that Clyde and the other orang-utans trained by the Berosinis were mistreated, although, whatever the truth of this, no one could suspect

Eastwood himself of having a hand in the mistreatment of any animal. The story died, but in 1991 the allegations arose again when Ottavio Gesmundo, a member of the Chippendales male dance group, took a video at the Stardust Hotel where the Chippendales were appearing with Berosini's orang-utans. The video was shown on American TV and caused a storm of protests from animal lovers. (In the UK, it was shown on BBC 1's *Inside Story*). Viewers saw Clyde and the other orang-utans being 'disciplined,' which included being beaten on the head with a cosh. Gesmundo had hidden his camera in a hatbox while Bobby Berosini disciplined the animals before they went on stage.

Inside Story's associate producer, David Perrin, said, 'Everyone who has seen the video has been appalled. It is really shocking, and shows how animals are exploited in captivity.' But it was Ottavio Gesmundo who ended up in court, being ordered to pay almost half a million dollars for 'invasion of privacy.' In a controversial judgement, a Las Vegas jury ruled that Berosini was doing what was 'necessary discipline.' A spokeswoman for the Berosinis said, 'We don't believe we were doing anything wrong. We had to discipline the animals to keep them quiet.'

Eastwood was aware of the case when it went to court, and a spokesman for him told the press, 'He was never aware of any abuse of the animals while he worked with them.'

Had Sondra Locke's parents known of Eastwood's respect for animals, they might not have been so apprehensive about their daughter's involvement with him. Said Pauline Locke, 'We have heard Clint's got a terrible temper and he once was so angry he punched a horse in the face. A man who could hurt a defenceless animal like a horse would do anything.'

The incident she was referring to never happened. The story had circulated after the filming of *Two Mules For Sister Sara* because of a scene in which Eastwood appeared to punch a horse. The horse was, in fact, trained to fall as Eastwood swung his fist in exactly the same fashion as actors do when filming fight scenes. But the Lockes were equally concerned about Sondra's continual refusal to acknowledge their attempts to communicate with her. 'I wish I knew that my child was safe,' said Pauline Locke, 'but she refuses even to talk to me or her father. Her dad and brother, Don, have both written her letters, but she has never answered any of them. It's clear she has been turned against her family by those people in Hollywood.'

Whoever 'those people in Hollywood' might be, it's doubtful they included Eastwood, despite his unconventional married life; to him, family was everything. For the time being, Clint and Sondra were deeply in love, although by the end of their relationship Sondra Locke would be making horrendous accusations against him.

Theirs was certainly a bizarre relationship; although she was in love with Clint, she was not separated from her husband. Their marriage of convenience remained convenient, and they often had dinner with Eastwood. Sondra reputedly claimed that she refused to leave Anderson because she didn't want to upset her Baptist parents. As far as Clint was concerned, he was in no hurry to get married again – if ever – and for the time being this strange triangle must have suited him.

To prove that she wasn't just a female foil for Clint Eastwood, Sondra Locke made a TV movie, *The Walls Came Tumbling Down*, a mystery thriller that also starred Loretta Swit.

As for Maggie, she got on with her life, avoiding the limelight now that Clint was gone from her home, and she concentrated on opening an art studio in Carmel, as well as operating a keep-fit studio.

Having spent the last several years shunning awards ceremonies, Clint was told by Jack Haley that the National Association of Theater Owners wanted to present him with a special award in recognition of his distinguished career. Delighted to at last be recognized, Eastwood agreed to appear on the live telecast of the ceremony.

On Monday, 11 February 1980, Eastwood, accompanied by Sondra Locke, arrived to collect his NATO award. The Master of Ceremonies, a member of NATO, began by announcing, 'Regardless of how film styles have changed over the years, we have observed a certain constant among our patrons. Moviegoers still gravitate toward men and women of exceptional style. We call them "stars." Tonight, the Board of Directors of NATO has designated one of our brightest stars as recipient of the distinguished career award. The gentleman who'll present this award is also a star. In fact, it's difficult to think of an actor more popular or of a greater stature than Mr William Holden.'

Holden stepped forward to rapturous applause, and said, 'Thank you, thank you very much. There are some who feel that perhaps there are too many award shows and they might possibly be right. But, with the feeling of respect and regard and friendship that I have for the recipient of the award of which I am to present tonight, I deem it an honour to be able to be here and do so. I'm here this evening to pay tribute to a man who most of you know as an actor, but I know him as a director – and a damn good one. The film we made together was called *Breezy*, and the director was Clint Eastwood.'

Holden paused as the audience applauded, and then continued; 'Now, there are few careers in Hollywood as solid as Clint's. He's gone beyond being an actor. He's one of the most respected directors we have with his own production company, and in short, he's a film-maker concerned with maintaining an image of strength and honesty, as did Gary Cooper and John Wayne with whom he has every right to be bracketed.'

Holden concluded, 'Here, compressed into a few minutes is a quarter of a century in the life of a man who loves his work.'

A montage of clips were then shown from almost every film Eastwood had made, and then the orchestra struck up with – not the theme from *A Fistful of Dollars*, oddly enough – but 'I Talk to the Trees' from *Paint Your Wagon* as Clint Eastwood stepped onto the stage and received his award.

'Thank you, Bill, thank you,' began Eastwood. 'Well, directing films wouldn't be that much of a problem if you always have guys like William Holden with you. It's been a pretty great lark and I want to thank the NATO group for voting me this award. I'm much too young, of course. This is the first opportunity I've had in the last fifteen years of thanking the ticket buyers, the people out there in the audience who picked me up on the plains of Spain and stayed with me through the streets of San Francisco and even when I had partners like an orang-utan, and got through my term on Alcatraz. No way can I thank you except try and do entertaining films in the future. I've been here for twenty-six years and I ain't won nuthin' – but this is nice!'

By this time preparations were under way for the next Eastwood film, *Firefox*, based on the bestseller by Craig Thomas about a new secret super-plane which the CIA steal from the Russians. It was to be something of a cross between a spy film and *Star Wars*.

'The novel was recommended to me by a friend of mine,' said Eastwood, 'and when he told me about it, I could see the possibilities for a film, but the problems were obvious from the start. A picture like this has elements in it which rely very heavily on the right people for key situations, more so than most films.' He also had the preconceived idea that the subject matter would limit the audience to pilots and those who were familiar with the unique technical jargon. Likewise, the plot structure seemed at first too sweeping.

'When I finished reading the book, the problems seemed less insurmountable because I had been thinking of individuals who might be able to help in each of the phases covered by the book. I decided I wanted to make the picture and that most of the details would fall into place once we put a team together and started pre-production.'

Another picture in the pipeline at this stage was *Honky Tonk Man*, which Malpaso had picked up for half a million dollars. Dave Turner, of the CEAS, was dismayed when he learned of the project and, when he had the opportunity to speak personally to Eastwood, asked him, 'Did you know that one of our British comedians plays a character called Honky Tonk and he's a poof?'

'A what?' asked Eastwood.

'A poof! A homosexual! You're not doing a Paul Newman and playing a poof, are you Clint? We can take your Bronco Billy, but I don't think the most earnest of fans could see you playing a homosexual.'

Eastwood laughed softly and said, 'No Dave, a Honky Tonk is a sleazy pub where they play Country and Western music and the main character is a kind of serious, tragic figure. It's kinda different, I guess.' And it *was* different; Eastwood would play a singer who is dying of tuberculosis.

In June of that year, Eastwood appeared before a court judge to defend his company's right to call *The Enforcer* by that name when an authoress claimed the title had been stolen from one of her books. The fact that Warner Bros had in fact made a film by the same name, starring Humphrey Bogart, in 1950, helped Eastwood win his case. He then set off for Wyoming, scouting for possible locations for an up-coming project, and spent the best part of July and August there.

In September he and Sondra travelled to France for the sixth American Deauville Film Festival. They arrived in the elegant French town of Deauville on the Normandy coast on Sunday 7 September, arriving on Warner Bros' private jet plane to find themselves facing a crowd of fans who mobbed them. That evening he made a personal appearance on the stage of the Casino where *Bronco Billy* was to be premiered. Said Barry Brown, Executive Producer of BBC's *Film 80*, 'He was charming, succinct and low key and the French audience gave him a rapturous ovation.'

The next morning Eastwood rose at dawn for a private and unscheduled tour of the beaches where Allied Forces had landed on D-Day. He had seen newsreel footage of the landings and wanted to experience the actual locations first hand. Consequently, he was late for a full day of non-stop TV, radio and press interviews. Reported Barry Brown for the Clint Eastwood Appreciation Society's magazine, 'Yet he found time to attend a packed press conference (for those unable to interview him personally) in the Casino's small theatre. It took eight minutes for the many photographers to take pictures of him at the table on stage before the conference could begin, and Clint reacted calmly and pleasantly without any sign of irritation.'

This was by far the most extensive publicity junket he had ever undertaken; no doubt he wanted to ensure that *Bronco Billy* didn't bite the dust in Europe as it had done in the States.

On Tuesday morning Barry Brown and *Film 80*'s presenter Barry Norman, who was there to interview Clint, were invited to join him for breakfast at the Normandie Hotel. 'He was refreshed and ready to go, dressed casually in his favourite, but obviously well worn, patterned sports shirt, and greeted us like old friends from England (this was only our third meeting).' They drank orange juice and then Eastwood quietly excused himself, went into the adjoining kitchen and ordered scrambled eggs. By ten a.m. the two Barrys were sitting in the hotel grounds with the camera crew waiting for Eastwood who had returned to his room to put on a jacket – the weather was a little too cool – and when he returned Barry Norman began his interview. 'Clint, his usual laconic, charming self, chatted to Barry in an intelligent, amused, laid-back manner,' said Barry Brown. Since then Barry Norman has been a great admirer of Eastwood the man, if not always Eastwood the actor. During the interview, Barry Norman, aware of the good work done by the Clint Eastwood Appreciation Society (of which Barry Brown and myself were honorary members), asked Clint what he thought about the British fan organization. He replied that he much appreciated the work that the CEAS did, and from then on Eastwood acknowledged the British-based society, accepting honorary presidency of it. The society's huge membership, devoted to their idol, discovered they had a figurehead who was sincerely interested in their activities. This consequently led to a number of visits to the US by members of the CEAS to meet Eastwood.

*

Barry Brown noted that after Eastwood and Locke left Deauville in the jet plane that had brought them, 'the town was never the same again for the rest of the Festival. That's charisma!'

Eastwood flew on to Finland to scout locations for his up-coming thriller *Firefox*; its subject made authentic locations out of the question. As he told Dave Turner, 'You can see why we can't film it in Moscow – I don't think the Russians would appreciate it!'

On the way back to the States, Eastwood and Locke stopped off in the UK to see Frank Sinatra in concert at the Albert Hall. Before the concert began, he phoned Dave Turner in Birmingham. The Turners had not expected any such call, and so Dave's wife, Jackie, had trouble believing that she was speaking to Clint Eastwood.

'Can I speak to Dave?' he asked.

'I'm afraid he's not in right now,' said Jackie, flummoxed by the what appeared to be a hoax call and knowing her husband was busy and didn't want to be disturbed. 'Can I help?' she asked.

'This is Clint Eastwood. Are you well?'

'Yes, I'm fine thank you. Is that Kevin? It *is* Kevin, isn't it.'

'No, this is Clint.'

'Wait a minute,' said Jackie, unconvinced. She told Dave, 'I think it's Kevin playing around.'

Dave picked up the phone. 'What are you doing ringing at this time?'

'Hi Dave, it's Clint!'

Dave paused for a moment. 'Kev, is that you, *Kev*? Kev, if that's you fooling around, I'll bloody murder you.'

'It's not Kevin. It's me, Clint Eastwood.'

'Clint, *really*? Is it really *you*?' He turned to Jackie and said, 'He says it's Clint.'

'Who's this Kevin?' asked Eastwood.

Dave explained that he was just a friend. And then he panicked a little. 'It really *is* you, isn't it?'

'Sure it's me. How are you? Jackie said you weren't in.'

Eastwood spent some time on the phone talking to Dave Turner, giving him details of his forthcoming productions and, finally, wishing them both well. 'If I don't see you before Christmas, both of you have a good holiday and I'll be talking to you.'

Few other major movie stars ever took such a personal interest in their fan clubs, and the CEAS became the most widely publicized film star appreciation society in Britain.

*

Firefox went into production in 1981 with Eastwood producing and directing, as well as starring, but this time not for Malpaso. However, he was producing as well as directing under a new banner, Robert Daley Productions, a company set up specifically so that Daley could make non-Eastwood films. Although the screen credits show Eastwood to be producing for the first time, he dismissed any suggestion that this was a new role for him behind the cameras. He said, 'I don't see the role of producer as anything especially different from what I've been doing over the years with the Malpaso Company. I like to get involved with each phase of production, regardless of what or what might not be a job category. I think the way our team is organized helps eliminate other decision making steps which can sometimes make a picture more costly or time consuming than necessary.'

Among his team was Fritz Maines, his long time friend, now promoted to the position of Executive Producer as well as serving as a Unit Production Manager. Of his friend and boss, Maines said, 'He was always a natural leader, but a natural leader with a different type of approach. He never had to look behind him because he always *knew* that they were there. And that holds true right now within the film business. Clint never looks behind him because he knows that the troops are there and that they're always performing, and if they're not performing he knows about it.'

Bruce Surtees was again Director of Photography, and Ferris Webster, with Ron Spang, was Film Editor.

For the first time since *Where Eagles Dare*, Eastwood was working with a predominantly European – and largely British – cast, including Freddie Jones, Ronald Lacey and Nigel Hawthorne.

Ronald Lacey told me, 'We all met Clint and he made everything perfectly clear from the beginning how he worked, and it was very comfortable; like working hard and being on holiday at the same time. Which for a lot of totally neurotic people who have all worked gruelling schedules, especially on the stage, was a blessing because there we were in what I called a multi-million dollar sea of calm. Clint is probably respected as much in Europe as a director as he is a movie star in all those Dirty Harry films and Westerns.'

As Eastwood had observed, there was no way the Russians would have allowed the film to be shot in Moscow, but the film did take in a number of European locations including Vienna, Austria and Greenland, while back in the States sequences were filmed in

Montana, San Diego and Los Angeles. The US Department of Defense, the Air Force, the Navy and the Marine Corps all gave their wholehearted co-operation to Eastwood.

His role was that of Mitchell Gant who has semi-retired from the military following a mental crisis resulting from his Vietnam experiences. It was the first time Eastwood had touched on the subject of Vietnam directly in a film. Gant finds himself recruited by the CIA to steal the 'Firefox,' the ultimate warplane developed by the Russians. It flies at six times the speed of sound, undetected by radar. Its integrated weapons system, adaptable to nuclear armament, is operated by pilot thought waves. Gant's mission is to penetrate Russian security, steal the plane and elude the sophisticated Russian air defence system.

This was a role that gave Eastwood a rare chance to show a greater range of emotions, as Gant battles against his mental problems to find the courage he needs to get the job done. But in most respects the part was tailored to his particular screen image. As he said, 'Gant is a loner and the very best at what he does. He has conflicts to deal with and problems to solve outside his area of expertise, but he never doubts himself. He is a professional, a technician and a patriot. I liked the guy and wanted to go through the changes he experiences.'

While filming in Vienna, Eastwood invited the book's author, Craig Thomas, and his wife to the location. 'I thought he might enjoy watching his idea become a film,' said Eastwood.

Thomas, who, until the success of his novel was teaching English literature, said, 'The Managing Director of Warner Bros in the United Kingdom met my wife and me at the airport and took us to the location. We were both nervous as kittens. Then this tall man with a moustache, and wearing a raincoat, came over and introduced himself as Clint Eastwood. He didn't think we would recognize him in his espionage disguise, but frankly there's not a lot of chance you aren't going to recognize Clint Eastwood, even if he's wearing a monkey suit.'

Eastwood explained to Thomas the initial doubts he had about the book becoming a film, but that upon reading the book he changed his point of view completely.

'He told me he was hooked when he read the book, which was very flattering,' said Thomas, 'especially since writing was really just a hobby to me when I started out, just like growing pot plants or collecting stamps. I never assumed I should or would be a writer, although I wasn't deterred by rejection slips.'

Standing by a gloomy canal throughout a chilly night, Craig Thomas and his wife forgot the cold as they were warmed by Clint Eastwood's own version of Hollywood there in Vienna. 'My wife and I stood there open-mouthed for ten hours watching the whole incredible process,' said Thomas. 'The nicest part of all was the amount of time Clint spent with us. He didn't have to bother because he had plenty to do, but the whole time we were there, when he wasn't working, he was with us. It was very considerate of him.'

The film's climax is an aerial special effects display in which Gant in the Firefox finds himself in a supersonic dog fight with the Russian Air Force. To produce this sequence, Eastwood contacted John Dysktra who works through his own independent company, Apogee. He had been responsible for the effects in *Star Wars* which won him an Academy Award, and had also worked on *Star Trek* and *Battlestar Galactica*. 'I met the guy, took a look at his operation, and gave him the job,' said Eastwood.

Dysktra and his team built nine versions of the Firefox; four large-scale models and four small-scale, plus one that was full size which measured 66 feet long, 44 feet wide and 20 feet high. 'It was built from a radio station broadcast-antenna skeleton,' said Dykstra, 'with a plywood and glassfibre skin. It has a complete running gear and can taxi up to thirty or forty miles per hour.'

Two of the larger models actually flew but the remaining models were used for blue screen composite miniature photography.

'We used a real live plane to duplicate all the manoeuvres whether it was involved with take-off, acceleration, dog fights or landings. We mounted a camera in the nose of a Learjet piloted by Clay Lacy, one of the finest stunt pilots in the industry. We also incorporated an inertial navigation system, which records flight motion and enables us to duplicate actual in-flight movement for staged matte shots, or background photography with the models. The impression of speed, which varies from 300 miles per hour to about 60,000 miles per hour, comes from exposing in-flight film at two frames per second and then playing it back at 24 frames per second. It's an awesome effect, tied into motion and cloud formation.

'This kind of special effects work can be maddeningly slow, complex and expensive, but Clint was the most open-minded and least sceptical of us all. *Firefox* is state-of-the-art in special visual effects, and Clint is the reason why.'

The film was released in 1982 and, as usual, the critics didn't take it to their hearts. Said *Variety*, 'Despite the tense mission being depicted, there's no suspense, excitement or thrills to be had, and lackadaisical pacing gives the viewer plenty of time to ponder the gaping implausibilities that skilful execution could have rendered irrelevant.'

'What is most curious about this farrago,' thought Richard Combs for the *Monthly Film Bulletin*, 'is that Eastwood, the actor and the director, should have walked through it all with scarcely a thought for each other.'

The French critics were confused, seemingly unable to distinguish between an Eastwood action film with humour and the comedy of *Bronco Billy* or *Every Which Way But Loose*. 'If *Bronco Billy* managed to maintain the illusion of self-parody,' said *La Revue du Cinéma*, 'one has to say straight out that *Firefox* is idiocy incarnate and easily oversteps the boundaries of involuntary humour. [The film] boasts a deadpan seriousness compounded by a disconcerting aura of conviction. And the joke sort of congeals around the depiction of a communist world peopled by the worst caricatures imaginable.'

'And what if *Firefox* were a comedy?' asked *Libération*. 'Well then, split your sides at the outlandish view of Soviet manners, laugh yourself hoarse over the wretched comrade first secretary whose first reflex after the Firefox is stolen is to ask Eastwood by radio if he would be so kind as to give back "something which doesn't belong to him," and lose any remaining vestiges of self-control over the scene where, landing in an ice field for a refuelling rendezvous with a US submarine, Clint's first words, fresh out of the cockpit, are a request that someone "check the oil and tyre pressure." A sufficient number of narrow escapes confirms that, like all great comedians, beneath Clint Eastwood's unruffled countenance lurks an irresistible urge to grin.'

Firefox was not a huge success, nor was it as bad a picture as the critics would have had the public believe, although the sci-fi special effects looked out of place in a film of this type; models may look realistic flying through space since few of us have seen real space ships in flight, but we've all seen planes in the sky, and the Firefox in flight did not look convincing.

Perhaps the critical backlash on this film harmed its commercial potential – perhaps the public just weren't ready to allow Eastwood to present himself, with his tongue in cheek, at the controls of a piece of futuristic machinery. Yet it is a film that precedes many of our more recent blockbusters that have had audiences flocking to cinemas between the mid-eighties to the present day – except that Eastwood hasn't starred in any of them; they usually feature the likes of Sylvester Stallone and Arnold Schwarzenegger.

Eastwood could console himself with the fact that he was still bankable – *Firefox* didn't lose money; it just didn't make as much as he or Warners would have expected – and he was able to continue living a life style that suited him. Although he was still legally married to Maggie in 1982, he enjoyed a stable relationship with Sondra Locke but was in all respects a free man. Sondra still had a husband at home to whom she regularly returned. Maggie, meanwhile, bought herself a new one million dollar home in Los Angeles and dated Henry Wynberg, former escort to Elizabeth Taylor. The gossip columnists intimated that, unbeknown to Maggie, Wynberg was making secret telephone calls to Taylor in an attempt to try for a reconciliation. Liz however was not interested, they said, as she was too busy trying to wrestle her former husband, Richard Burton, away from the alluring charms of Sally Hay who, thought Liz, was young enough to be his daughter. *That's* what the columnists said, and whatever the full truth, it was enough to supply readers with an ongoing real life soap opera.

That year Maggie's divorce from Clint became final. The alimony she won from him remains an undisclosed figure. It has been guessed at as being anything between $25,000,000 and $50,000,000. What was certain was that Maggie was determined to keep the whole affair private and amicable. It was an unconventional end to an unconventional Hollywood marriage. But now that Eastwood was free to marry Sondra – at least, if she were to get a divorce – he didn't. More babies were not part of Clint's plans – Sondra would later accuse him of forcing her to have abortions and a sterilization operation – and he saw no reason to tie the knot for a second time. By now Sondra was happy to tell the world that they were in love, but Eastwood continued to refer to her as 'a dear friend' and maintained his own home in Carmel – as he preferred to remain there and be near to his children – while she remained with Anderson. It later transpired that Sondra and Anderson lived in one of Eastwood's two Los Angeles homes while the other house, in Bel Air, was used by Clint and Sondra to spend time together. He had a new house now in Carmel, Los Ondas on San Antonio Street. A high fence ensured his privacy. The side windows were smeared with salt that blew in from the Pacific Ocean.

As to whether or not Sondra Locke actually objected to this set-up remains the subject of speculation, despite the accusations that later flew. According to one of the many 'close friends' that gossip columnists manage to dig up, it was Sondra who laid down the ground rules. 'Clint may not have liked the situation, but it was the only way she would share his bed. Gordon was with them all the time. He would travel to Carmel with them both and stay at Clint's mansion there. He was with them for breakfast and was still around at dinner time. It's amazing that Clint put up with that odd arrangement. He not only provided a lovely house, but so much more besides. He was forever buying the little trinkets that Gordon made for thousands of dollars – that was basically just a way of supporting him.'

However, another 'close friend' was reported as saying, 'Clint's never been faithful to the women in his life. But he has such a way with women, they never believe he's unfaithful.'

15

Make My Day

Producer Herb Wright wanted Eastwood to play Ronald Reagan's ancestor, eleventh century King Brian Boru. Wright had acquired the screen rights to Morgan Llewellyn's best-selling book *Lion of Ireland* which thrilled Reagan so much that the president called the author personally to offer his praise. Wright hoped that Eastwood would star, but Clint was his own man. He had turned down many films over which he would have no control, including *Apocalypse Now*, leaving the part open for Martin Sheen. Eastwood later noted that the huge amount of money spent on making the film would have financed the invasion of some country or other. And in 1983 a peculiar story circulated in the press that Eastwood had indeed helped to finance an action by military personnel!

It was said that he and William Shatner had financed the abortive attempt by mercenaries to rescue US prisoners still held in Indo-China. If true, it might well have been a noble act. However, there were those who claimed Eastwood and Shatner merely wanted the film rights to the action, had it proved successful. The actors were supposedly intrigued by Green Beret Lt Col James 'Bo' Gritz, the man who led the raid. Said one of those 'close friends' that the press invariably find, 'Clint would like to be this guy, and sending him to war and then playing him on the screen was the only way he could do it. In a manner of speaking, he probably sees himself as Lt Col Clint Gritz.' It is, of course, a very quotable quote, but I doubt that Clint Eastwood would back any kind of war, especially just so as to acquire the film rights.

In fact, Clint did get to make a similar kind of film, *Heartbreak Ridge* in 1986, and the exploits of Gritz may well have been the inspiration. If there was a fantasy for Eastwood to be someone like Gritz, it never showed. In fact, his soft spoken manner, warm but not overbearing charm and dry sense of humour seem to take people by surprise when they meet him. He has noted, 'I think people are disarmed when they find out I'm not Dirty Harry. I think they would rather have Dirty Harry.'

Writer Norman Mailer disagreed. He preferred the Clint Eastwood he met, and wrote, 'On first meeting he's one of the nicest people you ever met. He's very laid back. If you don't bother him, he will never bother you. In that sense, he's like the characters he plays in his films...I think you'd have to be around for a year before you saw his ugly side, assuming he has one.'

Clint went back to work, and again he was directing. In fact, he had now arrived at the stage where his decision about whether to direct or not depended largely on having a clear vision of what he had, and didn't then want 'to have to work with another guy and have to explain it to him.' *Honky Tonk Man* was unlike anything he had done before. He played an ageing, alcoholic country singer during the Depression era. Discovering he has leukaemia, he turns to his family and makes it his goal to make it to the Grand Ole Opry before dying. On tow, during his final journey, is his nephew who's determined to keep an eye on uncle. Portraying the nephew was Kyle Eastwood in his biggest part up till then.

Evidently, Clint hoped the film would propel Kyle into the acting business in a big way, but the film, while winning plaudits from more critics than usual, was a resounding flop at the box office, and did more harm than good to Kyle's chance of becoming a full-time actor. He would eventually embark on a career as a musician. Clint rather hoped that Columbia Pictures would give Kyle the starring role in their upcoming *The Karate Kid*. But the studio were unimpressed by Kyle in *Honky Tonk Man* and refused to cast him. Clint played what he probably figured would be his ace card; he offered to direct *The Karate Kid* for peanuts, as well as star in a movie of Columbia's choice, if they gave Kyle the lead role. This was the kind of offer no Hollywood studio would be expected to turn down. It was therefore something of a shock for Clint when they told him, 'no deal!' Clint had not worked at Columbia, and it now seemed certain he never would.

Filming of *Honky Tonk Man* took place entirely on location in Sacramento in the Sonoroa region of northern California, in Carson City in Nevada, and in Nashville, Tennessee. 'Shooting on location keeps you in touch with reality,' he said. 'It's easier that way. A small crew gets into the spirit of a film when it's working far away from studio soundstages. I choose my crew as carefully as I do my actors. I think that's why I've always had technicians who do a great job. When we move we do it together and we never stay in the same spot too long. I like to keep a rhythm going. I don't think I could work slowly if I tried.'

At more than two hours, *Honky Tonk Man* was far too long for those who didn't enjoy Country and Western music, even though the film had a generally successful mix of humour and pathos. Much of the appeal for Eastwood in making the film was the music and he laced the picture liberally throughout with musical greats such as Marty Robbins. Tragically, Robbins died only days before the film opened.

This was a picture, like *Bronco Billy*, which found its admirers among America's film critics. Richard Schickel wrote in *Time*, 'If there are any people left who doubt Eastwood's accomplishments as a screen actor, they had better come around for this lesson in underplaying a long, strong scene. In a season when everyone suffers the tyranny of the sentimental, one feels a special gratitude for people who do not know the meaning of the word cute.'

Eastwood's often seemingly immobile face had long been the topic of debate among film buffs, critics and Eastwood fans. What is true is that as time has passed, Eastwood has become a better actor (reaching his peak surely in *White Hunter, Black Heart*). But that he never ever understood the art of screen acting, as some have suggested, is something he refutes. 'If you look back through history, the people who've been the strongest in film were people who could express a lot by holding certain things in reserve so that the audience is curious to find out what the reserve is,' he said. 'You can see people who think they know what their face is doing because you can see them watching themselves as they're talking to you. If I thought about what my face was doing, I'd really get screwed up. I mean, nobody really knows acting. A lot of things just develop, they stay in your subconscious mind.'

Fans may well have been surprised to find no sign of Sondra Locke in the *Honky Tonk Man*. He had now made two films in succession without her, but had her back for his fourth Dirty Harry picture,

Sudden Impact in 1983. Cynics couldn't help but suggest that he returned to the role because of the disappointing returns on his last two films, particularly on *Honky Tonk Man*, but while there may be some truth in the suggestion that he needed a megahit, it should be remembered that *Honky Tonk Man* was not released until *Sudden Impact* had got under way. By now, *Film Review* noted, Eastwood was able to make his films on his own 'inflexible terms,' in which he received 60 per cent of all profits, leaving the other 40 to the studio. Presumably, this meant that Eastwood was entitled to his 60 per cent *after* the film had made its production costs back, and since he made his films on tight budgets with usually healthy returns at the box office, he was becoming increasingly wealthy. It was estimated that he would earn $30,000,000 from the profits of *Sudden Impact*.

This fourth Dirty Harry was more violent and ultimately unpleasant than the previous ones. Callahan investigates some curious murders which have a ritualistic significance; the victims, all male, appear to have been first shot in the groin and then through the heart. But once again Harry Callahan's methods find no favour at City Hall and he is sent out of town, to a small Californian coastal resort of San Paula where one of the victims came from and where they figure he can't get into trouble. But being Dirty Harry, he soon crosses the local Police Chief who refuses to give him any co-operation, and wants none in return. So Harry goes to work on his own, bringing him into contact with a young female artist, played by Sondra Locke, who turns out to be a rape victim who has taken the law into her own hands and is in the process of killing the men, and the woman, who violated her and her younger sister, now an inmate in a psychiatric hospital.

While investigating the murders committed by Locke, Callahan also has to dodge attempts on his life when he is held responsible by the underworld for the death of a gangland boss. This sub-plot was, 'a reversal that Harry hasn't faced before,' explained Eastwood. 'And it presents itself unexpectedly, without any connection to the central story-line. It keeps Harry off balance and adds another dimension to his list of problems. He's still the same character but we've added a few twists to make the film more interesting than its predecessors from a visual as well as a story point of view. For one thing, we've taken part of the action out of San Francisco and adapted it to Santa Cruz, which we call San Paulo. That gives Harry a different backdrop to work against.'

It has been suggested, however, that the film's location was taken out of San Francisco because the mayor of that city, Diane Feinstein, had vowed never to let Dirty Harry soil the good name of her police force again after *The Enforcer*, and blocked any attempt to make further Dirty Harry films there.

As far as Clint was concerned, the character was still one with something to say that the public wanted to hear. 'Harry stands out because of what he represents, especially now that the pendulum seems to be swinging in a more conservative direction. People are a little edgy about the rights of criminals taking precedence over the rights of victims. They are more impatient with courtroom procedures and legal delays. I think the public is interested in justice, and that's what Harry stands for. He's unique because he's stood for the same principles from the beginning, when it wasn't terribly fashionable.'

Clint knew exactly what he wanted with this film, and once again didn't want to have to explain it to another director, so he directed it himself. 'I wanted it to have a dark, sinister quality as well as action.' He surrounded himself with people he had worked with before such as Bradford Dillman as Callahan's superior, reprising his role from *The Enforcer*, and Pat Hingle, who was in *Hang 'Em High* and *The Gauntlet*. 'I want a team working with me who share my point of view and can move quickly, think ahead to the next set-up, the next scene or the next location,' said Eastwood. 'We don't want to cut corners – we just want to get the most out of what we're doing. I really don't differentiate between the actors and the crew. Everyone is there because they have a job to do and I assume it's going to get handled efficiently.

'As far as directing myself is concerned, I've done it in eight films and I'm comfortable with the process. At this point it actually makes things easier and more efficient. I'm also producing *Sudden Impact*, so there are fewer hurdles all the way round. Decision-making takes time, and usually, when you have lots of people involved in deciding one thing or another, it costs you days or weeks better spent elsewhere. I also want to be involved personally and this is the best way. I really enjoy what I do.'

The film, while hardly a classic, did deliver what has become Eastwood's most famous line of dialogue; 'Go ahead, make my day!' It was a line that was reprised later in the film; it had now become something of an Eastwood trademark to reprise a witty line, phrase or just a word. In *The Good, the Bad and the Ugly* it was 'There are two kinds of people in the world my friend; those with ropes around their necks, and those who have the job of doing the cutting,' which is later reprised with various definitions as to the two types of people in the world. In *Dirty Harry* it was 'This is the most powerful handgun in the world and would blow your head clean off, etc.' In *The Gauntlet* it was 'Nag! Nag! Nag!' Every Eastwood fan has his or her own favourite Clintism. 'Make my day' became the most legendary.

'"Make my day" came from the screenwriter, Joe Stinson,' explained Eastwood. 'Only thing I did is I reprised it at the end – that's my contribution. I saw the line as a goodie, so I said "Let's throw it right in there".'

He never expected the critics to be on his side with this film, but he might have been surprised that even a popular fan magazine such as *Photoplay*, so normally supportive of all he did, should attack him for the film's excessive violence. Editor Ken Ferguson noted that Clint had often spoken in defence of the violence in his movies and had said, 'If violence does serve a real purpose, and I'm not at all sure it doesn't, it is to give man a release through motion pictures that keeps him on a straight and narrow outside the theatre.'

Ferguson observed that at the first public screening of the film in the UK, there were members of the audience who revelled in the on-screen slaughter. 'I cannot help thinking Clint has lowered his standards,' wrote Ken Ferguson, 'by pandering to the taste of those who are turned on by screen violence, and I personally find it rather sad that his personal fortune will probably increase because of this over-indulgent, nauseating and brutal movie. The ending to his film is a morally disturbing one when Harry himself becomes an accomplice to an act that allows a killer to remain free and above the law. It's time Harry handed in his badge.'

Clint probably thought so too, if only because it was becoming more difficult to find interesting story-lines for Dirty Harry, and when the character was resurrected for a fifth time a few years later, in *The Dead Pool*, the whole thing smacked of desperation.

Another act of desperation was when Clint and Burt Reynolds announced in November 1983 that they were teaming up to make a 'buddy' movie. Again cynics were quick to point out that both stars had run into box-office trouble in recent years, and this was a distinctive marketing ploy. Filming was due to begin in February, but first the problem of billing had to be sorted out. Eventually they agreed that Reynolds' name would appear first on the film credits while Eastwood's would come first in TV and newspaper ads; that would all change before the film was in the cinemas. Blake Edwards was set to direct. But first Clint was to make *Tightrope*.

The film grew partly from the fascination he had with New Orleans as one of the world's most exciting cities. Perched on the Mississippi, just before the river divides to form the delta that empties into the Gulf of Mexico, it retains all the romanticism of the Deep South. Its distinctive architecture – its iron balconies, old cotton planters' town houses, the old stern-wheelers on the river, all help to keep the past alive. But it is the jazz – Clint has always been a keen jazz fan – and the Creole cooking that has *aficionados* from all over the world flocking to sample the sounds and the tastes and the other delights of New Orleans.

With all this as a colourful and atmospheric background, Eastwood was once again a detective, but this time one who is under pressure both at home and at work. His wife has left him and he makes a valiant effort to bring up his two children on his own. At work he has his superior breathing down his neck to solve a series of murders in New Orleans where prostitutes are the victims of a psychotic pervert. To make matters worse, public outcry over the murders is growing in volume, especially from Beryl Thibodeaux, founder of the New Orleans Rape Crisis Centre.

In an intriguing twist to the usual type of Eastwood hero cop, he becomes implicated in the murders when it becomes obvious that the killer appears to have an amazing knowledge of police procedures, keeping one jump ahead of the police. Also, one of his colleagues is aware that Eastwood is himself visiting prostitutes to satisfy his own kinky brand of pleasure. The killer, feeling confident as Eastwood fails to make headway, starts to taunt the police, sending coded messages that have Eastwood scurrying from one lead to another without success. In desperation, he seeks the help of Beryl Thibodeaux, and eventually they find themselves moving towards a romance. But then Eastwood's own tie is found around the neck of a strangled victim. The film builds to a tense and exciting climax as the killer invades the life of Eastwood, threatening the lives of those he loves.

Tightrope could be aptly described as Clint's first *film noir*, a taut thriller directed, not by Eastwood, but by screenwriter Richard Tuggle. No doubt, Eastwood was willing to give Tuggle his first stab at directing when Clint realized that here was a director to whom he didn't have to explain everything. The vision in this film belonged first to Tuggle. It was, as usual, shot on a tight budget, this time in New Orleans.

At a time when films were becoming steamier, with *Body Heat* and *The Postman Always Rings Twice*, Clint was happy to join the trend. A sample of the dialogue, between Eastwood and a prostitute, was:

'I'm wondering what it would be like to lick the sweat off your body.'

'I don't like the way you said that.'

'How would you like me to say it?'

'As if you didn't say it to someone every night.'

His leading lady this time was French actress Geneviève Bujold as Beryl Thibodeaux, and in her performance of a strong, independent-minded woman, she never allowed herself to be overawed by the screen presence of superstar Eastwood.

The film was largely liked by the critics. The *Mail On Sunday* thought it 'the most thoughtful thriller Eastwood has been in for years.' Al Clark's *Film Yearbook* Volume Four was cautious in its appraisal, acknowledging that 'Eastwood continues to explore interesting variations of his star persona in this intriguing thriller,' but felt the film 'never quite delivers on its promise despite authentically opaque cinematography by Bruce Surtees, due primarily to excessive caution and inexpressive staging by debit director Tuggle.'

Tightrope featured another of Eastwood's talents that had long gone unnoticed and, in this case, uncredited. Although Lennie Niehaus wrote the original score, Eastwood wrote the film's *Theme for My Daughter*, probably drawing inspiration from Allison who, in this film, was given her first major role as, naturally enough, one of his two daughters. He also had Kimber working for him during the making of this film, although Allison never knew it. While Allison performed before the cameras, Kimber worked in the production offices.

Kimber's fortunes had been mixed. She had fallen pregnant by her boyfriend, Anthony Gaddie, in 1983. Gaddie has said he did not know the child was his. 'I knew about Clint before I met Kimber because I was a friend of her mum,' he said. In order to qualify for the government grant to pay the bills for the baby's birth, she and Gaddie married.

'My father did not approve of me having the baby,' said Kimber. 'I was 19 and perhaps he thought I was too young.'

He did, however, give her a job. But she was disappointed because she'd been studying to become an actress and hoped her father would give her an acting job. Instead she found herself answering phones and running errands while Allison was given a part in the film. Eastwood was undoubtedly risking much by bringing Kimber into such a close proximity, especially with his legitimate daughter working alongside of him also. But at the age of 19, Kimber thought that her father had snubbed her in favour of Allison. 'We were all working together, but my father never introduced me to Allison,' said Kimber. 'I didn't see much of him either. He was filming nearby but he only strolled into the office a few times. I had been the one studying acting yet he used Allison in the film.'

It would appear, from what was to happen later when the world finally heard about Clint's other child, that Sondra Locke knew nothing about Kimber – or Roxanne.

In February 1984 Kimber gave birth to a son. She named him Clinton. Meanwhile Eastwood was filming his 'buddy' movie with Burt Reynolds, initially called *Kansas City Blues*. It was the stormiest film Clint had made since *Paint Your Wagon*, although it had nothing to do with star egos between himself and Reynolds. They had long been friends and worked well together – even their much-publicized discussions about star billing settled down when Reynolds finally allowed Clint's name to appear first in everything.

The on-set problems began when director Blake Edwards claimed he couldn't understand the leading lady, Clio Goldsmith, because of her 'Italian' accent. She was in fact British-born but had made some Italian films. She was replaced by Madeline Kahn. Further eruptions resulted in the dismissal of Edwards who then insisted his screenplay credit be changed to 'Sam O Brown' which was his way of saying 'S.O.B.' The new director, hastily brought in, was Richard Benjamin, the superb comedy actor who had previously directed *My Favourite Year* and *Racing With the Moon*. Then Marsha Mason quit, or was fired, or something, and Jane Alexander replaced her. Even the film's title got replaced, by *City Heat*. With all this going on, Clint was unable to visit his grandson. Maybe he actually had difficulty coming to terms with the fact that he was now a grandfather, and a secret one at that. Kimber was understandably upset that Dad didn't come to visit, but he sent flowers and balloons. 'He finally did see the baby when he was a month old,' said Kimber.

It was still impossible for Kimber to let the world know that Clint Eastwood was her father, even though she had named her own son after him. Behind closed doors, there was no getting away from the fact, as Kimber's husband, Anthony Gaddie, was to find. 'After we married, I wanted to forget all about him,' he said, 'but you couldn't escape him. Finally it helped to break up the marriage.' He and Kimber divorced.

City Heat, despite its backstage intrigues, was a film that was marketed to kick up a lot of interest, with the pairing of Eastwood and Reynolds. Not since Paul Newman and Robert Redford got together for their second outing in *The Sting* had so much excitement been generated by the teaming of two superstars. The cost of putting them in the same film was phenomenal, although sources disagree on the exact fee each was paid. One source suggested that Reynolds received $5,000,000 while Eastwood was to receive his usual massive percentage, while another source put Eastwood's figure at $5,000,000 and Reynolds's at $4,000,000. Whichever way you looked at it, it was a lot of money; no wonder the film's budget was something in the region of $25,000,000, an exorbitant amount for an Eastwood film.

The film was set in Kansas at the end of Prohibition and focused on a seedy world of bent cops, bootleg liquor, molls and dolls, pimps and pump action shotguns. Eastwood was again a detective, laconic, handy with his fists and deadly with his arsenal of firearms. Reynolds played his one-time partner, now a private eye who, when shot at, is more prone to duck while Eastwood would defiantly walk into the open to fire back. The one-time partners find themselves thrown together in their efforts to wade through a convoluted plot in which they try to clean up the town.

The success of the film basically relied on the chemistry between Reynolds and Eastwood. But it had been forgotten, or ignored, that Clint Eastwood was very much a charismatic star *on his own*. Virtually all past efforts to team him against others of equal star status had failed – *Paint Your Wagon*, *Kelly's Heroes*, *Two Mules for Sister Sara*. But perhaps the most disastrous element of the film was the poor screenplay which, at best, was only mildly amusing.

At a cost of $25,000,000, it had to take a phenomenal amount to turn a profit (usually, films have to earn around three times their production costs to make money). It raked in only $21,000,000 in America. Clint now found himself in the position of wanting, *needing*, a sure-fire hit. He didn't want to resort to another Dirty Harry picture. There was still one kind of movie that he could do better than anyone else at that time: a Western. Just how much he needed a hit became evident to him in August 1984 when he attended the world première of *Tightrope* at the Montreal Film Festival. It was obviously a film he had high expectations of, because while usually remaining unimpressed by reviews, he and Fritz Maines, in their hotel suite the morning after the première, scoured the newspapers in search of a favourable critique; it was also the day the film opened in a thousand theatres across North America.

'This isn't much,' he told Maines as he read through the review in a local newspaper. He picked up the *USA Today*. 'But take a look at this one.'

Passing the paper to Maines, Eastwood disappeared into the bedroom and returned a few minutes later to report that he had just talked to a friend in New York who told him that the *New York Times* seemed to like the film.

'That's great,' said Maines.

'Yeah, but the guy who told me this is a physician,' said Eastwood with a grin. 'So he might not be looking for the same things I'm looking for.'

He was dressed in brushed suede slacks, a green LaCoste pullover and he he had grown his grey-streaked beard for his first Western in eight years, *Pale Rider*. He was 54 years old and aware that, as he passed through middle age and headed towards his sixties, he had become something of a nostalgic memory for his original fans, not all of whom had remained with him. In some respects, Eastwood had a whole new generation of admirers; critics might not like all his films, but they did recognize his ability to diversify between his more personal films, like *Honky Tonk Man* and commercial films that had nothing to offer but mass entertainment. Suddenly, his earlier films were being reassessed. The *Dollars* films were now regarded by critics as minor masterpieces – indeed, Sergio Leone, who directed them, was now looked upon as something of a genius – and Eastwood's own seventies Westerns, *High Plains Drifter* and *The Outlaw Josey Wales*, were being appreciated anew.

'I guess earlier in the game I was too successful for my own good on a commercial level,' he said. 'Or for whatever reason you're just not as fashionable in a certain area for a period of time. But then people liked *High Plains Drifter*. That grabbed a lot of attention. Then *Bronco Billy*; a lot of reviewers seemed to like that film. I guess there are just enough different kinds of films along the way that people started saying, "Well, there is an element of versatility there."

'I'm at the stage now where several generations have fallen in love and fallen out of love sitting in a drive-in or going to some of these movies.'

A poll in America around that time showed that one in three young people voted him as the person they would most like to be – beating Mother Teresa and Ronald Reagan.

As far as Westerns were concerned, it was something of a dead genre. Or at least, it was dead but wouldn't lie down. The last really successful Western had been *The Outlaw Josey Wales*. Towards the end of the seventies, attempts to resurrect the genre failed, especially when Michael Cimino, launched as a director by Eastwood, wasted a fortune on *Heaven's Gate*. But Clint was not deterred by the death of the Western. 'There was no reason for me not to do another Western,' he said. 'I just hadn't done another because I hadn't found the right material.'

His avoidance of Westerns may have had something to do with his allergy to horses which he was reported to have developed. Apparently, he had to keep his pills handy alongside his six-gun. But he was confident, despite the scoffs and sneers, that if anyone could make a successful Western, *he* could.

'There are lots of things other actors can do that I can't and there's lots of things I can do that they can't,' he said. 'One of them is making Westerns.'

A Dr Don Graham of the University of Texas, an expert on the Wild West, had a theory for the demise of the Western. 'Westerns went out of favour because of the opposition to violence caused by the unpopularity of the Vietnam War. Also civil rights groups drummed up new sympathy for the Indians.

'But now there is a political atmosphere which stresses heroism and self-reliance. The time is ripe for the rebirth of movies which highlight these values. And Clint Eastwood, tall, handsome, fearless and skilful with a gun, epitomizes the sort of hero people are searching for today.'

Clint insisted that his decision to return to the Wild West was simply because he had found a good screenplay. And he certainly had. *Pale Rider* was written by Michael Butler and Dennis Shyrack and told the tale of a struggling community under constant attack by land-hungry marauders. A girl prays for a miracle to save them. Into their midst rides a mysterious stranger, even as the girl reads from the Book of Revelation, 'And I looked, and behold, a pale horse: and his name that sat on him was Death, and Hell followed with him.'

The stranger is a preacher, but one very handy with a club, and after rescuing one of the simple folk from a beating in town, he helps the community to learn to stand up for themselves. However, when a so-called 'Marshal' and his six deputies are sent for to wipe out the community, the preacher once more takes out the guns he has sworn never to wear again, and sets about wreaking personal vengeance on the Marshal – the preacher had survived the Marshal's bullets years earlier (or had he?) – while at the same time saving the community.

It was, in essence, a classic Western tale, best captured on film previously by director George Stevens in *Shane* in which Alan Ladd, a gunslinger who had hung up his guns, rides into a community ravaged by land grabbers, and finally takes up the gun again to save the community before riding away. What Eastwood did so brilliantly was to give the film supernatural and religious overtones. A girl prays for a miracle, as countless millions in a troubled world are doing, and she saw her prayer answered by a preacher. Whether it was a true miracle is open to debate. The fact remains, within the story-line, the girl believed it and the result was satisfactory to her.

Eastwood has suggested that his character is in fact a horseman of the Apocalypse, and like the Stranger in *High Plains Drifter*, this mystical theme has left the film open to much debate. The scars he carries from the Marshal's bullets may mean that he was simply lucky enough to survive – or he may have died and returned. All this mysticism made the film more than just a reworking of *Shane*, as Eastwood surely recognized it would. He explained, 'In the beginning there was the conflict between the independent miners and the all-powerful trust. To develop the Biblical parallels I ended up accentuating the supernatural aspect a bit.

'When it was a question of my character, I felt that we had to create a relationship in his past with an antagonist, the Marshal. That way the figure of the Stranger takes on an extra dimension. And it goes along with the idea of the horseman of the Apocalypse.'

Critics liked the film, but were not slow to recognize its similarities to *Shane*; they considered it to be something of a remake. Clint refuted such a suggestion. 'George Stevens took a classic Western myth with *Shane*, the stranger-comes-to-town story,' he said. 'I don't think it was anything new then, and now we've taken a different approach.'

He made the film, he said, 'on a gut instinct. I usually go with something when the whim strikes me.'

He felt it had all the ingredients of the old Westerns and reworked them to give the story a modern, eerie feel. 'There's a whole new generation that hasn't been captured by Westerns and I think I can drag them in.'

Eastwood directed with a sure hand, giving the film a visual style and poetic flow that, in my opinion, makes it a superior movie to even *The Outlaw Josey Wales*. He played a saddle tramp of his own age, too old for the young girl, played sensitively by Sydney Penny, too old (and too troubled – assuming he is of this world) to begin life anew with her mother, played by Carrie Snodgress.

Richard Dysart, of TV's *LA Law*, played the ambitious and ruthless businessman out to grab all the land; Michael Moriarty was the gentle but stubborn leader of the small community, and as Dysart's son was Christopher Penn, brother of Sean. In an interesting piece of casting was John Russell as the murderous mercenary Marshal. His wide-brimmed hat, hawk-nosed face and stylish clothing put one in mind of Lee Van Cleef, and indeed the biggest disappointment with the film is the fact that Eastwood did not cast Van Cleef in the role. Whether or not he ever considered it, he certainly chose an actor with similar features. Possibly it would have cost too much for Van Cleef in what was a minor role. But what a beautiful cameo it would have made.

As a matter of fact, back in 1980, when I interviewed Lee Van Cleef, he told me that he had an ambition to work again with Eastwood. 'I bumped into Clint a few years ago at a gaming table in Nevada.' (Eastwood may have been making *The Gauntlet* at the time.) 'I had a film property offered to me which I thought I might be able to interest him in, but something else came along. Maybe someday we'll get to work again. I'd be happy to be in a film he directed. We'll see.' Van Cleef died in 1989, never having fulfilled his wish to work once more with Clint.

Although reviews were good, critics were too preoccupied with comparing the film creatively to *The Outlaw Josey Wales* (which, they seemed to forget, they hadn't liked that much when it was first released in 1976). *Film Review*'s Neil Norman wrote, 'Once you've made a Western as definitive as *The Outlaw Josey Wales*, any further explorations of the genre are almost bound to be a disappointment. And so it is with Clint Eastwood's long-awaited return to the saddle.' Then he added, 'Not that *Pale Rider* is a bad film – quite the contrary – it is probably the best-filmed work of his career, capturing the snowy hills and the lamp-lit interiors of a gold rush community with tactile authenticity. You can almost smell the kerosene.'

Once again Eastwood made a rare contribution to the background score. It would appear there have been other films for which he has written music, but he would only admit, rather bashfully, that he wrote 'the *Theme for My Daughter* for T*ightrope* and the theme for *Pale Rider*; a few things. Making movies gave me an opportunity to utilize music that I liked.'

Pale Rider was Eastwood's finest Western since the Leone films. And it proved very profitable, resurrecting the genre and setting off the rise in popularity in Westerns which continues with the two *Young Guns* movies and *Dances With Wolves*.

16

The Mayor of Carmel

On the face of it, the love between Clint and Sondra was strong and enduring. But by 1985 she was growing restless at being just Eastwood's leading lady, and wanted to work. She had aspirations of being a director, and with Clint's wholehearted support, she directed and starred in *Ratboy* in which she played a window dresser who stumbles across a half-man, half-rat, and tries to turn him into a show-biz success by appointing herself as his manager. It was something of a cross between *ET* and *The Elephant Man*, and co-starred Robert Townsend, Christopher Hewett and Larry Hankin.

Her direction was thought to be technically competent, due in part to the fact that Eastwood surrounded her with many of his own regular crew. But the film was shown hardly anywhere.

'Clint was incredibly supportive,' she said. 'But he wasn't on set very much – he was very conscious of not imposing his presence. He's always been a big supporter of women's work. He enjoys hiring them, and he believes in giving them an equal chance. He likes films where women are strong on screen, too. They've usually been equal in his pictures, if not dominant.'

She may have been referring to her own roles as being dominant, but if so, she was underestimating Clint; no one dominated him on screen. But as far as her work on *Ratboy* was concerned, he was, he said, very proud of her. 'I thought she did a great job. She's never been the kind of actress to rush back to the trailer after her scene was over. She's always hung around the set asking questions, learning what everybody did. I would ask her opinion about a scene, and her ideas were really good.'

While Sondra was working on her film, and with *Pale Rider* finished, Clint could afford to sit back and relax a little, as journalist Douglas Thompson observed when he interviewed Eastwood at The Hog's Breath. He sat in front of a roaring fire and, thought Thompson, seemed absurdly indifferent to the fact that he's the man most people in the world would like to see.

'Look,' Eastwood told him, 'you see me relaxing. I am not working at the moment. This is a nice place to be. I don't care about doing so much now. In the old days I always felt I had to do more. Now it's time to make some comments with my work that I'm interested in making.'

He found he also had a few comments he wanted to make that had nothing to do with films. He wanted to build a small block of shops and offices on vacant land next to his restaurant. He applied for planning permission – and they refused to make his day.

It was just one more aspect of life in Carmel that he felt was being choked by stupid red tape. It was a nice quiet town, just as he liked it, but it had some regulations that were absurd, and nobody seemed able to get the local mayor, 60-year-old Charlotte Townsend, or the rest of City Hall, to change things to the way people wanted them. Women were banned from walking in shoes with heels higher than two inches! There were no neon signs, few parking spaces, no traffic lights, no house numbers and no postal service. Fast-food franchises were banned, as were frizbees. Children weren't allowed to play in the park, lovers couldn't park their cars along Carmel Beach between 6 pm and 6 am, there were few permanent public toilets and ice-cream cones were forbidden to be eaten while walking the streets. The town was becoming so squeaky clean, it was uncomfortable to live in. And Clint cared about it very much.

'Carmel is my home,' he said. 'I've lived here fourteen years, my two kids go to the local school and this is where I plan to live the rest of my life. But I don't want to spend those years arguing with the mayor and councillors who say "no" to everything the people here want.'

And so he decided to campaign against Charlotte Townsend for the position of mayor. The campaign bagan in March 1986, fought over a six-week period during which Clint set out to woo the votes of the people of Carmel. His election pledge was to unite the community. In April, the voters of Carmel made his day; they turned out in record numbers to give him 72 per cent of the poll, compared to Townsend who got just 27 per cent. After just one hour and twenty-five minutes after the counting began, the mayor of four years conceded defeat. A third candidate, Tim Grady, a part-time dish-washer who was standing on an environmentalist platform, polled less than one per cent.

After learning of his victory, Clint announced, 'I'm going to concentrate on making us a whole community together. I'm very happy. Now I just want to get on with the job.'

Getting on with the job meant going into semi-retirement from movies for a weekly salary of $50. Within 24 hours of his election victory he was being tipped to become a future Californian Senator and some pundits began fantasizing that he would eventually become President. Clint tried to put the rumours to rest, saying, 'My political ambitions begin and end in Carmel.'

He took up his post on 9 April, and held a press conference at which reporters wanted to know what he was going to do about the town's plastic portaloos. He told them, 'The unsightly portable lavatories are the least of my problems. I have to solve the problems of our local water shortage, lack of parking spaces, absence of public restrooms, and help local business develop within the constraints that local residents will allow.'

He confessed that being the centre of attention at the weekly council meetings in the tiny City Hall would not offer the same sense of excitement he found on a film set, but he added, 'It may sound boring to you, but *I* don't think so. I can get great satisfaction from addressing local issues, which have been ignored by the past administration. To help the community is very, very important, and, yes, it is interesting. I am sure it will hold my interest for two years.'

One local lady explained to him how delivery trucks blocked her driveway. 'Why don't you write to me about it?' he suggested, and pointed out, 'We will have a public forum every four months, where the residents of Carmel can discuss issues with my administration.'

Suddenly it was possible for members of the public to come and tell Dirty Harry their problems and find out what he was going to do about them. Law and order was an issue, but if they hoped he might clean up the town with a .44 Magnum, they were disappointed. He said, 'I will look at the problem of having no street signs at the junction of Fourth Street and San Antonio which has become dangerous. We don't want San Antonio to become the speedway of Carmel.'

He was also going to try to change ordinances 'that are plain stupid – like the one banning high heels over two inches tall.' With typical good humour he added, 'I can imagine a police officer coming up to a woman and saying, "Let me measure your heels. Go on – make my day." '

He leaned back in his mayoral chair and smiled. 'And all this on my first day in office. Tomorrow, maybe I will play golf. But I don't believe I will be bored with local affairs.'

After that, the quiet town of Carmel was not quite so quiet again. Clint Eastwood became a business for some in the usually reserved town of Carmel. A shop, called Clintville, sold Clint bumper stickers, Clint badges, Make My Night frilly knickers and Make My Night T-shirts, featuring a stetson hanging down on the bedpost and cowboy boots beside the bed.

On the first Tuesday of every month he was appearing live at council meetings. Before they started, the hall was searched for explosive devices and plain clothes cops received their final orders on security before mixing with the crowd. These meetings now attracted more people than could have possibly been interested in local problems. City Hall became so packed that many had to stand. Half the audience were locals – the other half were out-of-towners, Sondra Locke lookalikes, standing with mouths open wide, eyes fluttering, dreaming that their idol would notice them.

Journalist Simon Kinnersley, present at one such meeting, noted how on the street, Clint, in blue blazer and grey slacks, looked like any ordinary citizen, but on stage he took the place by storm with his charisma, style, and magnetism. It was like the Clint Eastwood Show. And you didn't even have to buy a ticket to get in. If the agenda made the Open University seem wildly exciting, noted Kinnersley, Clint brought it all to life. When he smiled, he lit up the hall. When someone talked too long, he frowned. That shut them up.

He seemed to know everyone who asked a question, calling them by their Christian names; they knew him well after living among them for nearly fifteen years.

'It's no big deal for the locals to see me,' he said. 'To begin with, it caused a bit of interest, but now most of them don't take any notice so I can live a perfectly normal life.'

According to the gossips, almost every hairdresser in California had run out of bleach as girls turned their hair blonde and threw off their high heels, despite the fact that they could now legally wear them, in order to be as much like Sondra Locke as possible. Leggy blondes, it was said, walked with a stoop while the very leggy blondes gave up!

But not everyone in Carmel thought him flavour of the month. His one-time partner in the Hog's Breath Inn, Paul Lippmann, was gunning for him, claiming that there were some Locke-alikes who got lucky. Eastwood fired back, dismissing Lippmann as a passing acquaintance whom he met only a handful of times. Mac McDonald, editor of the local weekly paper, the *Carmel Pine Cone*, said, 'They were quite good friends until they fell out. Now Lippmann is out to do him down, so there's sour grapes.'

Kinnersley observed how one young lady, Ingrid Hardy, a honey-blonde in her mid-twenties, spent an entire meeting sitting in the middle of the front row, transfixed by Clint. A fifteen-minute break had her up like a shot and over to the door with camera and autograph book in hand. Eastwood, said Kinnersley, singled her out in a second. The journalist asked him if he thought the girls brightened up the proceedings. 'Well, I've never really thought about it,' said Clint. 'They're just citizens of Carmel like everybody else here, so why should they be special?'

Ingrid, however, pointed out that she had driven for more than five hours to be there. He slipped an arm around her waist and told Kinnersley, 'I guess it's nice to have the girls here. I don't really think about them that much.'

Clint let her go, telling her, 'Come and say hello again when everything is over.' He watched her go, turned to Kinnersley, smiled, purposely said, 'Now, what did you say about the girls?' and winked.

Lesley Salisbury had also seen this kind of encounter. 'At least one woman will slip him her telephone number,' she wrote in *TV Plus*, 'Clint Eastwood has heard all the lines before. But you'd never know it. The fans get their autographs, the women get a friendly smile, followed by a quick, expert, appraising look – his "squinty" look, he calls it. And, if he likes what he's squinting at, the smiles get warmer....' But it was all tease – or in most cases, at least. When a female journalist asked him how sexy he thought he was, he asked her if she fooled about on her first date.

Whatever the audience may have been hoping for, those who were seriously concerned about Carmel's problems were pleased with what Clint had achieved so far, a year after his election. Neon signs were still not permitted, but children were allowed to play in the park, lovers could park their cars on the sea front, and you could eat an ice-cream in the street. He achieved these seemingly mundane things –

important issues, though, to the residents – through diplomacy, charm and having a knack for making people see sense.

He'd enjoyed his first year as mayor, he said. 'I've got another year to go before I have to stand for re-election, so there's a while before I have to make up my mind if I'm going to run again.'

When he was asked if he was setting his sights on the White House, he shook his head, tired of the question by now. 'No, I don't have any further ambitions in politics. I like doing this because it's positive and improves people's lives here in Carmel. Here we can do something, but I'm not sure that you can in the same way if you go higher in politics. It may not seem earth-shattering what we're doing, and sometimes it seems nitpicky when we argue for hours about a tree, but it's important to people.

'The idea of doing anything more politically doesn't appeal to me at all. I don't want to follow on from President Reagan. I get excited by every moment of this, but I don't think I would with all *that*. It can get a little stuffy at times, but I like to have fun doing it and have a few laughs. Although what we're doing is important, you still mustn't take it too seriously; you must remember to laugh at yourself.'

A few years later, he expanded a little more on the subject and suggested that there had actually been some discussion about going more into politics. 'I accomplished what I wanted to do. It was a two-year term whereas running for a council seat was a four-year term so that was the incentive for running for mayor. But I just did it because I was interested in my community and I had no long-range ambitions for being a politician. That's something that doesn't fit into the scheme of things for me, although a lot of people speculated at the time that because the President of the United States was a former actor that I was looking for an ambitious political life, but that's not the case.

'We had a lot of discussions at that time about going for State office, but most of the offices beyond being mayor of a small community required retiring from the motion picture business, and I had no intention of doing that.'

Down the street from City Hall the night Simon Kinnersley was there, the Hog's Breath Inn was filled with tourists hoping to catch a glimpse of the star. And they did, as he came in after the meeting. It was, after all, his local, but there was no girl in tow, not even Sondra Locke. In fact, noted Kinnersley, she had only been seen in Carmel once!

However, Dwight Coleman, one-time bartender at the inn, didn't help to quell the rumours. 'I've seen him with women,' he said. 'But it was always so nonchalant, I doubt if people even noticed. Clint is basically a shy person. He just isn't the type who can sweet talk the girls. But then he doesn't have to.'

Although Clint had still never won an Oscar – he'd never even been *nominated* – there were other honours for him. In September 1986, a newly opened drug clinic was named after him, and, accompanied by Kyle and Allison, he attended a TV special in aid of the clinic. Later, he learned that he had been voted Man of the Year by America's Variety Club.

After being away from a film set for a year, Clint got back behind the camera, and in front of it, in 1986 for *Heartbreak Ridge*. The title, when announced, sounded at first like a Western. But it was a tough story about the training of American Marines. Eastwood played a gunnery Sergeant called Tom Highway, a no-nonsense, hard-drinking traditionalist who has spent his life in the Marine Corps. He has served in both Korea and Vietnam with distinction and now wants to train fighting Marines. His life is complicated by his two Commanding Officers with whom he is in perpetual conflict, his ex-wife, and his new platoon, made up of men who have no real understanding of what it means to be a fighting Marine. Finally, he leads them in an attack on Grenada; not exactly one of the finer moments of US military history.

The film portrayed these men as being undisciplined and foul-mouthed; Highway had his job cut out for him. The US Marines, who gave Eastwood their support in the making of the film, objected to the portrayal of the recruits as men who use four letter words. They insisted that Marines did not swear and that the film was bad for their image! It certainly didn't harm Eastwood's image, or his pocket. He was said to have earned $6,000,000.

A strong cast included Everett McGill, Moses Gunn, Eileen Heckart, Bo Svenson and, more interestingly, Marsha Mason who had been one of those to depart *City Heat* during filming.

The film's title referred to the Korean battle where Tom Highway distinguished himself. It also refers to a contemporary turning point in his life in which he sees his career coming to a close. His tough-as-nails Sergeant who is obviously a good man to have in charge – a man his recruits come to respect and follow – allowed Eastwood a different kind of performance. Instead of just relying on his usual screen persona, he affected a gravel voice, a short back and sides and an on-screen age the same as his – 55-years-old – and produced such a thoroughly enjoyable performance that it was easy to overlook the fact that the film was so predictable. After all, the story, as *Pale Rider* was to Westerns, was as familiar as countless other war films, particularly *The Sands of Iwo Jima* in which John Wayne gave one of his better performances as a sergeant whipping recruits into shape for the climactic battle. Critics approved of this Eastwood film, and so did the audience when the film was released in 1987.

Clint went back to work as Mayor of Carmel for his final year of office, during which time a new scandal rocked America – Irangate. A newspaper report circulated that typified the kind of thirst the Press had for any bizarre angle on Eastwood's life. Like anyone else in America concerned with corruption in the system, he watched in fascination as Colonel Oliver North gave his evidence live on television. But according to the report, which smacked of sensationalism, 'He has never been so utterly fascinated by anything. He is living every moment of North's evidence as if he were there, facing the Congressional inquiry.' It went on to detail how Eastwood's three attractive secretaries called each one of his friends in order to find out who had missed North's testimony so he could send them a copy of the video he had made of the investigations. 'Clint is a man possessed,' said the report. 'He *is* Ollie North.' Looking beyond the report's assertions of any kind of obsession, and supposing that Eastwood did in fact tape the investigations, it is possible that he merely saw it as a germ of a movie – and one that didn't come to fruition.

In his official capacity as the Mayor of Carmel, he was present in September 1987, when His Holiness Pope John Paul II arrived at Monterey Airport. Clint was just one of twenty civic and church leaders to great the Pope on the latest leg of his American tour. Organizers had feared that Clint's presence might in fact upstage their visiting VIP. 'Clint wasn't there as a celebrity,' said a spokesman, 'but as a mayor representing his town.'

As the Pope walked down the line of waiting dignitaries, he came face to face with Clint Eastwood. The Pope seemed to know exactly who Clint Eastwood was, and as they shook hands, Eastwood's face crinkled into a huge grin and the Pope smiled – and then he moved on, later flying to San Francisco where gays and AIDS victims were planning demonstrations.

Eastwood was restless being just Mayor of Carmel and was itching to get back to making movies. So he did, but this time purely as director – and producer – with *Bird*, the film he'd been planning for much of his life. It was the true story of jazz legend Charlie Parker whom Eastwood had first heard when he was a teenager in Oakland, himself playing Dixieland piano. "I was proficient for my age,' he recalled, "but I didn't have the discipline at the time as I was too busy chasing the chicks and doing the things kids do.'

To portray Charlie 'Bird' Parker, Eastwood chose Forest Whitaker. It was a superb performance and won Whitaker a Best Actor award at the 1988 Cannes Film Festival where Eastwood, accompanied by Sondra Locke, turned up and where, after all the years I'd been trying to get an interview with him, I at least caught up with him at a press conference.

The American critics were almost unanimous in their praise of *Bird*. *Time* proclaimed Eastwood as 'a major American director.' The jazz buffs also liked it, especially as he used previously unheard tapes of Parker's playing which Clint came across when he visited Parker's widow. 'I didn't know of their existence when I started out, but I'd heard all the rumours over the years about lost tapes. I knew that people had recorded Bird where they had recorded his solos only and then turned off the tape. When I went to visit his widow, Chan, in Paris, I said, "Where is all of that stuff?" And she said, "Well I have some tapes that are really quite good because I used to tape Bird's solos." So she took me to the bank and got them out of the vault and went into a studio in Paris and transferred them as we listened to them. They were old tapes and some of them were crumbling a bit.' The quality of most of the solos were good enough to use, but the rest had to be rebuilt from scratch, resulting in a soundtrack that in effect was a new Parker recording.

Chan, in the film, is portrayed by Diane Venora, continuing his policy of casting actresses who were anything but traditional – such as Jessica Walter, Tyne Daly, Geneviève Bujold and Carrie Snodgress. 'I don't know if it's conscious or just upbringing, but it seemed like in the thirties and forties, women had a strong voice in motion picture making,' he said. 'Then, in the fifties, it kind of drifted into the girl-next-door-with-a-pony-tail type who never had much function in the story. But I tried in the seventies to have strong women roles: *The Beguiled*, *Play Misty for Me*. It's also from a selfish point of view that the stronger the woman's role, the better catalyst it is for the male protagonist – it works on a lot of levels.'

His ideal strong women of the screen included Barbara Stanwyck, Bette Davis, Joan Crawford and Katharine Hepburn. His ideal woman was, he thinks, Simone Signoret in *Room at the Top*. 'The most feminine creature on earth,' he said, 'yet she had moments of real toughness. She was all woman.' As for the women who came on strong, such as those who dyed their hair blonde and passed him their phone numbers, he said, 'I hate women who go around flirting and chirping like canaries.'

Getting behind the camera for the first time without being in front of it as well since *Breezy*, Eastwood felt in his element. The day will come, more than likely, when he'll no longer be acting, but directing only. But, unlike Alfred Hitchcock who said that 'actors are like cattle,' he has a healthy respect for actors, and finds his job made easier because of his own experience. 'Actors are like anyone else – you just have to make them extremely comfortable and very secure and they'll give you great ideas,' he said. 'It's easier for me to do that, being an actor myself. I can sense when they're not really ready.'

When casting, his prime concern was to look for people who get on with the job. 'There's one kind of actor who likes to show off his technique, go into another room, lean against the wailing wall, and let everyone know how he's getting ready. Then there's the other kind who just wants to go in and do the job. I like that kind better.'

The film itself was the first really authentic movie about jazz to come out of Hollywood. 'Jazz was a generally unappreciated music way back then,' said Eastwood. 'Parker could have played more commercial music and by doing that received much more acclaim. But he opted to push back barriers, stretch his genius despite the cost. He played the way he felt it, but he was a lone voice. He could have survived by playing safe but he didn't. Now every sax player in the world is influenced by him. Who knows why some people step out and pioneer? It was that dedication to his genius that interested me.'

Bird was also the first American film to deal with an inter-racial romance without melodrama or hysteria. 'The approach was just to do it straight,' said Eastwood. 'You have the same problems when you're married to anyone!'

Parker died at 34 having taken so much heroin during his life that the coroner said there wasn't a vein left to inject.

'I'd just like people to understand something about this American icon of jazz,' said Clint, 'what made him tick. He was living in the fast lane. Everything he did was in excess. He was going to soar high and fast but it was going to be a short existence. I guess everyone has a road down which they could have gone and become an out-and-out drunk or into some other form of self-destruction. But something in the brain says "that's enough," and you stop. The ones who do go right down that road are in trouble.

'I have known many people in all forms of the arts who were self destructive like Charlie. And they were not the genius he was. It seems you can't do anything about it.

'Parker himself may have been hooked, but he went out of his way to stop others from getting into the same thing. His philosophy was "do what I say and not what I do." That's depicted strongly in the film because he was acutely aware that he was adversely affecting a whole generation of jazz saxophonists; they thought that they *had* to indulge in drugs to be able to play like him. He just couldn't kick the habit himself, even though he was very discouraging of it.'

Eastwood himself is an advocate of clean and healthy living, taking no part in the Hollywood where cocaine is often served up with the coffee and doughnuts. 'We know what we want, and drugs play no part in our plans,' he said.

Bird was the first time that Clint was honoured with a major movie award as he received the Golden Globe for his direction. There was a trend for Golden Globe winners to become close contenders for the Oscars, but Eastwood didn't even get a nomination. The only Oscar *Bird* won was for Best Achievement in Sound. He was, however, honoured by the NAACP (National Association for the Advancement of Colored People) for his non-prejudice towards ethnic minorities in his work. To receive the award, he attended the ceremony which was televised in the States.

While Eastwood was editing *Bird*, he had three more months to fulfil as Mayor of Carmel. He decided not to run again. 'I did quite a bit as Mayor,' he said. 'Now other people can come along.' Being Mayor had been extremely time-consuming, and he had grown restless, wanting to get back to making movies again, and spending more time with Kyle and Allison while they were still teenagers. 'I have really enjoyed this, but I have to take care of personal stuff for a while. If you miss time with your family, you wonder if it's time you can get back.'

His successor to the Mayorship was Mrs Jean Grace, a 52-year-old pollution control expert and divorced mother of three. Clint welcomed her into office and they became friends. 'Clint is a very down-to-earth person,' said Mrs Grace, 'and we can be good friends because I can take his celebrity without being awed by it. He is a remarkably well-balanced person.' Immediately the gossip spread that they were romantically involved.

The fact that he turned up at Cannes with Sondra Locke seemed to be a public demonstration that they were as much in love as ever. When someone at Cannes dared to ask him about his alleged affair with Mrs Grace, he flashed an easy grin and said, 'Those stories are just rubbish.' Whatever the truth about his friendship with the new Mayor of Carmel, and despite the way Clint and Sondra hugged for the sake of the cameras, there were hidden problems that would soon surface and become public.

Talk of his viability to run for President would not go away. 'The White House stories are nonsense,' he declared. As far as politics were concerned, he said that whereas he had generally been conservative, his politics had shifted; 'In this last election, I surprised even me. You go through each issue and you vote in an individual way. I found myself voting for a Democrat on certain issues.'

However, he did say that his return to the political world couldn't be entirely ruled out for the future. 'Being mayor was a happy experience, but I don't think I'll miss it. And there are things I want to do in the movie business right now.'

If there were things in the movie business he really wanted to do, they must have been shelved for a while because he went into his fifth, and worst, Dirty Harry film, *The Dead Pool*; it really couldn't have been something he wanted to do *that* much. He said this one was different from the previous Harry films – 'more of a sleuth thing, a detective story with action sequences.' Which is not what Dirty Harry is really about. It was the kind of job Colombo or Kojak could have done with no less excitement. This new story featured Harry as a local hero after jailing a top crime lord. He finds himself in the spotlight of TV whose people follow him everywhere in the hope that they'll get high ratings if they're on the scene when he is eventually blown away.

His superiors want him in the newspapers, and the crime lord wants him dead. The 'dead pool' is a list of celebrities being systematically murdered, and includes as its highlight Harry himself.

The mysterious celebrity killer has blown one victim to pieces, agonizingly poisoned another and slashed the throat of another. One of his attempts on Harry's life involves the most unusual car chase ever in which Harry's car is pursued by a remote-controlled model car packed with explosives. It is the only really exciting scene in the film.

Directing once again, as well as producing, Eastwood tried to remain publicly enthusiastic about packing a .44 Magnum once again. 'It's fun, once in a while, to have a character you can go back to,' he said. 'It's like revisiting an old friend you haven't seen for a long time. You figure "I'll go back and see how he feels about things now." All Harry has ever wanted was to make some sense of the system.

'Originally, the part was written for an older man than I was when I first played it. He was a guy who had been on the force a long time, a mature guy who was fed up with what he saw happening to people. The laws were crazy, he was saying. A lot of people felt that way. That's one reason why the films are so popular.'

This time, though, the emphasis shifted away from Harry's unorthodox methods and wranglings with his superiors, and perhaps it wasn't just coincidence that San Francisco Mayor, Diane Feinstein, during her final months of office, agreed to allow Dirty Harry loose in the city's streets again.

Filming in the streets of San Francisco apparently did not please all the city-dwellers there. It seems that one neighbourhood were so angry they even went to court to try and stop cameras filming on their streets. But the man who was special assistant to the San Francisco police, Sergeant Gary Epperly, admitted, 'That was all our fault. Normally we canvass the neighbourhood to bring them into the show – meeting the cast, getting autographs, and becoming part of the film. One area just wasn't adequately surveyed by us, and the neighbourhood objected. But eventually Clint was allowed to film there after all.'

Despite the delays, Eastwood kept his cool under pressure. 'He was almost the most relaxed person on the set,' said one of his regular technicians. 'If things didn't always go the way we planned, he would make them work somehow, even if it took days. He wanted to get it right.' Ironically, the original title for *Dirty Harry* had been *Dead Right*. This fifth and last, *The Dead Pool* was a Dead Loss! It was time, he realized, to hand in his badge. He announced there would be no further Dirty Harrys. 'You can fall into a pattern of self-imitation and you'd have to have an awfully good script to take you away from that.'

Clint hardly wasted any time before going back to work. *Pink Cadillac* was an action comedy co-starring Bernadette Peters. He felt it had the right mixture of the traditional elements of an Eastwood film with some that were not so traditional. 'My character is a modern day bounty hunter – and is trying to find the girl who stole his favourite pink Cadillac. He's something of a drifter. He's a real cornball guy, wears disguises, imitates people. It's something different.'

The character he played, Tommy Nowak, was not unlike the true-life bounty hunter, or 'Skip-tracer,' portrayed by Steve McQueen in his last film, *The Hunter*, in that his job is to apprehend bail-jumpers. In style, it was perhaps closer to TV's *The Fall Guy*. And in its subplot involving Eastwood chasing after Bernadette Peters while being pursued by the 'Birthright' gang is hardly different from Eastwood chasing Sondra Locke while being pursued by the 'Black Widows' in *Every Which Way But Loose*.

Filming took his cast and crew up to the rural backdrop of the pine-covered hills of northern California. It was country he knew and loved, and his concern for the environment had him almost reaching for his broom at the end of one day's filming when he saw how much rubbish was left lying around – or rather he ordered two of his crew to clean up. 'I wouldn't want to think we were leaving all that junk.'

At the end of each day's filming he headed for his home in Carmel to view the dailies and then work out in his gym. But, not surprisingly, rumours emerged that he took Bernadette Peters home with him. The rumours dispersed just as quickly as they arose.

He seemed to be enjoying the self-imposed solitude in his life – even Sondra Locke seemed to be less in his company now that she was not appearing in his films.

'I find as I get older my priorities change,' he said. 'I get more libertarian in my outlook. I get more "Hey, I just want to be left alone".'

The loner instinct inside of him grew stronger in his fifty-ninth year, and he went through periods of, he said, 'liking to be around people and other times when I don't want to be around anyone. It's very easy for me to go off by myself for long periods of time. Sometimes you just don't want to talk or listen. Sometimes I go up to the mountains where you can almost hear the silence. It's almost caressing you. Caressing not only your ears but your mental outlook. I love sitting and watching the birds.'

Dirty Harry sitting on a rock watching birds? His screen image made it hard sometimes to forget that not only is the man a country hick at heart, but also an *actor* merely playing a part. And contrary to the image that he himself has perpetuated, by streamlining roles to fit his own screen persona, he said, 'I've always thought of myself as a character actor, rather than a leading man. But I suppose it's a left-handed compliment that people believe I'm like Harry Callahan – I must have been convincing.'

So convincing that the story arose around 1983 that he had acquired a permit so that he could carry a gun after telling police that he had received death threats – one rumour even had him under threat of kidnap. The image of Clint Eastwood in real life packing a .45 may be one that helps the public believe more strongly in the legend that he had by this time become. But he was prepared to laugh off the idea completely. 'If someone sits down and thinks about it, the idea of me carrying a gun is foolish. What would be the necessity of it? It's not quite as Wild West out here as it's said to be. I suppose if your life were in danger, you might carry a gun. But my life's not in danger. Still, I guess it's a sort of compliment when people confuse the actor with the role. It means you've done a good job.'

17

A Loner's Life in Hollywood

One day in 1989, Sondra Locke was directing on a film set when she received a letter from Eastwood's lawyer. It informed her that the locks on the doors of the Bel Air home she shared with Eastwood had been changed and that an attempt to enter the house could result in arrest. Her clothes had been put into storage and the Mercedes car that Clint had given to her as a present had been taken back. He had, she said, even confiscated her pet parrot Putty. As she read the letter, she fainted.

Later, at the home she shared with her husband, he persuaded her to sue for every dime she could get. She took his advice, but first gave Eastwood an ultimatum, to let her back into the house and agree on a financial settlement within 24 hours, or go to court. Consequently a long and bitter legal wrangle ensued.

Her last words to him, so it was reported, were 'Don't you remember me? I'm the woman who has loved you for years, acted as your wife and given you my heart.'

She complained, 'I had to move in with friends [presumably her husband], I had to borrow clothes and I had no idea where my pet parrot Putty was, or my car.' She asked a judge to force Clint to give her back her parrot or be cited for contempt of court. But her main aim was to get a share of Eastwood's massive fortune as well as two Hollywood mansions.

'I loved Clint for so long and I guess I still do,' she said. 'But right now all I can think of is revenge.'

Eastwood's sudden break-up with Sondra sent journalists flocking to Carmel and Hollywood looking for anyone who would say anything. 'Close friends' and 'Hollywood insiders' were quoted every which way. 'Clint has made no secret of his gross infidelity to Sondra,' a so-called insider was reported to have said by *Sunday* magazine. 'He would be sure that she stayed out of the way for weeks at a time while he went through one of his randy periods chasing – and catching – dozens of women. He told her it was just his nature and she would have to put up with it. So Sondra would simply go and stay with Gordon when there were lines of other women taking turns with Clint in Carmel or Los Angeles. He has no trouble in talking women into bed and he takes advantage of every opportunity. And Sondra would probably have put up with it indefinitely, but he simply tired of her.'

But other 'close friends' claimed that he had in fact asked her to leave Gordon and move in with him permanently. When she didn't, he finished with her for good.

He seemed, at this time, to be growing closer to his daughter Kimber. Early in 1989 he met her fiancé, 28-year-old Doug McCartney. A former construction engineer, McCartney was now running a valet parking company, and also taught soccer as well as playing for the local team in Denver. He and his future father-in-law took an immediate liking to each other.

Kimber had known Doug for two years, and it was no secret to him who her famous father was. He said, 'It makes no difference to me who Kimber's father is. I'm fond of her for who and what she is in her own right. She's really a lovely person.'

He had no qualms either about taking on a ready-made family. Kimber's son, Clinton, was now five. Said a friend of Kimber's, 'Little Clint is a quiet child who never strays far from his mother's apron strings. He is shy and softly spoken. He would rather sit with a book than race around the neighbourhood like other five-year-olds. I have never seen him with a toy gun slung on his hip playing cowboys and Indians. If you met him, you would never guess for a moment that he was Clint Eastwood's grandson.'

Eastwood ignored all the press brouhaha and set off for Africa to film *White Hunter, Black Heart*. For some years he had been planning a remake of *The African Queen*, in which John Huston directed Humphrey Bogart and Katherine Hepburn. While researching, he became fascinated by the behind the scenes stories as told by

Peter Vietrel (who co-wrote the screenplay of *The African Queen*) in his book *White Hunter, Black Heart*. So with *Bird* cinematographer Jack Green, *Firefox* designer John Graysmark, a cast headed by Marisa Berenson and 51 Zimbabweans, he set out to film Vietrel's book instead.

All the true life characters were to be portrayed, but under different names – e.g., John Huston became John Wilson – but there was no hiding the fact that this was a film about Hepburn, Bogart and Huston out in Africa making *The African Queen*. In the role of Hepburn was Marisa Berenson, her best film role in many years. Kevin Kline was originally slated to play Bogart, but the role eventually went to Richard Kanstone. Jamie Koss portrayed Lauren Bacall, Jeff Fahey (who had made *Impulse* with Sondra Locke) became Vietrel and as John Huston was Clint himself. The actor-director was in the somewhat bizarre situation of portraying a true-life actor-director, and affecting his most remarkable performance ever. He had said that he always saw himself as a character actor – now he was at last proving it.

In his novel, Vietrel characterized John Wilson as 'a violent man' yet admired the way that his 'personal mania for self-destruction' was offset by his 'almost divine ability to always land on his feet.' The book was, in fact, written while Vietrel was recovering from the rigours of working with Huston to finish the script (originally penned by James Agee) while on location. More than just a behind-the-scenes account of movie-making, the book, and the film, painted a portrait of a charming and in many ways an admirable man who also happened to be massively egotistical and capable of causing trouble for everyone around him.

Much of the story takes place prior to the filming of *The African Queen*, during which time Huston – or Wilson – seemed indifferent to the questions posed by Viertel about the rewrites, and disappeared at intervals into the jungle. He took off with a native tracker for days to fulfil what Viertel believed was his prime motivation to be in Africa – not to shoot a film, but an elephant.

Vietrel had actually written a screenplay based on his book and interested a number of producers, but most of them wanted to combine it with various sub-plots, presumably to take it away from its obvious background of real life film-makers. He came to write various other drafts – one with director Burt Kennedy, another with actor James Bridges – but he was never able to get the picture off the ground. Then it came to the attention of Clint Eastwood.

'It was drawn to my attention by a fellow I'd known years ago; I'd had a bit of a part in a picture he'd produced,' Eastwood explained. 'I got very curious about it, and so I read it on a plane and liked it. And so I took it to Warner Bros who also liked it and agreed to do it.

'I've ended up with a script that tries to incorporate everything in the book, all the major scenes and characters. So here we are, nearly forty years after Huston made his movie and several years since I got interested in the script.'

Filming began in June, 1989, and during the time in Zimbabwe, Clint personally piloted a helicopter to enable him to track a wild herd of elephants. Playing totally against type, Eastwood allowed himself for the first time to get beaten up on screen without coming back to wreak revenge. The man who gave him a pounding was British actor Clive Mantle who played Little John in the TV series *Robin of Sherwood*. Mantle told me, 'We had just finished shooting the scene and were sitting down, when Clint said, "My cameraman and I have just been talking and we can't think of another film in which I've been beaten up and the guy got away with it." '

Usually fight scenes are shot under the supervision of a second unit director or a stunt arranger, but Clint directed this fight scene himself. 'He had choreographed part of the fight,' said Mantle, 'and when we had shot all the planned shots, he ad-libbed the rest. He'd say "You punch me in the stomach," or "Let's try it if you kick me," and that way he put the scene together. He's made so many films and performed in so many action sequences, he can direct a fight as well as anyone.

'The scariest thing of all was when he gave me that look he gave Eli Wallach in *The Good, the Bad and the Ugly*. You know, that scowl of his. It would frighten anyone.

'The only thing that got me was that I'm about half his age, yet he is so fit that when we filmed that scene, by the end of it I was panting for breath – I was so exhausted, but Clint wasn't even sweating. You'd think he'd just been out for a walk.'

Even at the age of 59, Eastwood was in tremendous shape and for one scene he allowed himself to shoot the rapids of the Zambezi River. Only the crocodiles hoped he would fall overboard. He was filming a scene in which, as the Huston-figure, he had to shoot a scene for *The African Queen*. A boat, like the original used in the Bogart movie, was built at Pinewood Studios, designed and constructed to be tough enough to face the rapids and finally hurtle over the Kariba Falls.

Clive Mantle had been a fan of Eastwood's since his school days when he first saw *The Good, the Bad and the Ugly*. 'I had not met Clint before we went to Africa. He chose me, and the rest of the cast, by watching tapes of us. When we arrived on location we were so excited that we were actually going to meet *the man*. We had a couple of wonderful days, but I thought that when he arrived and took one look at me, he'd probably send me home. We were a bunch of English actors and we spent the time sitting looking out over the lake, having a drink or two. Evening came and we had run out of drinks, and it was my turn to go to the bar and get some. So I went off and bought a bottle of vodka and some tonics, and I was heading back when I suddenly saw Clint walking down the path towards me.

'I thought, *Oh my God*, he's going to sack me for being an alcoholic. So I just said, "Hi, I'm the guy who's supposed to beat you up." He sort of smiled and said, "Oh yep!" I said, "Did you have a pleasant trip?" and he said "Fine, thanks." I couldn't believe I was actually talking to this man who has got to be the greatest film star in the world. And he didn't send me home.

'He's an incredibly pleasant man. He's got a wonderful calm quality. Like he's got life really sussed. He is so relaxed, you get the feeling he could slow down the planet if he wanted to. He's one of probably only two or three men in the world that I could look at and say, "I would like a little of what makes him that way." I just wish some of it would rub off on me. He'd wander around with a beer and chat. He'd tell us about his early life as a steel-worker. But he was definitely the boss. There was absolutely no question about who was in charge, but he never had to raise his voice.

'He likes to work fast. But he doesn't rush anyone. If you feel you can do a take better, he'll let you do it. But he keeps himself surrounded by technicians that he knows well, because he trusts them to do their job properly. Some actors who direct use a stand-in in front of the camera while they set up the camera shot. But Clint lines up the shot he wants and steps into it, and does what he does brilliantly. He trusts his cameraman, Jack Green, to tell him if it went well or not.

'One evening he asked if he could join Alun Armstrong, Chris Fairbanks and myself for a drink in Alun's room. He brought with him crates of beer imported from all over the world. So we sat there trying all this different beer. And then he picked up a bottle and said, "This is my favourite beer in the whole world." It was a Newcastle Brown, and Alun, who's a Geordie, just couldn't get over it.

'When I asked him what he was going to do once he'd finished the film, he said, "I'm going to drink a little wine and watch a few sunsets."'

What Eastwood didn't know then was that when he did get back he would have to deal with a hornets' nest, for in July, while he was still on location and journalists were still prising 'close friends' and 'Hollywood insiders' out of the woodwork, someone blabbed about Roxanne, Kimber and little Clinton.

Newspapers around the world screamed the headlines 'DIRTY HARRY'S SECRET FAMILY.' Somehow reporters Annie Leask and Mike Kerrigan had managed to get hold of Kimber's birth certificate which showed her to have her mother's maiden name, but also showed that the father was Clinton Eastwood Junior. They set about tracking her down and found her working as a waitress at the Avenue Grill, a trendy restaurant in Denver, Colorado. When approached by the reporters, Kimber said, 'Yes, Clint Eastwood is my father. I must speak to him about this.'

She displayed mixed emotions, saying, 'I am partly shocked and partly glad it is all out in the open. I don't know what he will think about this. I have to talk to him and find out how he feels about it all.'

Kimber revealed that she had a son and said that Eastwood 'loves his grandson and sees him when he can.'

But who put the press on the trail in the first place? 'It could only have been leaked by someone who's been very close to Clint,' said an 'insider.' 'It was a secret he shared with very few people.'

The mole most likely was Frances Stevenson. On 9 July 1989, the *News of the World* published an article, said to be an interview with her, in which she made the preposterous claim that since blowing the whistle on Clint, she was in fear of him and warned him publicly that she was armed and protected.

She also claimed that Clint was obsessed with sex and particularly enjoyed bondage. The article had her describing how she caught Clint and Roxanne making love at her own apartment, and that she saw him sitting in a chair with his hands tied with a golden sash. Stevenson said she was a friend of Roxanne, and that Eastwood had begged her not to tell Roxanne about his other girlfriends.

Later Clint sued the *News of the World* and won. But he never denied that Kimber was his daughter. The money he received for damages he gave to charities, and the paper printed an apology, saying, 'On July 9, under the heading "Go on Clint, Make My Day", we printed articles containing allegations and suggestions about Clint Eastwood which we now know where untrue...' Despite this, the fact that Clint had his 'secret family' was now known to the world.

He heard the news himself while on location in Africa and was, fortunately, if only for the time being, out of circulation to all journalists. Finishing off the location, he went to England to complete the film at Pinewood Studios. For two weeks he filmed scenes in the mock up of Claridge's Hotel were Huston made the original film deals. Other scenes were also shot at West Wycombe House and Park, near to Pinewood.

While in England, he was snapped out and about in London with Jane Brolin, ex-wife of James Brolin. Meanwhile, back in Carmel, a 38-year-old mother of two, Jaclyn Reeves, announced that she and Eastwood were occasional lovers. Their relationship, she said, 'goes back a long way.' But she vehemently denied that he was the father of her children, quashing delight expressed in the newspapers who thought for a short while they had discovered a second secret family. But Jaclyn Reeves was living in a home owned by Eastwood and worked for Malpaso, complete with a company car.

'I have a gentle spot for women but, even today, I don't find it easy to share my feelings with them,' Clint has said. Consequently, especially in his post-Locke days, he was often to be seen at receptions or premières with an attractive but anonymous woman at his side. It might be just the daughter of a studio executive, or the wife of a friend, and she would invariably be the elegant type.

While in London that August, Clint had a secret rendezvous with ex-wife Maggie who was in the process of divorcing Henry Wynberg. They had remained friends and had even made plans to share a holiday together. They travelled to St Tropez where they were the guests of a Hollywood mogul at his villa. During the evenings they were seen at various night spots, fuelling the rumours that the two were in love again. For a while, if the press are to be believed, it looked as though Clint and Maggie would get back together again. They turned up one evening with friends at the swish Club 55 where the owner Patrice de Colmant observed, 'They were in great form – smiling and laughing. Everyone was very relaxed and happy and the Eastwoods seemed to be enjoying themselves.' But any remote chance of a reconciliation between them was more of a reporter's dream – they were good friends, had always remained so after what was surely Hollywood's most amicable divorce, and their friendship was simply enduring.

The same could not be said for his relationship with Sondra Locke who was said to be so furious to learn about Eastwood's third child that she made an incredible outburst in which she accused him of forcing her to have two abortions and a sterilization operation; she threatened to blow the lid off his *other* secrets. 'If he tried anything in open court, I've got my own ammunition.'

She claimed she suffered 'humiliation, mental anguish, severe emotional and physical distress,' during her years with him. In court papers, Eastwood denied the allegations.

'I felt so disappointed,' he said. 'And the disappointment was with myself. How could I have been such a bad judge of character?'

Ever in search of story, journalists traced Locke's parents in their modest farmhouse in the hills of Tennessee. Upon hearing the reports of their daughter's allegations, Pauline Locke said, 'It's obvious that Clint wanted to hurt my daughter. Otherwise he would not have done all those terrible things to her. He would not have made her pregnant, then forced her to have abortions. One of those children Clint made her abort could have been the grandson

I've always longed for. I hope Sondra gets every cent out of him.'

Alfred Locke was convinced that, having heard the myth that Eastwood carried a gun with him, Sondra must have been frightened enough of Clint to submit to having the alleged abortions. 'Sondra has always had a terrible fear of guns. I'm sure that is one of the reasons she was so frightened of Clint, that she would do anything that he told her. When Sondra was a little child and the hunting season was on, she would just shake and tremble at the distant sounds of gunfire. The very sight of a gun was enough to make her cry. I'm sure seeing Clint's gun all the time upset her very much and frightened her.'

Eastwood, meanwhile, maintained his dignity and his silence, speaking of the matter to no one. In desperation, reporters tried to get something out of Maggie who had become Mrs Henry Wynberg. 'I will not discuss this,' she told them bluntly. When asked if she would deny the stories of Clint's third child, she said, 'I'm not going to deny it – but I never discuss Clint's life or my own in public.' Even Sondra Locke's lawyers said they were unable to comment.

Clint's refusal to enter into public slanging matches typified his collected manner, and even when the legal fur was flying, he refused to rise to the bait of Sondra Locke's accusations of forced abortions and emotional betrayal. He was, however, determined that she wouldn't get a dime in her palimony claim. And he refused to stay hidden. Renowned concert pianist Byron Janis saw no reason why his wife, Maria Cooper Janis, daughter of Gary Cooper, shouldn't accompany their friend Clint to a function.

The picture of him that seems to emerge throughout all of this is a man who shrugged off his problems with a code of silence. But there is much more to Eastwood than a laconic nature, and in his mature years he wasn't afraid to admit, 'I'm as emotional as the next person – I probably cry easier than most, in fact.'

If the vision of Eastwood weeping at a time of crisis in his life seems to contradict his strong, silent image, he points out, 'Strong men are sensitive and aren't afraid of showing it. It's the people who are insecure about their manliness who are averse to showing their feelings.'

Kimber had been wanting to see her father since the news-story had broken. For her it was 'a tremendous relief. I no longer had the burden of keeping it all a secret,' she said. 'I even changed my name legally to Eastwood and I hoped that my father would at last acknowledge me publicly, so we could all get on with our lives.'

He took her to a restaurant; she wanted to tell him how she felt. 'We dined on beautiful food,' she said. 'I was more interested in our relationship and I begged him to spend more time with me.

'He said, "I am sorry, it's all my fault. I will make more time for you in future." I felt sure he meant it.'

And he probably did. But perhaps the pressure on him, from reporters and from the forthcoming palimony case, preoccupied him too much and Kimber said in an article in the *Sunday Mirror* on 8 April 1990, that she had not seen him since that meeting. 'I have tried to make an appointment to see him, but he always has other commitments.' She desperately wanted him to acknowledge her and said, 'The world is not going to turn against Clint Eastwood because he has an illegitimate child.'

In that, she was right. The news of his other daughter and past affair with Roxanne Tunis was a storm in a tea-cup.

Around this time he began seeing 38-year old actress Frances Fisher, who was said to bear a remarkable resemblance to Sondra Locke; that was more to do with wishful thinking by the Press. But she was small and blonde, and above all discreet.

It was becoming harder for him to keep his private life under wraps. Allison, now eighteen, hit the headlines after she was banned from driving after a drink-driving charge. The press would have had people believe she had a drink problem. Any reporter brave, or stupid, enough to ask Eastwood about his daughter's drinking was met with a chilly squint and stony silence.

In May 1990 Clint Eastwood became, unbelievably, 60 years old. In August he was in Cannes with his leading lady Marisa Berenson to promote *White Hunter, Black Heart*. There he met up with his long-time friend Ingrid Pitt.

'I was there with no make-up on,' she told me, 'and I looked just *awful*, and of all people, I come face to face with Clint. I said to him, "I'm sorry you have to see me like this!" He said, "It's okay because *I've* got more wrinkles!"

'And that humour we had between us was still there. The moment we saw each other it was, "Shall we?" – "No" – "Okay".'

*

Warner Bros in the UK had made the bizarre decision not to release *Pink Cadillac* but to put it straight out on video – it was considered too big a risk to release before *White Hunter, Black Heart* which they hoped would be a big prestigious hit. This was a policy hard to fathom since *Pink Cadillac*, despite its dreadful reviews in America, made the top five in the US box office ratings. In fact, Warners delayed putting P*ink Cadillac* on video until September 1991.

White Hunter, Black Heart was greeted by the British press with much acclaim. 'Eastwood's performance is a revelation,' wrote Derek Malcolm in *The Guardian*. 'He directed the film with great wit.' 'It is brilliant,' said Alexander Walker of the *Evening Standard*. Iain Johnstone of the *Sunday Times* thought Eastwood 'gave the finest performance of his career.' John Wilson, (aka John Huston) was, for Clint, a *tour de force*, and the film was outstanding. Yet surprisingly it was given a limited release in Britain as Warners tried to sell it on the more 'arty' circuit, premièring it at the Edinburgh Festival following its opening in Cannes. Eastwood obligingly followed the press junket Warners had arranged, first in France, then in Scotland where he told reporters, 'It is the right time for a film about environmental issues. We should know about the demise of wildlife like elephants and rhinos, and that man still gives the impression he was put on this earth to destroy everything.' Then he revealed his plans to make one last Western, *The William Munny Killings*. At the time of writing, the film has not gone into production, but the cast will include Morgan Freeman and Gene Hackman. There is also the possibility of Jeremy Irons being included. *The William Munny Killings* will be the realization of a much loved project he'd been planning for six years.

'It's about time I returned to the Wild West for one last confrontation with a lizard,' he said. 'It is something I want to do and I have a screenplay which I plan to start on in January. It's about a renegade cowboy who has been out of action for a while and comes back to sort out his life and make a last deal. It's going to be a stylistic film. But I won't be playing the Man With No Name 25 years on.'

*

Before that, however, he returned to familiar form in *The Rookie*, a violent action movie in which he played an ageing cop in Los

Angeles who finds himself with a young partner, played by Charlie Sheen. The older cop has to show the young rookie the ropes, and since their targets are a murderous big-time car thief (Raul Julia) and his gang, there is plenty of opportunity for shoot-outs and car chases.

Eastwood saw it as a change from playing the embittered Dirty Harry, and he was obviously prepared to accept that he was now one of Cinema's elder statesmen. 'He's not so much embittered like Dirty Harry, he's just the callous one. Obviously I'm beyond the age of playing the rookie, so I'm playing the senior cop who teaches the rookie the ropes.

'The young rookie comes along from a wealthy family and has no reason for entering the profession of law enforcement, but he wants to, and the older cop that I play can't understand it at all. He can't understand why anyone would want to be a cop unless they absolutely had to.'

When British TV chat show host Terry Wogan asked if he'd followed a tough fitness programme to cope with all the action in the film, he replied, 'I follow a regular regime of fitness, just trying to stay in fairly decent shape, but to keep up with Charlie Sheen and some of these younger guys, you gotta get out there and jog a little.'

Wogan then said, 'Should you be doing all that at your age,?' to which Eastwood replied with typical dryness, 'At 39, I don't see why not!'

Eastwood was impressed by the young Sheen, and comparing his own progression at Sheen's age, he said, 'I think these young men and women in films all around the world nowadays seem to be much further ahead than I was. When I think back at myself at Charlie's age – he's around 24, 25 – I don't think I knew a tenth of what he does. It's amazing how good some of these people are at such a young age.'

Clint was now at an age where he was working with a generation of actors who had grown up on his films. Said Martin Sheen, 'He's totally cool. I'm terribly starstruck with the man. The guy was one of my heroes growing up as a kid and I got to work with him. I was blown away.'

Even more overawed to work with him was Lara Flynn Boyle, the *Twin Peaks* actress who played Sheen's girlfriend.

She recalled her first meeting with him: 'I was in the wardrobe trailer talking about clothes when I heard this voice saying "Is Lara Flynn decent?" The wardrobe lady said, "Yes, she is," and in walked Clint Eastwood. I was starstruck. He shook my hand and said, "It's so good to have you here – you're wonderful on *Twin Peaks*." I just sat there with this huge smile on my face.'

Not so impressed to be working with Clint, though not necessarily unimpressed by the man himself, was Sonia Braga who, in a bizarre scene, rapes him. She said, 'Here I am, a 39-year-old woman wearing a jump suit and blasting an Uzi, acting like I'm in a Tom and Jerry cartoon.'

She summed the film up thus; 'Me and Raul Julia play the bad guys. We steal cars. Clint and Charlie are the good guys, the cops. That's it.'

Kyle Eastwood, by now working hard to establish himself as a professional musician, composed one of the themes used in the background score, having now given up acting altogether.

The critics were impressed by the way Eastwood had crafted the film, but generally hated its content. The *Daily Mirror* said, 'As director as well as star, Eastwood naturally dominated the proceedings. But the end result is a thoroughly unpleasant, though undeniably accomplished, piece of work.' The *Radio Times* found it 'well acted and made, but thoroughly reprehensible.'

The fact was, it was the kind of film that attracted people in 1990 and it was a commercial success. It was also Eastwood's best action film in years. Having reached the age of sixty and been a star for almost thirty years, Eastwood knew by now that in order to indulge himself in films like *White Hunter, Black Heart* and *Honky Tonk Man*, he had to satisfy his regular studio, Warners, with the occasional blockbuster.

Clint's long-planned Western didn't go ahead in January, but he still intended to do it the following summer. He did however receive a rather radical offer to make a cameo appearance in the planned TV series *The Young Indiana Jones*, the adventurer created on the big screen by Harrison Ford in *Raiders of the Lost Ark* and its sequels. Clint was being wooed to play the role of Illinois Jones, the long-lost elder brother of Indiana, and it was said the fee being offered was a phenomenal $10,000,000. Harrison Ford was being wooed to make a guest appearance while the main role of young Indiana would go to River Phoenix who played the same part in the opening scenes of *Indiana Jones and the Last Crusade*.

In February 1991 Clint won a most unusual award when America's oldest undergraduate organization – Hasty Pudding Theatricals – named him as its Man of the Year. He was handed the group's traditional trophy – a brass pudding pot – for making 'a lasting and impressive contribution to the world of entertainment.' It was all lighthearted fun and Clint entered fully into the spirit of the occasion by allowing two drag performers to put a huge bra, decorated with US flags, over his smart suit. Then he told the cheering crowd, 'I'll treasure this as one of the great moments of my life.'

But there were more serious matters to deal with. Sondra Locke's palimony suit against him was due to reach court, but behind the scenes her lawyers had been wrangling with his lawyers. During this time Sondra was struck by breast cancer; she said she thought it was as a result of stress following her break-up with Eastwood. She underwent two operations, and shortly after made a brave appearance at the première of *Postcards From The Edge* in Los Angeles.

On 9 March, with just a week to go before Eastwood and Locke were due to begin their battle in court, their lawyers reached a secret settlement, although no one was saying how much it was. Estimates reached as high as $50,000,000, but it was known that Sondra was to receive the deeds to the two houses she was fighting for. According to her lawyer, Norman Oberstein, 'Both parties are happy with the outcome.'

Shortly after Clint took Frances Fisher off to Colorado for the annual American Ski Classic. Clint took part in some celebrity races along with Martina Navratilova, Nadia Comaneci and Florence Joyner. The event was the first time he had been seen publicly with Frances who said, 'I've known Clint for two years now, and we've been going out together for over a year. He's a wonderful man and a special friend. It's just nice to be here together away from it all.'

Asked if she was in love with him, she replied coyly, 'Yes.' Did they live together? 'I don't think I'd be allowed to answer that one,' she said.

A skiing 'friend' with them in Colorado said that Clint was nervous about becoming emotionally embroiled again following his palimony battle. 'Clint's had a lot of girlfriends and a lot of problems with them. These days he doesn't like to commit himself, although Frances has been around for a year now.'

Eastwood refused to comment on his relationship with Frances but was happy to allow Mary Corbet of *Hello!* magazine to take photographs of the couple. Frances admitted that she was more a skater than a skier. 'My skiing's not quite up to Clint's standard, but he's helping me along.'

Eastwood, of course, had been skiing since his teenage days when he used to drive himself and his sister up into the mountains, and they taught themselves to ski. It has remained one of the passions of his life, as has the countryside, as has his need to be free and alone from time to time. Or to be more accurate, Clint Eastwood is actually a man who is a natural loner, but one who needs people from time to time. It has taken him 61 years to fashion his life exactly the way he wants it; he never wanted to be owned by anyone or tied down by conventions like marriage. While there will always be women in his life, it's most unlikely that he'll ever marry again. He is answerable to no one and although he still enjoys the company of his select and long-time band of buddies, often his favourite company is his own. He is a free spirit, tied down only by his love of making movies, but unburdened with Hollywood's way of life. He is Hollywood's loner, and has reached an age when most men dream of retiring. Yet he looks not only back over a career that has made him a legend, but also forward to a future in which the legend will undoubtedly grow.

He has joined the ranks of John Wayne and Gary Cooper but also the likes of Alfred Hitchcock and John Ford. As an actor-producer-director, he is second to none. No film star before him has achieved what he has, and at the current time no one in the foreseeable future will. Actors have produced their own films – Kirk Douglas, John Wayne, Burt Lancaster – some have directed some of them – Laurence Olivier, Paul Newman and the afore-mentioned stars. But not one has managed to become such a multi-million dollar corporation, producing *every* film he stars in, and directing virtually all of them.

There is more to come – and no one will be surprised if his 'one last Western' is followed at some time or another; or if he continues to act for a further decade. But if he does reach a point where he decides to call it a day as an actor, he'll continue to produce and direct. There is only one reason he'd retire completely.

'I guess I'll take periodic little sabbaticals and try and improve my golf, but for the most part I'll keep working. I enjoy working. I've been lucky enough to have a nice long-running career and I still enjoy it. And I guess when the day comes that I don't enjoy it, I'll put my feet up and relax.'

Filmgraphy

Revenge of the Creature 1955. Universal-International. John Agar, Lori Nelson, John Bromfield, Robert B Williams, Nestor Paiva, Grandon Rhodes, Dave Willock. Produced by William Alland. Directed by Jack Arnold. Screenplay by Martin Berkeley. Photographed in black and white by Charles Wellbourne. Music by Joseph Gershenson. 81 minutes.

Tarantula 1955. Universal-International. John Agar, Mara Corday, Leo G Carroll, Nestor Paiva, Ross Elliott. Produced by William Alland. Directed by Jack Arnold. Screenplay by Robert M Fresco and Martin Berkeley. Photographed in black and white by George Robinson. Music by Joseph Gershenson. 80 minutes.

Lady Godiva 1955. Universal-International. Maureen O'Hara, George Nader, Eduard Franz, Leslie Bradley, Victor McLaglen, Rex Reason, Torin Thatcher, Henry Brandon, Grant Withers, Arthur Shields, Alex Harford. Produced by Robert Arthur. Directed by Arthur Lubin. Screenplay by Oscar Brodney and Harry Ruskin. Photographed in Technicolor by Carl Guthrie. Music by Joseph Gershenson. 89 minutes.

UK title: *Lady Godiva of Coventry*. It emerged as the second half of a double bill.

Francis in the Navy 1955. Universal-International. Donald O'Connor, Martha Hyer, Richard Erdman, Jim Backus, Myrna Hansen, David Janssen, Clint Eastwood. Produced by Stanley Rubin.

Directed by Arthur Lubin. Screenplay by Devery Freeman, based on the character 'Francis the Talking Mule' created by David Stern. Photographed in black and white by Carl Guthrie. Music by Joseph Gershenson. 80 minutes.

Never Say Goodbye 1955. Universal-International. Rock Hudson, Cornell Borchers, George Sanders, Ray Collins, David Janssen, Shelley Fabares, Raymond Greenleaf, Frank Wilcox. Produced by Albert J Cohen. Directed by Jerry Hopper. Screenplay by Charles Hoffman, based on a screenplay by Bruce Manning, John Klorer and Leonard Lee, from the play *Come Prima Meglio Di Prima* by Luigi Pirendello. Photographed in Technicolor by Maury Gertsman. Music by Joseph Gershenson. 96 minutes.

The peculiar credit 'based on a screenplay' is correct! It was in actual fact a remake of the 1945 $2,000,000 weepie *This Love of Ours*, scripted by Manning, Klorer and Lee, which in turn was a remake of MGM's *As You Desire Me*, starring Greta Garbo in 1932.

Star in the Dust 1956. Universal-International. John Agar, Mamie Van Doren, Richard Boone, Leif Erickson, Coleen Gray, James Gleason. Produced by Albert Zugsmith. Directed by Charles Haas. Screenplay by Oscar Brodney. Photographed in Technicolor by John L Russell Jnr. Music by Frank Skinner.

The First Travelling Saleslady 1956. RKO-Radio. Ginger Rogers, Barry Nelson, Carol Channing, David Brian, James Arness, Clint Eastwood, Robert Simon, Frank Wilcox, Daniel M White, Harry Cheshire. Screenplay by Devery Freeman and Stephen Longstreet. Photographed in Technicolor by William Snyder. Music by Irving Gertz. Lyrics by Hal Levy. 92 minutes.

Escapade in Japan 1957. RKO-Radio. Teresa Wright, Cameron Mitchell, Jon Prevost, Roger Nakagawa, Philip Ober, Kuniko Miyake, Clint Eastwood. Produced and directed by Arthur Lubin. Screenplay by Winston Miller. Photographed in Technicolor and Technirama by William Snyder. Music by Max Steiner. 93 minutes.

Ambush at Cimarron Pass 1957. Regal. Released through 20th Century-Fox. Scott Brady, Margia Dean, Clint Eastwood, Irving

Bacon, Frank Gerstle, Dirk London. Produced by Herbert E Mendelson. Directed by Jodie Copelan. Screenplay by Richard G Taylor and John K Butler, from a story by Robert A Reeds and Robert W Woods. Photographed in Regalscope and black and white by John M Nickolaus Jnr. Music by Paul Sawtell and Bert Shefter. 73 minutes.

Lafayette Escadrille 1957. Warner Bros. Tab Hunter, Marcel Dalio, Etchika Choureau, David Janssen, Paul Fix, Veola Vonn, Will Hutchins, Clint Eastwood, Bill Wellman Jnr, Jody McCrea. Produced and directed by William A Wellman. Screenplay by A S Flesichmann, from a story by William A Wellman. Photographed in black and white by William Clothier. Music by Leonard Rosenman. 92 minutes.

UK title *Hell Bent for Glory.*

A Fistful of Dollars (original Italian title *Per Un Pugno Di Dollari*) 1964. Jolly Film (Rome), Ocean (Madrid), Constantin (Munich). Clint Eastwood, John Welles (Gian Maria Volonte), Marianne Koch, Pepe Calvo, Wolfgang Lukschy, Sieghart Rupp, Joe Edger, Antonio Prieto, Jose Calvo, Margherita Lozano, Aldo Sombrell. Produced by Harry Colombo (Arrigo Colombo) and George Papi (Giorgio Papi). Directed by Sergio Leone. Screenplay by Sergio Leone and Duccio Tessari. Based on the story *The Magnificent Stranger* by Sergio Leone. Photographed in Technicolor and Techniscope by Massimo Dallamano. Music by Ennio Morricone. 100 minutes.

Because the film was originally released in Italy with many of the European names changed on the screen credits to read like American names, Sergio Leone is credited on original Italian prints as Bob Robertson. His real name was used for US and UK versions. All current prints still credit music to Dan Savio. So many of the actors' names were Americanized that it has become virtually impossible to match the real names to their aliases. The film's title itself is slightly incorrect in the screen credits; it reads simply as *Fistful of Dollars* – someone forgot to put the *A* at the beginning.

For a Few Dollars More (original Italian title *Per Qualche Dollari In Piu*) 1965. Produzioni Europee Associate (Rome), Arturo Gonzalez (Madrid), Constantin Film (Munich). Clint Eastwood,

Lee Van Cleef, Gian Maria Volonte, Josef Egger, Rosemary Dexter, Mara Krup, Klaus Kinski, Mario Brega, Aldo Sombrell, Luigi Pistilli, Benito Stefanelli. Produced by Alberto Grimaldi. Directed by Sergio Leone. Screenplay by Luciano Vincenzoni and Sergio Leone (dialogue by L Vincenzoni), from the story *Two Magnificent Strangers* by Sergio Leone and Fulvio Morsella. Photographed in Technicolor and Techniscope by Massimo Dallamano. Music by Ennio Morricone, conducted by Bruno Nicolai. 130 minutes.

The Good, the Bad and the Ugly (original Italian title *Il Buono, il Brutto, il Cattivo*) 1966. Produzione Europee Associate. Clint Eastwood, Lee Van Cleef, Eli Wallach, Aldo Giuffre, Luigi Pistilli, Rada Rassimov, Enzo Petito, Claudio Scarchilli, John Bartho, Livio Lorenzon, Antonio Casale, Sandro Scarchilli, Benito Stefanelli, Angelo Novi, Antonio Cass, Aldo Sombrell. Produced by Alberto Grimaldi. Directed by Sergio Leone. Screenplay by Age-Scarpelli, Luciano Vincenzoni and Sergio Leone, from a story by Luciano Vincenzoni and Sergio Leone (English version by Mickey Knox). Photographed in Technicolor and Techniscope by Tonino Delli Colli. Music by Ennio Morricone, conducted by Bruno Nicolai. 'Ballad of a Soldier' lyrics by Tommie Connor. 180 minutes (US: 155 mins, UK: 148 mins).

Le Streghe (The Witches) 1966. A five-episode film, the last episode, called *Una Sera Come Le Altre*, featured Silvana Mangano and Clint Eastwood. Produced by Dino de Laurentiis. Directed by Luchino Visconti, Pier Paolo Pasolini, Muaro Bolognini, Franco Rossi, Vittorio de Sica. Screenplay by Cesare Zavattini, Fabio Capri and Enzo Muzzi. Photographed in Technicolor and Panavision by Giuseppe Rotunnio. Music by Piero Piccione and Ennio Morricone. 110 minutes.

Hang 'Em High 1967. Leonard Freeman Productions-Malpaso. Clint Eastwood, Inger Stevens, Ed Begley, Pat Hingle, Ben Johnson, Charles McGraw, Ruth White, Bruce Dern, Alan Hale Jnr, Arlene Golonka, James Westerfield, Dennis Hopper, James MacArthur. Produced by Leonard Freeman. Directed by Ted Post. Screenplay by Leonard Freeman. Photographed in DeLuxe Color by Leonard South and Richard Kline. Music by Dominic

Frontière. 114 minutes.

Coogan's Bluff 1968. Universal-Malpaso. Clint Eastwood, Lee J Cobb, Susan Clark, Tisha Sterling, Don Stroud, Betty Field, Tom Tully, Melodie Johnson, James Edwards, Rudy Diaz. Produced and directed by Don Siegel. Screenplay by Herman Miller, Dean Riesner and Howard Rodman, from a story by Herman Miller. Photographed in Technicolor by Bud Thackery. Music by Lalo Schifrin. 94 minutes.

Where Eagles Dare 1969. Winkast-MGM. Richard Burton, Clint Eastwood, Mary Ure, Patrick Wymark, Michael Hordern, Robert Beatty, Anton Diffring, Donald Houston, Derren Nesbitt, Ferdy Mayne, Peter Barkworth, William Squire, Neil MacCarthy, Brook Williams, Ingrid Pitt, Vincent Ball. Produced by Elliott Kastner. Directed by Brian G Hutton. Screenplay by Alistair MacLean. Photographed in Metrocolor and Panavision by Arthur Ibbetson. Music by Ron Goodwin. 155 minutes.

Paint Your Wagon 1969. Paramount-Alan Jay Lerner Productions. Lee Marvin, Clint Eastwood, Jean Seberg, Harve Presnell, Ray Walston, Tom Ligon, Alan Dexter, William O'Connell, Ben Baker, Alan Baxter, the Nitty Gritty Dirt Band. Produced by Alan Jay Lerner. Directed by Joshua Logan. Screenplay and lyrics by Alan Jay Lerner, adapted from the musical play by Paddy Chayefsky. Photographed in Technicolor and Panavision 70 by William A Fraker. Music by Frederick Loewe. Music for additional songs by André Previn. Background score by Nelson Riddle. 164 minutes.

In the UK Clint Eastwood sang *I Talk to the Trees* on the flip side of Lee Marvin's No 1 hit *Wanderin' Star*.

'I'm not queuing up to do another musical although I must say I enjoyed making that one because no one had the pretence of being legit singers who were all of a sudden bursting into song. Everyone played their songs as their characters' – *Clint Eastwood in 1991*.

Kelly's Heroes 1970. The Warriors' Company (Hollywood)-Avala Films (Belgrade)-MGM. Clint Eastwood, Telly Savalas, Don Rickles, Donald Sutherland, Carroll O'Connor, Hal Buckley, Gavin MacLeod, Len Lesser, David Hurst, Ross Elliott, Karl Otto Alberty, Perry Lopez.

Produced by Gabriel Katzta and Sidney Beckerman. Directed by Brian G Hutton. Screenplay by Troy Kennedy Martin. Photographed in Metrocolor and Panavision by Gabriel Figueroa. Music by Lalo Schifrin. 143 minutes.

Two Mules For Sister Sara 1970. Universal-Malpaso. Shirley MacLaine, Clint Eastwood, Manolo Fabregas, Alberto Morin, Armando Silvestre, John Kelly, Enrique Lucero. Produced by Martin Ritt and Carroll Case. Directed by Don Siegel. Screenplay by Albert Maltz, from a story by Budd Boetticher. Photographed in Technicolor and Panavision by Gabriel Figueroa. Music by Ennio Morricone. 116 minutes (UK: 113).

The script by Albert Maltz was a rewrite of one of Budd Boetticher who was originally slated to direct the film.

The Beguiled 1971. Jennings Lang/Universal-Malpaso. Clint Eastwood, Geraldine Page, Elizabeth Hartman, Jo Ann Harris, Darleen Carr, Mae Mercer, Pamelyn Ferdin, Melody Thomas, Peggy Drier, Pattye Mattick, Charles Briggs, George Dunn, Charles Martin, Matt Clark, Patrick Culliton, Wayne 'Buddy' Van Horn. Produced and directed by Don Siegel. Screenplay by John B Sherry and Grimes Grice, from a novel by Thomas Cullinan. Photographed in Technicolor by Bruce Surtees. Music by Lalo Schifrin. 105 minutes.

Play Misty for Me 1971. Universal-Malpaso. Clint Eastwood, Jessica Walter, Donna Mills, John Larch, Jack Ging, Irene Hervey. Produced by Robert Daley. Directed by Clint Eastwood. Screenplay by Jo Heims and Dean Riesner, from a story by Jo Heims. Photographed in Technicolor by Bruce Surtees. Music by Dee Barton. *Misty* composed by Errol Garner. 105 minutes.

Dirty Harry 1971. Warners-Malpaso. Clint Eastwood, Harry Guardino, Reni Santoni, John Vernon, Andy Robinson, John Larch, John Mitchum, Mae Mercer, Lyn Edgington, Ruth Kobart, Woodrow Parfey. Produced and directed by Don Siegel. Screenplay by Harry Julian Fink, Rita M Fink and Dean Riesner, from a story, *Dead Right*, by Harry Julian Fink and Rita M Fink. Photographed in Technicolor and Panavision by Bruce Surtees. Music by Lalo Schifrin. 101 minutes.

Joe Kidd 1972. Universal-Malpaso. Clint Eastwood, Robert Duvall, John Saxon, Don Stroud, Stella Garcia, James Wainwright, Paul Koslo. Produced by Sidney Beckerman. Directed by John Sturges.

Screenplay by Elmore Leonard. Photographed in Technicolor and Panavision by Bruce Surtees. Music by Lalo Schifrin. 87 minutes.

High Plains Drifter 1972. Malpaso-Universal. Clint Eastwood, Verna Bloom, Marianna Hill, Mitchell Ryan, Jack Ging, Stefan Gierasch, Ted Hartley, Billy Curtis, Geoffrey Lewis, Anthony James, Dan Vadis, Paul Brinegar, John Quade. Produced by Robert Daley. Directed by Clint Eastwood. Screenplay by Ernest Tidyman. Photographed in Technicolor and Panavision by Bruce Surtees. Music by Dee Barton. 105 minutes (UK: 102 minutes).

Breezy 1973. Malpaso-Universal. William Holden, Kay Lenz, Dennis Olivieri, Jamie Smith Jackson, Marj Dusay, Roger C Carmel, Shelley Morrison, Eugenie Peterson, Joan Hotchkis, Scott Holden. Produced by Robert Daley. Directed by Clint Eastwood. Screenplay by Jo Heims. Photographed in Technicolor by Frank Stanley. Music by Michel Legrand. 107 minutes.

Magnum Force 1973. Warners-Malpaso. Clint Eastwood, Hal Holbrook, Felton Perry, Mitchell Ryan, John Mitchum, David Soul. Produced by Robert Daley. Directed by Ted Post. Screenplay by John Milius and Michael Cimino. Photographed in Technicolor and Panavision by Frank Stanley. Music by Lalo Schifrin. 124 minutes.

Thunderbolt and Lightfoot 1974. Malpaso-United Artists. Clint Eastwood, Jeff Bridges, George Kennedy, Geoffrey Lewis, Catherine Bach, Gary Busey, Jack Dodson, Gene Elman, Burton Gilliam, Roy Jenson. Produced by Robert Daley. Directed and written by Michael Cimino. Photographed DeLuxe Color and Panavision by Frank Stanley. Music by Dee Barton. 115 minutes.

The Eiger Sanction 1975. Malpaso-Universal-Jennings Lang. Clint Eastwood, George Kennedy, Vonetta McGee, Jack Cassidy, Heidi Bruhl, Thayer David. Produced by Robert Daley. Directed by Clint Eastwood. Screenplay by Warren B Murphy, Hal Dresner, Rod Whitaker, from a novel by Trevanian. Photographed in Technicolor and Panavision by Frank Stanley, John Cleare, Jeff Schoolfield, Peter Pilafian and Pete White. Music by John Williams. 125 minutes.

The Outlaw Josey Wales 1976. Malpaso-Warners. Clint Eastwood, Chief Dan George, Sondra Locke, John Vernon, Bill McKinney, John Vernon, Paula Trueman, Sam Bottoms, Geraldine Keams, Woodrow

Parfey, Joyce Jameson, Sheb Wooley, Royal Dano. Produced by Robert Daley. Directed by Clint Eastwood. Screenplay by Phil Kaufman, Sonia Chernus, from the novel *Gone to Texas* by Forrest Carter. Photographed in Technicolor and Panavision by Bruce Surtees. Music by Jerry Fielding. 135 minutes.

The Enforcer 1976. Malpaso-Warners. Clint Eastwood, Tyne Daly, Harry Guardino, Bradford Dillman, John Mitchum, John Crawford. DeVeren Brookwalter. Produced by Robert Daley. Directed by James Fargo. Screenplay by Stirling Silliphant and Dean Riesner. Photographed in DeLuxe Color and Panavision by Richard Glouner. Music by Jerry Fielding. 96 minutes.

The Gauntlet 1977. Malpaso-Warners. Clint Eastwood, Sondra Locke, Pat Hingle, William Prince, Michael Cavanaugh, Carole Cook, Mara Corday, Douglas McGrath, Jeff Morris, Samantha Doane, Roy Jenson, Dan Vadis. Produced by Robert Daley. Directed by Clint Eastwood. Screenplay by Michael Butler and Dennis Shyrak. Photographed in DeLuxe Color and Panavision by Rexford Metz. Music by Jerry Fielding. 109 minutes.

Every Which Way But Loose 1977. Malpaso-Warners. Clint Eastwood, Sondra Locke, Geoffrey Lewis, Beverly D'Angelo, Ruth Gordon, Walter Barnes, George Chandler, Roy Jenson, James McEachin, Bill McKinney, William O'Connell, John Quade, Dan Vadis. Produced by Robert Daley. Directed by James Fargo. Screenplay by Jeremy Joe Kronsberg. Photographed in DeLuxe Color by Rexford Metz. Music supervision by Snuff Garrett, conducted by Steve Dorff. 114 minutes.

Escape From Alcatraz 1979. Malpaso-Paramount. Clint Eastwood, Patrick McGoohan, Robert Blossom, Jack Thibeau, Larry Hankin. Produced and directed by Don Siegel. Screenplay by Richard Tuggle, from the book by J Campbell Bruce. Photographed in DeLuxe Color by Bruce Surtees. Music by Jerry Fielding. 112 minutes.

Bronco Billy 1980. Warners-Second Street. Clint Eastwood, Sondra Locke, Geoffrey Lewis, Scatman Crothers, Bill McKinney, Sam Bottoms, Dan Vadis. Produced by Dennis Hackin and Neal Dobrofsky. Directed by Clint Eastwood. Screenplay by Dennis Hackin. Photographed in DeLuxe Color by David Worth. Music by Snuff Garrett, 116 minutes.

Any Which Way You Can 1980. Malpaso-Warners. Clint Eastwood, Sondra Locke, Ruth Gordon, Geoffrey Lewis, William Smith, Harry Guardino. Produced by Robert Daley. Directed by Buddy Van Horn. Screenplay by Stanford Sherman. Photographed in DeLuxe Color by David Worth. 116 minutes.

Firefox 1982. Warners. Clint Eastwood, Freddie Jones, David Huffman, Warren Clarke, Ronald Lacey, Kenneth Colley, Nigel Hawthorne. Produced and directed by Clint Eastwood. Screenplay by Alex Lasker and Wendell Willman, from a novel by Craig Thomas. Photographed in DeLuxe Color and Panavision by Bruce Surtees. Music by Maurice Jarre. 136 minutes.

Honky Tonk Man 1982. Malpaso-Warners. Clint Eastwood, Kyle Eastwood, John McIntire, Verna Bloom, Alexa Kenin, Matt Clark. Produced and directed by Clint Eastwood. Screenplay by Clancy Carlile from his novel. Photographed in Technicolor by Bruce Surtees. Music by Steve Dorff. 122 minutes.

Sudden Impact 1983. Malpaso-Warners. Clint Eastwood, Sondra Locke, Pat Hingle, Bradford Dillman, Michael Currie, Albert Popwell, Paul Drake. Produced and directed by Clint Eastwood. Screenplay by Joseph C Stinson, from a story by Earl E Smith and Charles B Pierce. Photographed in Technicolor and Panavision by Bruce Surtees. Music by Lalo Schifrin. 117 minutes.

Tightrope 1984. Malpaso-Warners. Clint Eastwood, Geneviève Bujold, Dan Hedaya, Allison Eastwood, Jennifer Beck, Marco St John, Rebecca Perle, Regina Richardson. Produced by Clint Eastwood. Directed and Written by Richard Tuggle. Photographed in Technicolor by Bruce Surtees. Music by Lennie Niehaus. 114 minutes.

City Heat 1985. Malpaso-Deliverance-Warners. Clint Eastwood, Burt Reynolds, Jane Alexander, Madeline Kahn, Rip Torn, Irene Cara, Richard Roundtree, Tony Lo Bianco. Directed by Richard Benjamin. Screenplay by Sam O Brown (Blake Edwards) and Joseph Stinson, based on a story by Sam O Brown (Blake Edwards). Photographed in Technicolor by Nick McLean. Music by Lennie Niehaus. 97 minutes.

Pale Rider 1985. Warners. Clint Eastwood, Michael Moriarty, Carrie Snodgress, Christopher Penn, Richard Dysart, Sydney Penny, Richard

Kiel, Doug McGrath, John Russell, Charles Hallahan. Produced and directed by Clint Eastwood. Screenplay by Michael Butler and Dennis Shyrak. Photographed in Technicolor and Panavision by Bruce Surtees. Music by Lennie Niehaus. 115 minutes.

Heartbreak Ridge 1986. Malpaso-Warners-Jay Weston. Clint Eastwood, Marsha Mason, Everett McGill, Moses Gunn, Eileen Heckart, Bo Svenson. Produced and directed by Clint Eastwood. Screenplay by James Carabatsos. Photographed in Technicolor by Jack N Green. Music by Lennie Niehaus. 130 minutes.

Bird 1988. Malpaso-Warners. Forest Whitaker, Diane Venora, Michael Zelniker. Produced and directed by Clint Eastwood. Screenplay by Joel Oliansky. Photographed in Technicolor by Jack N Green. Music by Lennie Niehaus. 161 minutes.

The Dead Pool 1988. Malpaso-Warners. Clint Eastwood, Patricia Clarkson. Liam Neeson, Evan C Kim, David Hunt, Michael Currie. Produced by David Valdes. Directed by Buddy Van Horn. Screenplay by Steve Sharon, from a story by Steve Sharon, Durk Pearson and Sandy Shaw. Photographed in Technicolor and Panavision by Jack N Green. Music by Lalo Schifrin. 91 minutes.

Pink Cadillac 1989. Malpaso-Warners. Clint Eastwood, Bernadette Peters, Tim Carhart, Michael Des Barres, John Dennis Johnston. Produced by David Valdes. Directed by Buddy Van Horn. Screenplay by John Eskow. 122 minutes.

To date, the film has not been released theatrically in the UK (February 1992).

White Hunter, Black Heart 1990. Warners. Clint Eastwood, Marisa Berenson, Jeff Fahey, George Dzundza, Clive Mantle. Produced and directed by Clint Eastwood. Screenplay by Peter Vietrel, James Bridges and Burt Kennedy. Photographed in Technicolor by Jack N Green. 112 minutes.

The Rookie 1991. Malpaso-Warners. Clint Eastwood, Charlie Sheen, Raul Julia, Sonia Braga, Tom Skerritt, Lara Flynn Boyle, Pepe Serna, Marco Rodriguez, Pete Randall, Donna Mitchell. Produced by Howard Kazanjian, Steven Siebert and David Valdes. Directed by Clint Eastwood. Screenplay by Boaz Yakin and Scott Spiegel. Photographed in Technicolor and Panavision by Jack N Green. Music by Lennie Niehaus.

Index